KV-578-811

Bending Reality

Bending Reality

The state of the media

Edited by James Curran, Jake Ecclestone,
Giles Oakley and Alan Richardson

Pluto **Press** in association with the
Campaign for Press and Broadcasting Freedom

London   Sydney   Dover New Hampshire

First published in 1986 by Pluto Press Limited,
The Works, 105a Torriano Avenue, London NW5 2RX
and Pluto Press Australia Limited, PO Box 199, Leichhardt,
New South Wales 2040, Australia. Also Pluto Press,
51 Washington Street, Dover, New Hampshire 03820 USA

Copyright © The individual authors, 1986

7 6 5 4 3 2 1

90 89 88 87 86

Phototypeset by AKM Associates (UK) Limited,
Ajmal House, Hayes Road, Southall, Greater London
Printed and bound in Great Britain by
Cox & Wyman Ltd, Reading

British Library Cataloguing in Publication Data
Bending reality: the state of the media.
1. Mass media——Great Britain
I. Curran, James
302.2′34′0941   P92.G7

ISBN 0 7453 0148 7

Contents

Notes on contributors

Melissa Benn is a freelance writer and has written for the *New Statesman*, *New Socialist*, *Spare Rib*, the *Guardian* and *Women's Review*.

Tony Benn is the Labour MP for Chesterfield, a member of the Labour Party National Executive Committee and former cabinet minister.

Cynthia Cockburn is a researcher in Social Science at City University, London. She is the author of *The Local State* (1977), *Brothers: Male Dominance and Technological Change* (1983) and *The Machinery of Dominance: Women, Men and Technological Know-how* (1986).

James Curran is Head of the Department of Communications at Goldsmiths' College, University of London. He has edited and contributed to six books on the media including (with Jean Seaton) *Power Without Responsibility* (rev. edn, 1985).

Liz Curtis is the author of *Ireland: the Propaganda War* (1984). She works with Information on Ireland, a voluntary London-based publishing group.

Anna Durell is the Campaign Officer with the Campaign for Homosexual Equality. She has worked on the Lesbian and Gay Switchboard and is a former columnist on *Capital Gay*.

Jake Ecclestone is Deputy General Secretary of the National Union of Journalists and former FoC of the *Times* NUJ Chapel. He was a member of the original Steering Committee of the CPBF.

Peter Golding is a Research Fellow at the Centre of Mass Communications Research, University of Leicester, and the author of several books on the mass media including (with Philip Elliot) *Making the News* (1979).

Stuart Hall is Professor of Sociology at the Open University and is the author of numerous studies on the mass media including *Resistance Through Rituals* (1976) and *Policing the Crisis* (1978).

Richard Keeble is a lecturer in journalism at the City University and has worked as a journalist in both the local and trade union press.

Loretta Loach is a journalist on *Spare Rib* magazine and has written for *New Socialist* and *New Statesman*. She was National Organizer of the CPBF from 1984 to 1985 and Chair from 1985 to 1986.

Andrew Lumsden is news editor on the *New Statesman* and was one of the founders, in 1972, of *Gay News*.

Bel Mooney is a journalist, broadcaster and novelist. She has written three novels, presented three television interview series and written for a wide range of newspapers and magazines.

Geoff Mulgan works in the Cultural Industries Unit of the Greater London Enterprise Board.

Graham Murdock is a Research Fellow at the Centre for Mass Communications Research, University of Leicester and the co-author of several books on the mass media including *Televising Terrorism* (1984).

Nell Myers is the Press Officer for the National Union of Mineworkers.

Giles Oakley is a television producer on the BBC's *Open Space* programme and vice-chair of the CPBF. He is the author of *The Devil's Music – A History of the Blues* (2nd edn, 1983).

Mike Power is a printer with the *Daily Mail* and is a member of the National Council of the CPBF.

Alan Richardson is a researcher with the Society of Graphical and Allied Trades. He worked as a trade union journalist on the NATSOPA journal from 1979 to 1982 and is a member of the National Committee of the CPBF.

Jean Seaton is a senior lecturer in sociology at the South Bank Polytechnic and is the author (with James Curran) of *Power Without Responsibility* (rev. edn, 1985).

Colin Sparks is a senior lecturer in media studies at the School of Communications, Polytechnic of Central London, and has published essays mainly in the field of Cultural Studies.

Marc Wadsworth is a television journalist. He is vice-chair of the Labour Party Black Sections National Committee and was a member of the NUJ Race Relations Working Party. He is on the National Council of the CPBF.

Adrian Wilkes is a Campaigning Consultant and a volunteer campaigner with the Campaign for Freedom of Information. He has written widely on health and safety, the media, and freedom of information.

Ken Worpole works in the Cultural Industries Unit of the Greater London Enterprise Board. He is the author of *Dockers and Detectives* (1983) and *Reading by Numbers* (1984).

Phillip Whitehead is a television producer and former Labour MP. He is a Visiting Fellow in Television at Goldsmiths' College, University of London and was a member of the Annan Committee on Broadcasting. His most recent television series was *The Writing on the Wall* for which he also wrote the accompanying book.

Introduction

This book has been organized into three sections. The first examines the ways in which the media represent – and misrepresent – what is happening in the world. The second debates what concrete steps should be taken to rectify these distortions, and the third considers alternative approaches to campaigning for reform.

The book begins with a striking general essay by Stuart Hall, in which he considers the different influences that make the media the way they are. Some of his arguments are developed by Colin Sparks, whose essay challenges the conventional notion that the media are independent of the state if they are rooted in the market and free of public regulation. Between these two general commentaries are a number of case studies or observations based on personal experience of media reporting. The intention of these essays is not to imply that there is an objective reality that the media fail to record. There are, of course, a number of different facets of reality that can be registered depending on which 'facts' are selected, and how they are contextualized and interpreted. But a common theme in this section is that the media regularly portray in a negative and sometimes crudely pejorative way a wide range of minorities from gays and blacks to peace campaigners, Irish nationalists and trade union activists. The media also negatively stereotype women, as Cynthia Cockburn and Loretta Loach argue, in a way that has no real equivalent for men.

Many books about the media – and indeed many political speeches on the subject – go no further than a general indictment of the media. In the second section of this book, we attempt to carry the argument forward by considering concretely what can be done to improve the media. We begin with a critical survey by James Curran of the different approaches and proposals that have been advanced for reforming the media. This is followed by essays focusing on how we should respond to the new communications revolution, how public service broadcasting can be reinvigorated, what lessons should be learnt from the media interventions of the Greater London Enterprise Board set up by the GLC, and how pornography and images that denigrate women should be dealt with.

The last section of the book reviews some of the issues involved in organizing and mobilizing public pressure for media reform. It starts with an account of the origins and development of the Campaign for Press and Broadcasting Freedom. This is followed by a general discussion of how the concept of freedom can be repossessed by the Left, the lessons and experience of the right of reply campaign promoted by shop floor workers in Fleet Street, how freedom of information can be promoted through legislative reform, and finally how the resources of the Left can be more effectively organized in developing a significant socialist presence within the media.

Most books on the media nowadays are written by professional academics. This book is different in that it is authored by people working in the media (whether as journalists, broadcasters or on the shop floor), by people who have no connection with the media save as consumers, and by professional students of the media. It arises out of the activities and concerns of the Campaign for Press and Broadcasting Freedom, to whom the authors and editors of this book donate their royalties. We hope that it will contribute something, however modest, to the efforts of all those who seek to raise the standards of British journalism.

Part I: Whose Reality?

1. Media power and class power

Stuart Hall

For many people, the very idea of a campaign for greater press or media freedom in Britain today must seem like a contradiction in terms. Don't we already *have* freedom of the press? Isn't it, indeed, one of the jewels which adorns the crown of English liberties? Isn't freedom of opinion one of those precious 'Western values' which distinguishes *free* societies like ours from *totalitarian* ones like theirs? Does it not mark the crucial difference between 'us' and, say, Eastern Europe, where the state runs everything and dissidents run the risk of a spell in a distant mental home; or places like Chile or South Africa, where critics of the regime are likely to wind up amongst the list of the permanently 'disappeared'? The assumption that things are different 'over here' is so much taken for granted in Britain that we can only start by trying to dismantle some of the ideas which hold this consoling myth in place.

Of course, the media in our kind of system *do* operate differently, as compared with countries where no freedom of expression and opinion whatsoever exists; and there is little point in arguing otherwise. Critics of our system sometimes argue that such differences don't exist – or that, anyway, they are so superficial as not to *really* matter. This seems to me a mistaken strategy. This view is an exaggeration, a simplification, which only convinces those who are already convinced. Only those who have not encountered General Pinochet's little team of 'censors' face-to-face at three in the morning can afford the luxury of arguing that our fragile and limited structures of civil and political rights 'don't essentially matter'. This argument flattens every significant difference and distinction into a false uniformity. It doesn't square with the perceptions that most ordinary people have of the media. Most damaging of all, it doesn't actually explain how our system operates so as to limit and constrain which ideas circulate and which do not, and so as to determine what can and can't be said in our society.

In fact, we very well know that in liberal-democratic class societies like ours, the constraints and limits operate *in* and *through*, not in spite of, the 'freedoms'. It is *because* the 'freedoms' we have are of a very particular type – because what is formally free is, in fact, limited by the very real dispositions of power in society – and because, in reality, some can operate these freedoms to their profit while others cannot, that things are as they are. Unless we can convince people of this, we cannot expect them to see beyond the simplified alternatives of 'free market' or 'state domination' to which the rhetoric of Thatcherism and the New Right are anxious to confine us. How the 'freedom' we have actually operates is what needs explaining. People who are seriously in the business of challenging the state of affairs in Britain cannot, opportunistically, collude with any and every exaggeration provided it casts the *status quo* in a bad light. We have to provide those who are, by and large, at the receiving end of 'media power' with a convincing account – an adequate understanding – of how that power *really* works. Only then will we know why and how the situation needs to be changed. More significantly, only then can we win broad, popular-based support which, in our situation, is our only leverage for change. It is to this general objective that the essays and articles in this volume are addressed.

'Freedom' is a word which is always invoked in the abstract. But 'freedoms' are always specific, in time, place and history. In opposition to the old aristocratic rule, the old system of patronage and privileges, the rising middle classes *did* establish certain 'liberties'. Not because they were disinterestedly committed to the cause of liberty and the torch of freedom for everyone; more because the formation of public opinion and the constitution of a 'public sphere' in which the press played a critical role was one of the key sites where they forged their claims to social power. They were committed to the 'right' to have their own, substantial 'opinions' freely and widely circulated. And they cast this ambition in the language of the 'rights of man' (the rights of women had to wait for another two centuries). The driving force for this was, of course, the rise of the market and the increasing domination of commercial capital over all other forms of property and influence. From that point onwards, certain 'rights' have proceeded together: the right to 'publish and be damned'; the right to own property, to speculate in the market, to attract the biggest share, to cater profitably to existing public taste, to invest in the manufacture of opinions, and to reap the rewards. Today, we are still (so far as the dominant modes of organizing the cultural industries of modern society are concerned) at the later monopolistic phase of that exceedingly long march of market forces through history. Why was it worth anyone's while to undertake it? Because, then as now, opinion and influence, the power to represent and the power to dominate, knowledge and power, have marched together. Capital and the market tied them to one another in powerful ways which we have still to disentangle.

Rights and freedoms are also historical. Defined by one group or class, in one historical situation, they are likely, in the dialectic of history, to be expropriated and put to new and different uses by another group or class in another historical epoch. If there is an aspect of the 'freedom of the press' worth defending and expanding on today, it is that created in the struggles, first, of the unstamped press, the 'poor men's guardian'; later, the working class and Chartist press; later still, the alternative press, linked to the causes of social emancipation. Their cause is not widely sung or given thanks for today in Fleet Street. Nevertheless, they enunciated the fundamental social right to forge social needs and aspirations in their own language, to construct new relationships between speaker and audience and to give public voice to the rising ambitions of new kinds of men and women hitherto dispossessed of cultural power. They set a new kind of demand in place on the historic agenda of social movements – the right of access to the machinery of cultural power, the expropriation of the cultural expropriators. Ours is the same story, the same struggle – in new conditions, about a hundred years on.

Against the old system, the rise of the marketplace of opinion created a fluidity, an openness which had not previously existed: just in the same way as the end of feudal rights and of serfdom created a mobile and free labour force – 'free' of course only within the new forms of exploitation of labour power. The system was finally stabilized under the regime of capital and the market. Those who were most free to make their opinions heard and felt, who commanded the means of representing the lives and needs and causes of others, were those who could command the capital resources, set to work the technologies, harness the means of distribution and dominate the channels of communication by virtue of their power over the marketplace of free opinions. Technically, in such a system, *anyone* could 'become a press lord' or 'own a television station or two'. Actually, not 'everyone' did – only 'someones'.

In such systems the ordinary folk at the receiving end of the process

do have power – only of a vastly reduced and limited sort. They have
the power of the sovereign consumer – to buy or not to buy, to listen or
to switch off. They have every English person's inalienable right to
choose between the *Mail*, the *Express*, the *Sun* or the *Star*. I suppose
this *is* 'consumer choice' of a kind, though it isn't a choice which
noticeably expands the mind or diversifies to any significant degree the
range of opinions allowed to circulate publicly. Freedom, for most of
us most of the time, is the freedom to switch off, or to choose this cable
company over that, or this video list in preference to that. Meanwhile,
as production costs soar beyond the reach of any but the largest
multinationals, and as the conditions of competition become more
monopolistic, each alternative tends more closely to resemble than to
differ from the other. Under modern forms of monopolistic competition, more means more of the same – the direct opposite to the myth of
market competition and freedom. Yet, ideologically, the principle of
market freedom has never been so well identified with diversity of
opinion and variety of viewpoint, maximizing the range of experiences
which get expressed. Definitions of social and political reality are
produced afresh every day from the extremely narrow band of
accounts from which these understandings of the world are stitched
together. The technology which, in a certain version of this great myth
of progress, should be the agent of our final liberation has become
steadily more expensive and, in its forms of social and economic
organization, more dominant as it has become intrinsically more
flexible. The more flexible, interchangeable and multi-purposed are the
technologies, the more obvious are the ways in which their incorporation into the cultural industries is designed to cut off, rather than
to exploit and develop, their essentially open and more democratic
possiblities.

Does all this matter? It does, because – more and more, in our
society, but actually in every society known to us – ideological power
matters profoundly. We understand this better the more we know how
the whole process of media reporting and construction works. We
know that even news journalism, with its addiction to the clean
separation of 'fact' and 'opinion' and its taboo on editorializing; or
photo-journalism, with its addiction to hard-hitting realism; or
television, with its pervasive window-on-the-world effect, do not
simply transcribe reality to us in great unassimilated lumps through
our daily dose of newspapers or our nightly diet of television. They *all*
work by using language – words, text, pictures still or moving;

combined in different ways through the practices and techniques of selection, editing, montage, design, layout, format, linkage, narrative, openings, closures – to represent the world to us. Some of these ways we call 'factual': some 'investigative'; some 'fictional'; some merely 'entertaining'. No matter. They all work and can only work because they are able to construct the world for us meaningfully in discourse. They are the *machinery of representation* in modern societies. What they exercise is the power to represent the world in certain definite ways. And because there are many different and conflicting ways in which meaning about the world can be constructed, it matters profoundly what and who gets represented, *what* and *who* regularly and routinely gets left out; and *how* things, people, events, relationships are represented. What we know of society depends on how things are represented to us and that knowledge in turn informs what we do and what policies we are prepared to accept.

Some things, people, events, relationships *always* get represented: always centre-stage, always in the position to define, to set the agenda, to establish the terms of the conversation. Some others sometimes get represented – but always at the margin, always responding to a question whose terms and conditions have been defined elsewhere: never 'centred'. Still others are always 'represented' only by their eloquent absence, their silences: or refracted through the glance or the gaze of others. If you are white, male, a businessman or a politician or a professional or a celebrity, your chances of getting represented will be very high. If you are black, or a woman without social status, or poor or working class or gay or powerless because you are marginal, you will always have to fight to get heard or seen. This does not mean that no one from the latter groups will ever find their way into the media. But it *does* mean that the structure of access to the media is systematically skewed in relation to certain social categories.

However, this factor on its own does not adequately describe how the system works because, of course, in certain roles, *some* of those marginal categories get 'accessed' all the time. There are certain representational places they regularly and routinely occupy. And this structured visibility, of course, gives the machinery of representation – the media – precisely that illusion of balance, comprehensiveness and even-handedness which underwrites its claims to legitimacy. If you are a trade unionist battling, once again, to explain why you are 'holding the nation up to ransom', you can have a regular spot. Gay people are OK as buffoons in *Are You Being Served?* but not as serious people, looking like other 'normal' folk, advancing a serious case about sexual politics. Blacks are all right dancing, singing and clapping hands in their usual natural ecstatic joy, or costumed behind a guitar, or soberly dressed, taking a responsible view of life or tearing up the paving stones. Poor people can alway be 'vox popped' into place, worth fifty seconds for a quick quote. They lend social problems the air of authenticity. But on the terrain of their own definitions of who they are and what they want – on the ground of their own, intrinsic social rights to speak about the world as they experience it or to imagine the world as they might one day like to see it – each of these social categories has to work constantly against the grain of the machinery of representation.

There are, certainly, breakthroughs within this edifice. Our media system is a 'leaky' one, and we must beware of giving a definition of it which is too monolithic. Indeed it 'leaks' all over the place, like a badly patched-up roof, because it is subject to such contradictory pressures. It must keep, feed and expand its hold on mass audiences while being fundamentally oriented, in terms of how it sees and explains things, within the perspectives of those who control the power structures of society. That is why one of its characteristic voices is that of the ventriloquist, trying to speak the language of the latter apparently through the mouths of the former. What else is the 'plain man's speech' of the popular press but this impossible attempt to talk out of both sides of its mouth at once? In its relentless search for novelty, the machinery of representation is pulled towards every single rupture or crack in the social fabric – while hustling like crazy to stitch it all up or shove it back into place behind the wallpaper. Face to face with the deliberate decimation of the coal industry and the destruction of the ways of life of the mining communities and with yet another concerted effort to lower the costs of technological decline on to the shoulders of working people, the machinery of representation is skilled at transplanting every event into the language of violence – while cramming its pages full of denunciations of violence. In the very act of 'hard-hitting' the Minister, it gives the game away to him in a subtle of-course: 'Of course, Minister, since state pensions for old people are now too costly for a country like this to afford . . .' Balanced interview: game, set, match. Yes, there are breakthroughs and, when they occur, they are real and important. Because we are stuck with an over-monolithic account of how things work, we are driven in our sectarian and ultra-leftist way to talk as if *nothing* matters or makes a difference except the one, final, Big Breakthrough, one which seldom comes, but meanwhile protects our revolutionary rectitude. It is much more difficult to engage in the back-breaking job of pushing and supporting a whole range of 'openings' while at the same time criticizing their weaknesses and limitations. How many of us have actually said recently what we all know: that, despite its many failings and its retreats under pressure, opportunities for minority and marginalized points of view have widened not narrowed since the advent of Channel 4? I would stand with that judgement. Nevertheless, regularly and routinely, day after day in the press, night after night on television, week after week in the journals, we find the same categories, the same repertoire of images, the same systems of representation, the same structure of presences and absences, stresses and weaknesses, the same explanatory frameworks, the same pictures connoting the same chains of association, the same plots and narratives, the same links and smooth transitions, *tending* to repeat and reproduce a certain definition of the world, in and amidst the infinite 'diversity' of our great British media institutions, effortlessly to the end of time.

How is that tendency so systematically and routinely sustained? No single factor, in my view, can explain it. There is no one 'cause' which can prescribe and limit a system as complex and diverse as the one which has grown up on the basis of modern technologies in modern industrial societies like ours, sitting as they do at the pinnacle of a global communications industry. The 'pattern' is produced at the point where a number of different factors or forces converge: it is determined from several directions at once. The word which we most commonly use to describe it is 'bias'. But the concept is woefully inadequate and in many ways misleading. It suggests deliberate and wilful, self-conscious bending of the rules. Of course, a good deal of deliberate, conscious 'bending' goes on all the time. And yet I am convinced that, if everyone in the system stopped 'bending' it tomorrow, the emphases and structured 'absences' in the media would continue.

One clear and pervasive factor is the structure of ownership and control. This is not, as some people think, a sufficient explanation of the way the ideological universe is structured, but it is a necessary starting point. It gives the whole machinery of representation its fundamental orientation in the value-system of property and profit. It prevents new kinds of grouping, new social purposes and new forms of control from entering, in a central way, into the production of culture. It opens the whole field of representations to the economic pressures of the global multinationals which now straddle the communications industries in each nation-state, reducing those states to pygmy status. Then there is what is sometimes called censorship, which is only the tip of the iceberg of steady surveillance, which in turn is only the tip of the iceberg of that now routine broadcasting process of patrolling the frontiers of opinion. Under Thatcherism, this kind of ideological 'policing' has attained new heights – or depths, depending on how you look at it. Thatcherites themselves were surprised, recently, to find that the overt forms of 'intervention' were so scandalous that even the professional journalists themselves were moved to revolt. The steady 'consultation' between the departments of state and the media are not, of course, exhausted by the example in which the Minister phones and tells someone to take off an unseen programme. Indeed, that sort of thing is so 'unusual', i.e. so brutal in its openness, that it provokes the flaccid liberal conscience into life, because it is in danger of blowing the cover on the niceties, the delicate and sensitive protocols, which 'normally' govern such discrete exchanges.

These elements of covert and overt regulation, coupled to the massive power of capital, explains much in terms of how an ideological climate is constructed and maintained. But, in themselves, they are an insufficient explanation. There is also the way in which the hierarchy of *power* in the society is reproduced, in the media, as a structure of *access*. Or how the respect for, orientation towards and reproduction of power in the media surfaces as a set of limits and constrictions on knowledge. That is how, without a single Ministerial or MI5 intervention, 'topics' come to be defined, agendas set and frameworks deployed which ultimately define the 'sayable' and the 'unsayable' in our society. The area of what is considered as 'reasonable talk' about anything, as the appropriate and inappropriate registers, as the intangible boundaries which rule the inclusion or exclusion of certain things, certain points of view, is one of the most powerful of the ways the media's regimes of truth come to be established.

We know far too little – and often have far too conspiratorial an account – of how these discursive boundaries operate. How can we pinpoint, in the endless, diverse, flow of 'talk' in the media, the precise ways in which the state stands as the 'definer of the limits of political reality' for the media: circumscribing the force-field within which, alone, things are allowed to become legitimately 'political'? Beyond that limit – its reverse side – is 'violence' – and the media have helped over the years to constitute the discourses of violence into their own, distinct, regime of truth. Any act or event which can be transposed into the register of 'law and order' – a skill at which most media professionals are extremely adept – can, by that very shift in register, be inoculated against any possible moral, political, sociological or historical argument. 'Law and order' – the stock-in-trade of popular journalism – neutralizes every other language into which social questions could be cast.

It is not only in the arena of 'hard news' and reporting in the normal sense that these ideological mechanisms operate. A great deal of what might be considered 'subversive talk' ('sound' would have been a more accurate term, for much of it is musical) can 'freely' circulate on our pluralistic, hedonistic, post-modernist culture, via the media, without delivering a single, serious, subversive *charge* simply because it takes place and is constructed in the category of 'entertainment', 'drama', 'diversion'. The segregation of the 'serious' from the 'pleasurable', like the separation of 'the private' from 'the public', is one of the most important boundary-maintaining, limiting, mechanisms through which the high energy impulses which circulate through the tubes of our wired-up society are systematically de-fused. The de-politicization of 'pleasure' – or the neutralizing of cultural politics – is one of the cultural industry's greatest unconscious achievements. The simple notions of 'bias', which we trade in as ways of explaining how some of these effects are achieved, don't begin to touch the levels at which these processes are operating.

Is there a way forward for us? There clearly is. It requires a struggle on two fronts at once. We have to widen accountability; to bring the irresponsible forces under control; to expose and monitor; to open the air-waves to a kind of two-way traffic or dialogue; to resist the closures, of a hundred different kinds, which now operate to keep the channels of communication clogged. At the same time, it is clear that we have ourselves to project a more positive long-term goal of what kind of alternative 'communicative society' we envisage. We may need and require state intervention and regulation to break the monopoly and stranglehold of capital over the communications industry. But I hope we are past believing that the old, paternalist forms of 'state authority' are likely, in the decades to come, to be forces for a more open and two-way traffic in the exchange of ideas. Many of those public service institutions have become over time 'guardians' of an alternative set of vested interests, protectors of their own pyramids of power; as terrified of 'two-way flow' as the communications moguls. And yet, in societies like ours, the democratizing thrust is ultimately unstoppable. Along with that will come an ever-increasing plurality and diversity of views and experiences, a recognition that the only 'unity' which matters is founded on the recognition of difference, which must be reflected in how we conceive the media functioning in the twenty-first century. I remain convinced that the steady and unremitting application of the principle of democracy – a conversation in the media as wide and diverse as society itself – is the most explosive force we can apply to the world of the media. Only in that context does the term 'freedom' cease to be theirs and start being *ours*.

2. In whose image?

Cynthia Cockburn and Loretta Loach

During the last ten years women have felt a great deal of anger about our treatment by the media. What exactly does 'sexism in the media' add up to, and what can be done about it?

Complaints tend to fall under five main headings. First, women are rendered strangely invisible in the media – where are we? Second, where women do appear as the subject of news stories or features, the images are mostly limited and stereotyped. Third, we are used quite unscrupulously as sexual commodities. Fourth, violence against women is reported in a way that seems more hostile to the victim than the aggressor. And finally, because of the generally 'heterosexist' orientation of the media, 'the reader', 'the viewer' is assumed to be heterosexual.

Let's take these points in order. Women's invisibility derives partly from the way the English language works and partly from the way news and 'interest' is constructed by the media. With a language like ours, who needs discrimination? The woman who heads the Equal Opportunities Commission is known as its 'chairman'. Most textile workers are women, yet what they are manufacturing is 'man-made' fabrics. Forty-two per cent of working people are female yet what they contribute to the national product is 'manpower'. Little wonder that the woman in the street feels somehow out of sight. The media have merely to practice normal English usage and women neatly disappear from view.

Black people protest, too, that all the expectations and allusions in press, radio and television ignore their presence and their contribution to economic, social and political life. That is just what happens to women – so black women are doubly invisible.

Many of the everyday things that women do, and do well, are somehow not newsworthy. Achievement and striving is news, keeping the home fires burning is not. But even when women's achievements cannot be denied they are ignored or brushed aside. Consider the poor coverage received by the cleaning staff at Barking Hospital whose action against privatization was maintained longer than the miners' strike that monopolized the headlines for a year. The striking miners may have been media bogeys but they got coverage. Women are ignored.

The second point is stereotyping. Just as ethnic groups are ascribed racial characteristics without any regard to the differences between individuals – all Japanese are 'inscrutable', all Africans are 'physical', all Jews are 'avaracious', and so on – so sexual stereotypes portray women as essentially one thing, men as essentially the opposite. Women are soft, weak, emotional and irrational. Men are strong, brave, ambitious and logical. Both sexes come across as shallow cardboard cut-outs. Anyone that does not fit the stereotype is an oddity, an exception.

When lesbians and gay men are mentioned in the media at all, it is because they are gay. The significance of the story lies in the fact that they are homosexual. They are represented as oddities and often as a danger. (Witness the homophobic treatment of AIDS infection stories.) It is assumed that anyone who is homosexual thinks of nothing but sex and aims to seduce and convert others. And it is assumed that heterosexuals are not like this.

It is not just people that get stereotyped. Jobs, roles and activities too get stamped with a gender. When a woman crosses the line and gets into a 'masculine' position this is reported as an exception, so reinforcing the general rule. 'Council gets petticoat management', 'engineering feels the soft touch'. The very many jobs that we do, the different kinds of contribution we make to society, our immense variety, are rarely acknowledged or celebrated. We get the impression that women live in one world where they are concerned with the trivia of life. Men live in the real world – technical matters, business and politics are their domain.

The third point of criticism of the media is perhaps the one that causes more distress and anger among more women than any of the others. In the pin-up calendars, the *Sun*'s Page 3 photograph, in magazines as culturally distinct as *Materials Handling News* and the *Observer* colour magazine, in video nasties and art cinema, women's bodies are routinely exposed, held up to view, an offering to men's prurience. Our bodies are divorced from any sense of ourselves as people. It is as though it is taken for granted that women exist for nothing other than men's sexual enjoyment. We are used to sell motorbikes, building materials and other commodities. In fact, we *are* commodities.

The fourth point: violence. Violence is the very stuff of news. On television, radio and in the press, war, terrorism, disaster and murder are dominant themes of news programmes. Yet much violence by men against women is not taken seriously, and goes unnoticed and unreported. Only extreme cases are classed as news. When woman-killing, woman-battering and rape are reported, the men who commit these crimes are often represented as rarities, as abnormal, mad or deviant. The fact that the great majority of murders and all rapes are specifically crimes of masculine sexuality and that male violence exists on an epidemic scale is never openly stated in the media.

Besides, the reporting of sexual murders and rape is, in an aghast kind of mode, often actually salacious and titillating. The physical characteristics of the woman are given – she was 'blonde', she was 'attractive'. Surely, the report implies, she invited trouble. She led the man on. She really 'wanted it'. The media, like the law, implicate women in the violence committed against them by distinguishing between 'good' and 'bad' women (e.g. prostitutes) whose fate was the logical outcome of their way of life.

The portrayal of women on posters, in newspapers and in film as sex objects, and the prevalence of male violence against women, are not unconnected. Women are represented as passive, as frail (particularly if they are old) and as potential victims. Tabloids often print a rape story directly adjacent to a 'sexy' pin-up. The person to whom an advert often seems to be directed is a male, appealed to as 'voyeur'. The unspoken message: women are available.

Finally, heterosexism. Sexual relations are, second only to violence, the staple diet of the media. Heterosexuality is always assumed. The man who is addressed by the film-maker, the broadcaster, the journalist, is assumed to desire women. The woman reader, viewer or listener is assumed to desire men. The truth is far removed from this. Ten per cent of people do not consider themselves heterosexual. They feel marginalized by the assumptions that are made about them.

Everyone suffers from stereotyping in the media but men suffer less than women. There is a negative side to the stereotyping of women that has no counterpart in the stereotyping of men. Men's supposed qualities are rated socially higher than those of women. Women are not just sugar-and-spice, we are lumbered with a baggage of bad qualities too: the nagging wife, the neurotic spinster, the possessive lover. Above all, we are *stupid* – think of all those dumb blonde cartoons.

Stereotyping of homosexuals is carried to absurd lengths. Lesbians are portrayed as 'butch monsters'. Women's movement activities can often be discredited by the media simply by being associated with lesbianism. Conversely, lesbians are discredited by being associated with events and activities that are given negative media treatment because they show women being strong. Examples are the Greenham Common women's peace camp and the Greater London Council's women's committee. In all these kinds of ways, heterosexism is a big part of the 'sexism in the media' problem.

Of course, not every editor, journalist, director or script-writer is, personally, a misogynist. There are many women and men in the industry who dislike its sexism, and would like to eradicate it. Individuals however have little influence against the system. The BBC, independent television companies, the public and private radio stations, newspapers and magazine publishing, are institutions much like any other. They reflect the patterns of power in society. In a world where economic, social and political power resides in the hands of men, where women are systematically subordinated, it is not surprising that the media tend to legitimate this state of affairs. The media don't originate women's oppression. They do however hold a particularly influential place as generators and purveyors of the ideology of sexism – they give a lead to people on how and what to think.

Besides, much of broadcasting and all of the press is frankly a business. It is oriented to profit and it deals in commodities. To the capitalist media, culture, drama and news are commodities. It is not surprising then that women are often treated as commodities too.

However much the individual media worker struggles to change the media, she or he is up against proprietors who are often dictatorial, often monopolistic. She or he is answerable to a hierarchical management structure with a vested interest in the status quo. Besides being male, these hierarchies are white. Both women and black people are dismally represented in employment in the media, particularly at the upper levels where policy is made.

The production process in broadcasting, television and publishing also works against new ideas and new ways of doing things. Media workers are often racing to meet deadlines, having to pack their news into a cripplingly short span of words or seconds. In these conditions a kind of shorthand is called for, and one is driven to the use of formulae, including stereotyping. The way news is defined, focusing on events and action rather than everyday processes, focusing on powerful individuals rather than ordinary people, pushes men into the limelight; pushes women into the shadows. You may see or hear a woman 'witness' interviewed on tape or film, for instance, but what she says will most likely be evaluated, commented upon and put in context by an 'expert' in the studio. That expert is nearly always a man.

We should not exaggerate the influence of the media. We should not suppose that it has a one-to-one effect on the audience. People do not go out and rape and kill because they read about such things in the newspaper or see them in a film. But when media messages fit in with and reinforce values that are very widespread in society, the effect is cumulative and powerful.

Sex differences, the physical differences we are born with, are slight indeed in comparison with the exaggeratedly contrasted genders we acquire as we live and learn. Girls grow up to be compliant and subservient, boys to be aggressive, to aspire to leadership. Even the curious and destructive forms taken by masculine sexuality are learned, not given by nature. The media play a part in this teaching process, a social construction of gender, placing men and women in spheres that, like those of *apartheid* are separate and unequal.

The effect on us all is damaging. Men internalize the masculine image and feel inadequate if they are not the macho type that is portrayed as ideal. As women we struggle to look the way the fashion plates tell us we should. Sexism here merges into other forms of oppressiveness. We disrespect and discount the old, the 'overweight', the disabled – anyone who doesn't fit the model of the desirable woman as men define her. The overall effect is to control women, to limit our scope, to keep us in 'our' place and to make us fearful.

Today, after fifteen years of the contemporary women's movement, there is more consciousness than there was of the bad treatment women receive in the media. The *Guardian*'s 'Naked Ape' column can be seen as a media exercise in self-criticism. But how effective is it? Naked Ape may blush, but Andy Capp is every bit as cocky. It sometimes seems that while women's consciousness has grown, the tide in society has been flowing against us. The growing permissiveness of the twentieth century, culminating in the sexual revolution of the 1960s, while it has helped to end the sickness of repressed sexuality and Victorian morality, has had negative effects too. Sexual liberty has been deformed into male sexual licence. The result is that images of women that would formerly have been seen only in soft porn appear with scarcely a comment in up-market colour supplements and down-market tabloids. In a way that is quite contradictory, it is now difficult to urge respect for women and restraint in the media without being condemned as censorious or prudish. Mary Whitehouse and the women's movement are light years apart in philosophy, but the practical line that divides us is a fine one.

When it comes to using the media however, the Mary Whitehouse experience is more of a success story than that of feminists. Access for Mary Whitehouse is only available because her beliefs, while outspoken, generally inhabit the accepted range of 'democratic' opinion: she desires the strengthening of the existing constraints in our society to arrest what she sees as a period of moral decline. By contrast, most journalists and broadcasters see themselves as liberals, and would defend the status quo in journalism, considering themselves a bulwark against so-called extremists from either wing. Feminist critiques of the media are far more extensive and challenging than either of these positions.

There is a material and ideological imbalance in the structures of the mass media which favours the white, male, middle-class establishment. This is reflected in the patterns of ownership, control and employment in the industry. 'Men control the means of expression – from the press and broadcasting to advertising, film, publishing and even criticism – by occupying dominant positions within them, and by using the power this gives them to convey the ideas and values of a patriarchal order.'[1] The dominance of men in the industry is undoubtedly the single biggest obstacle to our achieving change in the way in which the media views us.

In 1975 the ACTT published a report called 'Patterns of Discrimination'. It found that, of the 150 grades covered by union agreements in film and television production, 60 per cent of women employed were in these three grades: production secretary, continuity 'girl' and production assistant. In more than half the grades not one woman was employed and in skilled and technical jobs women counted for less than 10 per cent. There has been no real need to revise this study because according to the ACTT Equality Officer, 'In ten years virtually nothing has changed.'

In 1984 the Women's Employment Working Party of the Directors' Guild decided to investigate their own profession because of a growing concern among members that women were being discriminated against. Thirteen major independent television companies were asked for staff employment figures. The Independent Television Companies Association (ITCA) prevented the release of this information to the guild and only one company replied. 'We have thirteen male staff directors and employed seven freelance directors during 1983 all of whom were male.' In 1983 ITCA figures for independent television revealed that out of a total of 301 directors only 28 were women.[2] The interim report of the working party concluded that the 'continuing bias towards male directors encouraged the presentation of male experience and concerns as central and relegated the experience and views of women to the peripheral areas of "women's programming" '. One major initiative which was expected to change this in fact highlighted the numerous problems and contradictions women face working in a system which is overwhelmingly male and hierarchical.

Channel Four had been the television development on which many feminists had pinned their hopes. It held the promise of a new, distinctive ingredient in British broadcasting which on the surface at least seemed favourable to us. A group set up in 1979 to strengthen women's organization in the industry began to lobby around the new channel. Initially, the Women's Broadcasting and Film Lobby (WBFL) concentrated on the inclusion of training provisions for women in the broadcasting bill. However, this, and their request for the appointment of a woman specifically to oversee positive action, both went unheeded. Fortunately, they were more successful in their most innovative and original proposal for a weekly current affairs programme 'made by women but not only for women'. It was to deal with economic, social and political issues from a women's perspective.

Now at last we were to have an opportunity to see the world from the point of view and experience of women. It was expected that this would challenge the hackneyed news values which informed the tired, traditional practices of male journalists. So, for example, the International Feminist Bookfair or the UN Decade for Women would, on this agenda, be regarded as a newsworthy item in itself and not something requiring a peg on which to hang it. Moreover, the lives and experiences of the majority of women who don't see themselves as feminists could also become important material for journalists.

The all-women production team called Broadside were in complete agreement on this new programming strategy but the method by which they wanted to run the enterprise was vetoed by Channel Four's conventional requirements. Jeremy Isaacs asked that they appoint an editor, preferably a woman, who had extensive experience in current affairs. It was admitted by Channel Four that no such female person existed, precisely because of institutionalized bias against women in the industry. But that did not lead them to adjust the criteria for the appointment.

The appointment of an editor also ran contrary to the political aspirations of Broadside who wanted power and control to rest with the production company as a whole. Relations of production in television are enormously hierarchical and competition is the soul of the business. In this scenario any new initiative, particularly one whose aim was to transform the content and practice of programming, would inevitably experience more than the customary difficulties and strains.

Broadside were a talented group of women whose previous existence in an all-male institution had bred within them deep frustrations. They saw release in this new, all-women venture but it was an imaginative leap that even the innovative promise of Channel Four could not accommodate. After sixteen programmes the channel decided to abandon its commitment to a women's weekly current affairs programme – suggesting that it would be misleading to assume it ever held such a commitment in the first place.

The institutions of press and broadcasting are alien and impenetrable to the mass of women. Confronted with such power it is easy to feel demoralized and cynical about the possibilty of change. But the ideology and outlook of the trade unions are themselves responsible for making women vulnerable to feelings of defeat. When 'Patterns of Discrimination' was published ten years ago there were no women officers in the ACTT; today there are only four. In 1984 an NUJ survey in Fleet Street revealed that 'few women sit on chapel committees and fewer still hold official union posts'. The *Sun* has a chapel committee of thirteen men and one woman, the *Mirror* has a chapel committee of 24, three of whom are women, and at the *Guardian* there is one woman on a chapel committee of sixteen.

The NUJ survey also showed that the proportion of women to men employed on national newspapers fell as low as 7 per cent in some cases and never rose above 11 per cent overall. At the *Sun* there are 40 general news reporters; only three of them are women. At the *Guardian* there are 35 general news reporters; nine of them are women and of the 35 news subs only one is a woman. At the *Sunday Times*, they have a general news reporters' team of nine; all of them are men. Fleet Street of course is almost an exclusively male terrain both in the newsroom and in the wine bar. But the situation is little better in other sections of the industry. Women at the BBC for example see the organization as a 'man's club in which women are seen as stereotypes and often assumed to be secretaries, wives and mistresses'. Many women do work in press and broadcasting companies, but outside the editorial areas, in cleaning and catering: low-paid, anti-social and unglamorous jobs.

In the last ten years or more an awareness and recognition of women's disadvantage in this field has begun to be established. Even the director of personnel at the BBC commissioned a report on women's employment. It recommended the appointment of a women's employment officer to 'monitor the progress of women staff' and 'interpret the spirit as well as the letter of the Equal Opportunities Policy'.

Where such change is detectable, it can be attributed to pressure from a number of independent women's organizations which grew up in the early seventies and some of which are still active. All of these groups have at different times and with different emphasis campaigned for change throughout the industry with suggestions for positive action policies in training and recruitment. (See p. 26)

The political strength of these campaigns lies in their shared if tacit belief that to have individual women in positions of power will not in itself solve the problems of unequal employment practices nor how we are portrayed in the newspapers and broadcasting media. In fact, the successful few often tend to 'defend existing structures and practices with even more conviction than their male counterparts and deliberately disassociate themselves from feminism, the women's liberation movement and other women'.[3] This is sad but hardly so surprising. The philosophy of the women's movement is in fundamental contradiction to a system which thrives on competition, rich rewards and a strict division of labour.

The feminist challenge to the way our media operate aims directly at the heart of patriarchal values and at the means by which they are reproduced. Because these values are so estabished, it is often quite beyond the imagination of men to understand and accept the nature and importance of this critique.

The editor of the *Observer*, Donald Trelford, was asked on a BBC radio programme if there was any occasion on which he could not send a woman reporter. No, he replied, except that as women get older they are less willing to go on overseas assignments because of family commitments. 'Logically,' he said, becoming aware of a contradiction, 'there is no reason why these should bind women more than they do men but they do.'

There is a value which middle-class men place on their work that is derived from the power it gives them. It is a value so intense that it can often mean more to them than life itself. An assistant producer at the BBC was quoted in their report: 'Women care more about the quality of their lives than for promotion and, unlike most men, do not think ahead about the next step. Men think in terms of careers; women think of jobs.'[4]

Men's attitudes and the conditions and practices which reinforce and perpetuate them give us some insight as to why so many women in the media feel uncomfortable and alienated in their working environment. Their private anxieties in this area are entirely connected to the difficult social world they inhabit. The media world is one where money, prestige and power are the order of the day and in this competitive male club private feelings of personal inadequacy are unwittingly nurtured and developed. The potential for feminist solidarity is impeded by these conditions. The identity of women becomes fragmented and turned inward or turns into competition with other women and with men. It becomes impossible to imagine that other women experience lack of confidence or difficulties. This further isolates women, often creating profound feelings of defeat, disillusionment and personal failure.

The vibrant women's movement of the 1970s helped build a sense of identity and strength which gave women the confidence to understand their situation politically and begin organizing for change. There was activity on many levels, involving direct action, spray painting hoardings, demonstrations, occupying newsrooms for the right of reply and the more ponderous process of lobbying the unions for positive action.

The feminist media that also emerged during this time did much to influence the editorial content of print and broadcasting journalism and, uniquely, allowed women to express and discuss the issues that concerned them. An important component of this was the growing voice of black women. Urvashi Butalia, in an article on Asian women in the West, said that as black and Asian women 'have begun to fight in the streets and in their homes, a parallel fight has taken place in the arena of the media. For access to information and the use and control of information to gain solidarity and strength is crucial to any movement.'[5] When *Outwrite* was established in March 1982, this was one example of women from different ethnic groups rejecting the mainstream media and opting to 'run and control their own media forms rather than allow men, whatever their colour, to take control'.

It had taken the anger of a mass movement of women to shift the distressing pattern of discrimination that the media both reflects and creates. The changes that have been made are significant but by no means commensurate to either the extent of dissatisfaction being voiced or the energy and commitment that went into achieving reform. One reason for this, which can be generalized beyond the media, is that women were excluded from the institutions which fight for change. They were confronting the double burden of employers' prejudice and that of their brothers in a trade union movement whose habits and concerns were based on the historical assumption that its members were and always would be male.

On a different level, a new kind of Conservative government and a period of severe economic decline restricted the opportunity for real, material change and ideological influence. The crisis of the early 1980s began to affect our capacity for renewable and confident struggle. Problems also began to develop in the movement's self-definition as a unified and effective force as individual women achieved a measure of power and were used by those resistant to change to undermine criticism.

By the mid-1980s, so the media tell us, the feminist revolution had ended. They were misrepresenting a period of great change for the women's liberation movement, as for other social change and liberation groups. Feminists need to clarify and understand the nature of these changes because it affects how the media view us and how we view ourselves. This will inevitably involve some reassessment of our aims and strategy for changing the institutions of press and broadcasting.

The communications industry is being transformed rapidly by technological developments and right-wing political change. The expansion of cable and satellite television, de-regulation of local radio, the dismantling of public service broadcasting and the structural changes in the ownership and control of our newspapers all have fundamental implications for women and other groups in our society whose concerns, lives and identities go unrecognized in the media. A new and urgent response from feminists is required to begin the second phase of what we have always expected would be a long revolution.

We would like to thank Anne Karpf for her help and suggestions.

References

1. Anna Coote and Bea Campbell, *Sweet Freedom*, Picador, 1982, p. 189.
2. *Direct Magazine*, April 1985.
3. Helen Baehr, *Media, Culture and Society*, No. 3, 1981, Academic Press.
4. Monica Simms, *Women in BBC Management*, 1985.
5. *ISIS Journal*, Geneva 1985.

Women and the media – campaigns and resources

Women's Media Action Campaign Against Sexism in the Media. Also publishes a newsletter – c/o AWP, Hungerford House, Victoria Embankment, London WC2.

Women's Monitoring Network, c/o AWP, Hungerford House, Victoria Embankment, London WC2. Groups and individuals monitoring media sexism.

Women in Media – 18 Bowyers Walk, Beckton, London E6 (01-380 0517)

Equality Council, c/o NUJ, Acorn House, 314 Grays Inn Road, London WC1 (01-278 7916). Complaints on media material should go to the NUJ.

Advertising Standards Authority, 2-16 Torrington Place, London WC1. Official body to complain to about printed advertisements.

ACTT Committee on Equality, c/o Sandra Horne, Association of Cinematograph, Television and Allied Technicians, 2 Soho Square, London W1 (01-437 8506)

Campaign for Press and Broadcasting Freedom – 9 Poland Street, London W1V 3DG (01-437 2795). Campaigns against bias in the media.

Women in Publishing – c/o 3 Roden Street, N7 6QJ

Black Women in the Media – c/o Outwrite, Oxford House, Derbyshire Street, London E2

WEFT – Unit A12, Metropolitan Workshops, Enfield Road, London N1 (01-254 6536). Multiracial women's media resource centre in Hackney. It is in the process of setting up a 16 track sound studio and screening space.

For the CPBF code of conduct on sexism in the media, see p. 242 below.

3. Sexual stereotyping in the media

Anna Durell and Andrew Lumsden
Speaking with one voice

As to the present situation I think you must be perfectly clear about the matter. Homosexuality is against the Christian law of morals and is rightly regarded as a social menace if it becomes in any sense widespread. There is an accumulation of evidence that homosexuality is becoming a real social evil, and I know cases where homosexuals are enticing men and persuading men who are not by nature homosexual at all into this practice. You will have seen what the magistrates have said. Quite obviously society must protect itself against this as against any other anti-social moral perversion. This is hardly the moment at which to put in a plea for a better law or for public sympathy. I hope that all homosexuals will stop at once to realize that whatever their physical infirmities or their natural tendencies any indulgence of them is against Christian morals and the public welfare. They should seek priest and psychiatrist for help. (Geoffrey Fisher, Archbishop of Canterbury, in a letter dated 3 November 1953, and discovered by a gay man in a second-hand book in summer 1985)

Here's a curious thing that happened in Fleet Street in the summer of 1985: Kelvin McKenzie, editor of the *Sun*, Britain's biggest-selling mass-circulation daily, was giving evidence to the Press Council. He complained that gay people are harassing Fleet Street. Good news, of course, if it were true. But all that had occurred was a complaint by a gay man that the *Sun* on 28 September 1984 had published a 'queer-baiting' editorial. The Press Council astounded everybody – certainly it astounded the few lesbians and gays who followed the matter – by finding in the gay reader's favour. It had been 'improper and extremely offensive' of the *Sun* to 'advocate discrimination against homosexual people and encourage employers to discriminate'.

Well, fancy. McKenzie's office hadn't been trashed; he hadn't been personally insulted; no one had occupied the newsroom; the windows

hadn't been painted with graffiti; his reporters hadn't been rendered
miserable in their favourite pubs by furious activists (though it wasn't
long afterwards that furious blacks demonstrated outside the *Sun*
against its coverage of the relations between the races in Handsworth,
Birmingham). The *Sun*, in return for advocating open season on
homosexuals, had been hit over the head with the Press Council's
feather duster, and felt 'harassed'. The most interesting thing about
McKenzie's cry that he feels gays have been 'harassing' him in the
carefree conduct of his paper is that it may even have been more or less
true. Such cries from the heart, cries almost for sympathy, seem always
to be wrenched from the powerful whenever an audible sign of protest
reaches them from the sat-upon – from the white police chiefs
'harassed' by 'uppity niggers' in Alabama in the 1960s, from male
establishments 'harassed' in the 1970s by 'women's libbers', from
separatist gay men 'harassed' in the early 1980s by 'lesbians'
(pejorative).

It could be that McKenzie, taking him both in his own right and as
the type of all who run the mass media, does not understand why
anything his paper has ever done about lesbians or gays should be
thought specially offensive. It's only at intervals, not constantly, that I
can think with hatred of straights such as McKenzie, rendered brutally
dim-witted by their sexual ignorance though they are. Except when
absolutely enraged, I tend rather to think of the editors of *all* Britain's
front-rank media – 'prestige' media as much as 'popular', the *Guardian*
and *Question Time*'s as much as the *Sun*'s and Radio 2's – as James
Baldwin says of racist whites: as 'deluded children – the slightly mad
victims of their own brainwashing'. (*New Society*, September 1985) It
really is so easy to imagine that 'deluded child' McKenzie, or Peter
Preston of the *Guardian* (who most richly of all editors, in view of the
Guardian's liberal pretensions, deserves to be hauled before the Press
Council for indifference to the lesbian/gay readership) ask in perplexity
why offence repeatedly given to homosexuals should be thought any
different to offence cheerfully given to shoals of heterosexuals, from
the Royal Family princelings up. After all, newspapers and programmes
are *supposed* to be cheeky, to get people going, to stir it up.
Unobjectionable media must surely be dead media.

It's worth pausing – in fact it's essential to pause – over the media
defence, when attacked for their moral standards, that they have an
editorial and commercial obligation to be 'lively', and that causing
offence to sensitive interests and individuals is the very trade itself, *is*

journalism (a defence bound up with the argument that readers and audiences must be able to trust the 'editorial independence' of a medium). Let's defend the *Sun* itself and its brand of British media homophobia. In February 1985, at the height of the last round of AIDS-related gay-baiting, the harassed McKenzie's paper ran a front-page tale about how a gay man and his lover had been tossed out of a working men's club because of paranoia that they might give everyone AIDS. The *Sun* didn't only print the facts accurately (or so the man who informed the *Sun* told me). It put a happy picture of the two male lovers on the cover. To 'a mad victim of straight brainwashing', a 'deluded child', that of course was circulation-boosting shock-horror. To gays it's coming out. Catch a 'newspaper of record' or 'quality liberal' doing as much except to illustrate a 'problem' article or a lower-depths descent into the world of the gay disco. So vulgarity, as anyone knows who has vainly searched the 'great' papers and programmes for the faintest warmth or scruple towards homosexuals, can by fits and starts be more liberating in its mindless sensationalism than can suffocating 'good taste' and 'reponsibility'. Vulgarity, in February 1985, did more to shift the then Health Minister Kenneth Clarke over AIDS than anything the 'qualities' had seen fit to print or broadcast on the approach and arrival of the disease.

A DHSS grant to the gay-founded AIDS-counselling service, the Terrence Higgins Trust, is directly traceable to the horrors perpetrated by the *Mirror*, the *Star* and the *Sun* when, wholly motivated by the circulation war, they threw the whole country and every other branch of the media into panic about the 'plague'. Furthermore, a (miserly) release of AIDS-related funds to the medical profession in late August 1985 appears to be directly traceable (can it just have been coincidence?) to an impolite disclosure by the *Sun*'s brother-paper, the *News of the World*, only days before, that Lord Avon, son of a former British Prime Minister and himself a former minister in Mrs Thatcher's government, had died of AIDS – not that his death-certificate had said so – and that he'd been gay.

Add to these uncovenanted benefits, when populars yell up-front what establishment media merely whisper to one another, and think too indelicate for their columns or their air-time, the activities of 'agony aunts'. Almost to a woman they have for years been streets ahead of newsrooms and features departments in their realism about the existence, needs and normality of the country's zillions of lesbians and gay men. There *is* some defence for, there are things to be said on behalf of, those 'populars' which take all the stick for queer-baiting, while the immense sins of omission of 'quality' media, who allow no open lesbians or gay men to talk to their readership or audience, slide past unremarked. Only when some heterosexually identified columnist, some Paul Johnson or Auberon Waugh, fills his empty space out of an empty head with another gibe against 'homosexualists' is this embargo breached.

Journalism isn't a nice business. All media exposure of heterosexual activity as of homosexuals as often as not ends up leaving even those of its subjects who thought they wanted it smarting and fed up. What, if anything, in the British media is peculiarly vicious to lesbians and gays, causing us to 'harass' such fragile plants as the editor of the *Sun*? Actually, xenophobia (fear of strangers) and misogyny (including fear of 'feminine' attributes in men) are so thickly woven into the popular *and* quality approach to lesbians and gay men that it's unnerving to try to detach 'homosexuality' as a self-contained topic on which coverage might be – let's speak mildly about it – improved. The 'deluded children' in charge of the bulk of the UK's media know so little of the culture, history, or present lives of gay people (or if they do know, being lesbian or gay themselves, learn on the way up the career ladder to keep their mouths shut) that *their* 'homosexuality' (topic on an agenda) is rarely recognizable to me as *my* 'homosexuality' (experience).

Touchingly frail as most campaigns to move the media seem to be, including articles such as those in this book, some steps can be taken to tease out what is exceptional about the gay condition in the media. We have been put to a very particular servitude: 'we' lesbian and gay people, not lesbian and gay media employees, though the bulk of the latter are forcibly enslaved to passing as straight. We aren't regarded as existing in our own right. If we were, there would be 'out' reviewers, critics, interviewers, and 'name' reporters scattered across quality and popular media alike in rough proportion to the numbers of us in media employment. We are subject-matter, but are not, with the very rarest exceptions, permitted to be principals, writing or broadcasting in our real sexual persona. Journalistic objectivity is defined as the declared or taken-as-read heterosexual experience. 'Liberal' opinion, as in the *Guardian*, is that lesbians and gays should at best be spoken *for*; the fundamentalist consensus, as in the *Spectator*, that lesbians and gays should only be spoken *against*.

There is so much speaking *against* us, and some speaking *for* us – arguments conducted entirely, across the spectrum of the media, as if between self-assured heterosexuals – that we are plainly useful for something. Our servitude varies in function over different decades. The most recent version of it can be said to date, I think, from the then newly elected GLC leader Ken Livingstone's 1981 speech to Harrow Gay Unity, when to the vast excitement of the press he promised that lesbian and gay groups would be encouraged to seek (*Sun*speak) 'ratepayers' money'. The era of using lesbians and gays to vilify Left politicians and Labour overall had begun.

What creatures can they be, these homosexuals (I write 'they' not 'we', for these are the media's homosexuals) who are powerful enough to persuade some career politicians to offer them funds and legal reforms – and yet so rare that readers of mass circulation dailies are presumed, save by the 'agony aunts', to have none in the family, none as friends?

Here they are: 'striding the camp with their butch haircuts, boots and boiler suits' or 'built like a tank . . . always wearing men's-style clothes'. Who would recognize themselves or their best friends from such a description? Many gay men, in fact. Particularly sportsmen, professional soldiers and (real or pretend) construction workers. But according to Sarah Bond in the *Daily Express* of 10 April 1984 and Dianne Robinson in the *Liverpool Echo* of 29 May 1985 these are descriptions of lesbians. The images have a quaintly old-fashioned air; but then they are drawn, not from life, but the pages of Havelock Ellis.

The notion of the homosexual as 'invert' was created for political ends – Ellis and his circle were social reformers. It was also how some of those involved once saw themselves. 'Stephen' in *The Well of Loneliness* (1928) is a gawky, unfeminine creature whose urge to a 'male' lifestyle is covertly attributed to biological and psychological causes. Like most special pleading the ploy failed. Instead of establishing a wildlife reserve where those to whom Nature had been unkind could live free from social and legal penalties, the reformers, with their notion of 'inversion', erected a zoo. Imprisonment and/or social ostracism remained a terror for any of the same sex who expressed open affection, and popular writers – and the media in entirety – latched onto the idea of 'the homosexual' as a bizarre, and very rare, sub-species.

In the minds of lesbians and gay men (at least) this image had been replaced as long ago as the end of the 1950s with something far simpler and yet more diverse. The male characters in the 1962 Dirk Bogarde movie of homosexual blackmail, *Victim*, aren't 'women trapped in men's bodies' or, for the most part, 'effeminate' – not at least to the 1980s eye watching a box re-run – although one of the men does cry, and they talk about emotions a lot. So it's striking that the 'gender-swap' image flourishes in the press 25 years later, put to a servitude – a function of deriding lesbians – so far removed from the kindly intentions of those who originally speculated that 'inversion' is the reason why I am, why we are, homosexual.

This image flourishes alongside other stereotypes which flatly contradict the concept of inversion. The *Sun*, for example, even manages to confuse itself. On 16 April 1984, under the headline *Whip-girl's lesbian love child*, it revealed the 'amazing secret' that a murdered prostitute 'was a "father" ' (i.e. that her woman lover had a child), adding, in case readers should miss the point, that ' "Daddie" . . . also rode a motorbike'. The very next day, the *Sun* abruptly reversed her assigned 'gender', redescribing her as 'Torture queen . . . Miss Whiplash', who 'regularly had visits from "butch" girlfriends'. No wonder the *Daily Star* in June 1985 in an 'exclusive interview' with Judy Nelson, 'a stunning blonde mother-of-two' and 'all-American girl next door', described her and Martina Navratilova's relationship and sexuality as 'exciting world curiosity' and 'never fully explained'. Wot, stunning blonde be a lesbian? Never!

The image of gay men as 'pansies' manages to survive in forced marriage with other myths of startling incongruity: of the gay as sexual predator, and as security risk. The *Sun* as ever shines. Alongside that same autumn 1984 editorial (subject of the successful Press Council complaint) which praised Rugby council for banning gays from council jobs, there appeared a cartoon of a man in a bowler hat, corset, fishnet stockings, and high heels, being turned away from an employment exchange with the recommendation that he try the Ministry of Defence. Quite how, if we gays are so blatant, we manage to infiltrate Security Services, and persuade the reputedly moralistic agents of the KGB to take us seriously, isn't explained.

Are journalists simply foolish, or as amoral as they're painted – or do they consciously aim to disinform their readerships and audiences about one of the reasonably prominent surrounding realities of human erotic life? Whatever the cause or multiple of causes, the message off page and screen remains antediluvian and clear: those things called lesbians and homosexuals and so on are weird. So weird that while you (presumed heterosexual) may, if 'liberal', feel sorry for *them*, and if illiberal, be disgusted by *them*, the one thing you can be sure of is that no one would ever mistake you yourself for one (they are or become so weird) nor could anyone whom you have parented, or whose own child you are, or of whom you are fond or admiring, possibly be one. As a message, it is, it must be, in flat denial of the personal experience of all but the most reclusive or doctrinaire heterosexual of readers or viewers.

It is interesting to test the way in which so remarkable a message as the media's about lesbians and gays can be sustained even through the growing awareness of the lesbian or gay. I was raised in the 1950s. The images which haunted the twilight fringes of my own consciousness were precisely those of the 'female invert' and her male counterpart, the permed and perfumed ageing 'boy'. I separated what I knew of myself from what 'society', energetically promulgated through the media, alleged homosexuals to be. I never for a moment took to myself the accusation 'weird' or 'abnormal' for the simple ecstasy I felt in the company of certain schoolfriends. Having strong feelings – briefly – for fellow students or pupils is of course tacitly accepted in the shape of 'pashes' or 'crushes', but even though I guessed that my own feelings were of a different quality and duration from those of some of my friends, I didn't equate that with being 'homosexual'. I was normal. I just happened to fall in love with . . . whoever.

I knew that 'lesbians' desire women. But I saw theirs as a possessive, domineering appetite, hopelessly warped by the pathetic aping of (stereotyped) masculinity. Although school and college brought me into proximity to some two thousand women, I only met or got to hear of two lesbians. They, the most courageous of the 'out' so often being those homosexuals who most nearly conform to the prejudicial picture of what the homosexual *is* (and who accordingly find it hardest to hide), were of course tall, clumsy, and bossy. They confirmed my worst, induced, fears about what it means to be lesbian or gay, and threatened my fragile identity. I avoided them like the plague. The notorious gay male dons, the 'queeny' old men, for old men they seemed, were apparently another affirmation of what it is, and all it can can be, to be homosexual.

So far, the political intentions of the media of the 1950s (only fractionally changed today) had succeeded. I and my contemporaries who were, shall we say, non-heterosexual, didn't identify ourselves as or with 'lesbians' or 'queers'. We nursed our romantic despairs in secret, worked hard on love affairs with the other sex, and very often got married, had children (frequently in reverse order, that). Most of the marriages failed. Marriages do, but these for very true reasons of incompatibility. That some succeeded is a tribute to the adaptability of human beings under stress; and probably an index of the low expectations of self-fulfilment most women had before 1970.

There was, and there is, a sharp difference between some of what the male-growing-up-as-homosexual and what the female-growing-up-as-homosexual imbibes almost subliminally from the media, and it relates to the (in)famous ancient teaching that women scarcely possess innate sexuality – only sexuality tangential to men. Where the everyday occurrence of free-choice sexuality between women is virtually never 'noticed' in the press, the same is far from true of gay men. Whatever disinformation appears elsewhere, and however venal each local paper's motive in carrying the stuff, there are forever court reports about gay men on 'indecency' or 'obscenity' charges. The average gay male teenager, desperate for clues to the gay identity, can at least gather, as many a young gay woman can't in regard to sex between women, that sex between men is going on somewhere, perhaps even on a grand scale. Many young men promptly do the logical thing – hooray! – and go out looking for it. And find it.

However grotesquely the lawyers and the local papers (or national media, when a celebrity is caught) will have depicted both the 'criminal' and the 'act', and however timid this form of press collusion with the criminal law may have made the apprehensive, inexperienced, gay youth, the gay man – and naturally the gay woman when she finds her way – discovers a world of emotion and joy infinitely distant from the 'dirty' deeds dragged before magistrates. Saturated with what the media tell, and don't tell, parents aren't inclined to hear their own children's stories of homosexual reality – or perhaps as commonly, children presuppose that incomprehension in their parents, and can't bring themselves, perhaps even out of modesty, to speak. Free exchanges of common sense about homosexuality stay prohibited, the gay's knowledge stays concealed from parents, teachers, workmates and neighbours, who may never know that the average 'homosexual offender' is their son, their pupil, their colleague, or that nice boy next door. But gay men and women know it, and think the law and the press both an ass. The circle of misinformation revolves, giving further impetus to, and taking further impetus from, the media.

A breakthrough was available to everyone from about 1972, and the most clamant criticism of the UK media then, and still, is that they never applied even the basic journalistic techniques of enquiry to reporting it. Lesbians within the women's movement and gay men (and women) within the Campaign for Homosexual Equality and the Gay Liberation Front groups reworked the self-identity of, and offered a realistic public identity for, the sometime 'homosexuals' of folklore. We carried out those bitterly resented smash-and-grab raids on the language: rejecting 'homosexual' with its overtones of the 'clinical', reclaiming the word 'lesbian', and foisting onto the world at large the previously coded term 'gay'. There were of course demonstrations, conferences, marches, but above all we broke silence – we told people, anyone, everyone we met, just who and what we are. 'We', said one famous banner of the era, 'are the people our parents warned us against.'

All of this passed without competent analysis from any principal sector of the UK media, who largely confined themselves to publishing laments on the 'abuse' of that invaluable word 'gay' (which had never seemed invaluable to anyone till gays subjected to whole vocabularies of others' invention, took it). 'Gay'? An outrage, the parrot-squawks decreed: these people are neither daring nor debonair, but miserable *buggers*. (That itself is a medieval term of abuse, seemingly derived from Roman Catholic xenophobia against Bulgar 'heretics'). As usual, women's experience was drowned in a swamp of male myths about male sexuality. For the straight men's stroke-mags, *Whitehouse*, *Rustler*, *Knave et al.*, sexual acts between women are mere titillation for men – foreplay inviting the male voyeur to 'do the real thing'. The less overtly pornographic media deploy lesbianism's supposed 'maleness' to trash the aspirations of other women: of Women's Liberation, women's tennis, Greenham, Myra Hindley's parole application, any and every adoption of equal opportunities policies by local councils.

It has sometimes seemed as if the cult of Boy George and the 'gender benders' stimulated by the mass audience papers and programmes signals a dawning acceptance of some of the stereotype-busting undertaken by lesbians and gay men. Perhaps indeed something of freedom in dress and look, for the young of both sexes, has been gained. But the cult is invariably of success; and it is of success in the entertainments business. The *Sunday Telegraph*, in a second leader some years ago bewailing the era of gay liberation, openly stated how welcome the homosexual temperament has always been *when it is amusing*. Many gay men, and maybe some unknown lesbians too, *amuse* readers with columns, and listeners or viewers on programmes, to this very day, without any open acknowledgement, on any occasion, of their true sexuality. Blacks have rhythm. Gays have humour. Is it fanciful, anyway, to suppose that the pop world 'gender benders' titillate rather than challenge because, just like 'real' women, they can always be overborne, silenced, kept in their place?

Lesbians and gay men can't fail to be struck by the extraordinary anxiety the professionals of journalism display towards this common-place of life: homosexual desire. An anxiety wholly at odds with their preferred professional self-image of fearlessness, of news-gathering, of analysis. The impression is inescapable: that for a generation since the early 1970s the overwhelming majority of journalists, quality and popular (supposing there to be any real dividing line) have lent themselves to the artificial prolongation of old vested interests of power. The bulk of the media and their staffs behave as if they were under siege – 'harassed', in Kelvin McKenzie's word – and we must suppose that indeed that is how they feel. The *mortmain* of ageing propaganda about sexual 'respectability' flinches at each shock from the lesbians or the gays, but it is false; it is only galvanism. On this topic, the media stay dead.

As was seen with AIDS, all that can be said on *behalf* of the *Sun* and its competitors, and which I have said – how in their ungenteel way they at least compelled better public attention – pales beside the fact that everything was reflex. The newsroom knee, tapped by the word 'gay', kicked out. So did the cruder columnists' knees. For some it was a heaven-sent (and some called it that) chance to throw some mud that might stick, to link deviation with contagion. A chance to sweep gay men, lesbians and all who break bread with us out of the workplace, out of the council chamber, out of Parliament.

Yet simultaneously ours is a generation which has seen several local authorities and major trades unions and (in 1985) the TUC and Labour in conference pass resolutions prohibiting discrimination against lesbians and gays in general and persons with AIDS in particular. We have an 'out' gay member in the House of Commons. We have lesbian and gay publishing houses; 'mainstream' publishers with gay lists; an excellent variety of news and feature periodicals; very able voluntary organizations such as the London Gay Switchboard and the Terrence Higgins Trust; an unprecedented spread of leisure facilities; articulate spokespersons and 'ordinary' individuals by the dozen. Yet at the time I write, in autumn 1985, there is not *one* 'out' lesbian or gay writing or speaking direct to the public in all the length and breadth of Britain's flagship media.

In 1878 the *Times* got the terms of the Congress of Berlin onto the London streets even while the treaty was being signed and while details were supposed to be secret. In 1985, some 16 years after the demolition of the old presumptions about homosexuality, this news has yet to be released by the editorial floors of the major print and broadcasting institutions. A battle won . . . despatches delayed.

4. Racism in broadcasting

Marc Wadsworth

Black people pay millions of pounds a year to sustain British television and radio but we have little to show for it. No black television or radio stations have been granted a franchise to cater for the three million people of African and Asian descent settled in this country. Yet Northern Ireland, with a population roughly a third of that, can boast its own television and radio channels. Instead of independent channels broadcasting bosses have opted for facile tokenism – one black governor each on the BBC and IBA ruling bodies and low-budget 'ethnic' programmes.

Given the huge number of unused frequencies on the air waves, the situation in radio is least defensible. Multi-racial cities like New York have scores of legal radio stations aimed at minority as well as mainstream audiences, yet in London the choice is between just three Home Office-licensed stations – Capital, BBC Radio London and the all-news London Broadcasting Company (LBC). At the heart of the problem is the desire by the monolithic and out of touch BBC and IBA to achieve super audience ratings and big profits rather than a multiplicity of choice. Small groups of the politically powerless like black people suffer marginalization as a consequence. Sops like LWT's *Black on Black* and *Eastern Eye* (both screened by Channel Four) and the BBC's *Ebony* are served up to pacify black critics.

A fourth television channel was founded in 1982 to provide space for minority perspectives. Like the launching of 'ethnic' programmes on television and radio, its advent was an admission of the failure of the mainstream to fully reflect all views. There is no substitute, however, for black-run programmes and press operating independently and confidently – outside but influencing the mainstream. The central flaw in white-run 'ethnic' programmes which attempt to straddle the demands of both the white and black audience is pointed up by the criticism from black commentators that they do not truly reflect the communities their trendy bosses claim they are for. Linton Kwesi

Johnson, of *Race Today*, notes that the initial black and Asian
enthusiasm for television's 'ethnic' programmes began to wane as it
became more and more apparent they lacked guts and did not reflect a
sense of commitment to the black community but rather opted for a
'safe' balanced approach. The contempt in which LWT's white
executives themselves held the shows was revealed in a leaked
confidential memo from *Black on Black* and *Eastern Eye* supremo
Jane Hewland who wrote of the programmes 'winning brownie points'
for the station. The secret document, called 'Strategy for Ethnics'
(*sic*), was drawn up in response to the inevitable crisis of confidence in
the programmes. Hewland said: 'The current personnel are increasingly unwilling to work on the shows.' Channel Four commissioning
editor Farrukh Dhondy's solution was to say goodbye to LWT and
buy in a new strand of black programmes, which promise to be
'committed', from the newly formed independent production company
Bandung.

The problem with *Black on Black* and *Eastern Eye* was that their
producers, Trevor Phillips and Samir Shah, never had any intention of
taking up the cudgels on behalf of Britain's black communities. Their
view of 'good television' in no perceptible way differed from LWT's.
They were clearly smitten by the South Bank sophistication of their
television betters and elders; falling into the trap of believing that
polished production was more important than content and commitment. *Black on Black* was preoccupied with giving large helpings of
light entertainment and trivial news coverage a middle-class gloss.
Defending this, Phillips said:

> *Black on Black* has worked hard to demonstrate that there is both
> depth and variety in the black community; and that however we
> speak and dress, wherever we work or live, we share a common
> heritage. After 400 years of being caged by other people's stereotypes
> of us, it seems madness that we should begin to impose new ones on
> ourselves.

The television bosses should have taken the bold step of giving us a
unified current affairs programme of interest to black Britons of
Afro-Caribbean *and* Asian descent. This should then have been
supplemented with 'specials' which focused on a particular culture and
light entertainment. The principal success of *Black on Black*, *Eastern
Eye* and *Ebony* was that they provided a seed-bed for black talent which

might not otherwise have been introduced to the industry. But even this process has its critics. Institute of Race Relations director A. Sivanandan claims middle-class black people with television aspirations formed themselves into industry lobby groups like the Black Media Workers Association (BMWA) with the intention of enhancing their own prosperity. The BMWA, founded in 1982, still exists but Sivanandan writes of its demise as

> the fall coming after the white media made room for them in ethnic slots – since when they have gone back to being Afro-Caribbeans and Asians. None of these give a fart for ordinary black people, but use them and their struggles as cynically as any other bourgeois class or sub-class. The BMWA, in the short period of its fight-to-get-into-Channel-Four existence, never did anything for the lower ranks of black workers or, for that matter, demanded to make political black plays or programmes that would have improved the lot of ordinary Afro-Caribbeans or Asians – unless exposing the foibles and manners of one's own people to white voyeurs.

Sivanandan's blunderbuss blast at black bandwagonners fails to pinpoint the reason for the formation of the BMWA – combating institutional racism in broadcasting and press, one of the most secure bastions of white, middle-class values and personnel. The BMWA's main fault is the absence of a coherent set of objectives but it has nonetheless won some concessions from Channel Four and unions like the ACTT and NUJ in regard to job and training opportunities. Leading lights in the association like Gary Morris say they set about dispelling the myths propounded by BBC and IBA employers – first, that too few suitably qualified black people apply for jobs and, second, that those given a chance did not prove professional enough. The BMWA ran a series of courses for black would-be broadcasters. Morris says: 'Training for us constitutes part of our attack on the white bias so firmly entrenched in the mainstream media industry.'

Institutional racism is much more insidious than the overt racism we experience daily in the news media. It is responsible for denying able black workers jobs in the communications industry. I believe, as someone who could be described as part of the black token presence in mainstream broadcasting, that the greater employment of black people is the key to eradicating the white media values which make a nonsense of the claim that Britain is a multi-racial, multi-cultural society. Mere goodwill which results in white liberals scheduling the minority slot 'ethnic' programmes fronted by company-minded black personnel cannot supplant the need for a substantial presence of *conscious* black media workers.

The need is for properly trained black workers both in the mainstream and running our own operations. The *Voice* newspaper, a black weekly, says there should be proportional representation. As London is more than 15 per cent black this figure should be reflected at all levels of the workforce of companies based in the capital. In a criticism which could relate to any British radio or television station, the *Voice* asks LWT: 'Why does a station that includes a large ethnic audience not have a comparable representation on its programmes? And why, after three years of black programmes, are there so few black behind-the-scenes technicians?' Gary Morris believes the only way you solve the appalling under-representation of black workers in the industry is by introducing American-style 'quotas'. Though race quotas in any way strictly enforced are illegal, one or two local authorities serving catchment areas with a large black population have established 'equality targets'. Hackney Council, for instance, aims to employ 35 per cent black staff in all departments. This system is correct because nothing is achieved without specific objectives. Equality targets must logically flow from the ethnic monitoring of a given workforce which shows up under-representation or no representation of black workers.

Ethnic monitoring – a necessity – is currently in vogue as the cornerstone of often otherwise empty broadcast industry equal opportunities policies. The spur was provided surprisingly by the Commission for Racial Equality who, in 1979, wrote to the BBC and four of the big ITV companies with large black audiences to get them to introduce such a programme of action. Six years later it is possible to record that, of the 15 ITV companies that exist (including Channel Four), just five had declared themselves 'equal opportunity' employers. They are Central, Thames, Granada, TV South West and LWT. The BBC and Channel Four fell into line some time later. Ethnic monitoring was launched incompletely at all but Thames. With some this meant just monitoring external applicants; the BBC only monitors those applicants called for interview.

Thames, which according to people like Channel Four's former black commissioning editor Sue Woodford has the best record on equal opportunities for women, introduced the most thoroughgoing method of external and internal ethnic monitoring following intensive and often protracted consultation with management, unions and their Equal Opportunities Committee. The progress, achieved over more than a year, was painfully slow because of stalling by the NUJ chapel and sections of the ACTT. Where the commitment to equal opportunities has moved beyond just lip-service, as at Thames, this has been at the insistence of groups of workers. Two pressure groups – a women's committee and a black/Asian committee – played leading roles. I founded what is understood to be the only such black workers' group in a broadcasting company after discovering that equal opportunities at Thames had previously meant solely combating the under-representation of women. There was no race dimension to the policy even though black people made up only just over one per cent of the staff.

Trade union resistance to such changes is well documented. Indeed, TUC general secretary Norman Willis was moved to warn: 'There is a danger that unions are losing the initiative to employers in this area and are running the risk of appearing to obstruct equal opportunities rather than press for them.' Unions must end employment practices, sometimes operated with the connivance of their officials, which act against the interests of black workers. These include 'word of mouth' recruitment, internal advertisement of vacancies and the insistence on unnecessary qualifications. For example, a Thames TV consultant, reviewing job opportunities for women, discovered the insistence on 'O' level maths and physics for camera operators. Yet many of the white men in the job themselves did not have these qualifications. When unions help draft company house agreements, they must insist on the inclusion of a clause which commits management to a programme of equal opportunities complete with targets. If these minimal measures are pursued with vigour then the old customs and practices which are discriminatory can be eradicated, opening the door to greater black employment. The TUC and CRE codes of conduct for employers are relatively feeble weapons in this battle, but they are a start.

It is easy for individual black 'success' stories in broadcasting like myself to sit back contentedly believing we have filled the vacuum created by union inactivity on equal opportunities by forming a black workers' committee which, like the BMWA, fights for black jobs. But the reality is that the struggle is on a much broader front. As Bennie Bunsee, a black employment specialist, states: 'We must combine the struggle for equal opportunities with that of the struggle against racist images in television and the media in general.'

Controller of BBC 1 Michael Grade also makes the link between equal opportunities in employment and programme-making. A new-generation BBC boss, Grade says there won't be any real change until more black people are employed behind the camera. He believes the BBC, with Moira Stewart reading the news, is not doing badly in front of the lens. But a few months previously the corporation's only two black women television reporters were sacked as part of a programme of staff cuts in news and current affairs. Furthermore, Grade, a defector from LWT, presided for more than a year over a comedy, *Mind Your Language*, he now accepts was racist. He says it was he who insisted its run should not be extended. But only after LWT had enjoyed 12 months of profits from the programme.

In television drama, the demand from progressives in unions and black actors themselves for 'integrated casting' as a means of tackling the problem, is gaining ground. This means that black actors are cast in all roles and not left to fill the merely stereotypical. Preethi Manuel found, in her research into the representation of black people in television drama, that black actors nearly always play black characters. Roles frequently occupied were as low-paid workers, students and law-breakers – for example as a garage mechanic in *Crossroads* (ITV), nurse in *Shroud for the Nightingale* (ITV), students in *Grange Hill* (BBC1), railway worker in *King* (BBC1), mugger in *The Gentle Touch* (ITV), armed robber in *The Bill* (ITV).

Black people are seldom cast in contemporary roles commanding respect. In *Play for Today – The Amazing Miss Stella Estelle* (BBC1), Mr Jones, the black headmaster, is positively portrayed. And in *The Brief* (ITV), Lisa is a black American peace campaigner. But both are supporting roles.

Job opportunities are considerably lessened by the absence of integrated casting. And even the handful of black actors who are in employment – 2.25 per cent of the total in television – have their job prospects eroded still further by the continuing crime of white actors being blacked up for key roles like Othello. Michael Bates played Rangi Ram in *It Ain't Half Hot Mum* (BBC). Black children under 12 were present in just five of the 643 programmes monitored by Manuel, though schools programmes and, to a lesser extent, commercials, are beginning to tackle the imbalance. Apart from anything else, in a multi-racial metropolis like London, it is good broadcasting practice.

Some critics argue that the picture in television and radio news and current affairs is grimmer. Two incidents of which I have practical experience serve to illustrate the point. The first involved National Front organizer and student Patrick Harrington. For months this fascist had a regular walk-on part on television news programmes because anti-racists at the North London Polytechnic barred his entry to the college. Journalists, failing even to observe the NUJ's guidelines on reporting fascists and thereby demonstrating the virtual impotence of the code, engaged Harrington in sterile dialogue. His comment on the actions of the anti-racist pickets. His response to the day's court ruling. Harrington, capitalizing on the exposure by smartening his dress and steering clear of his repugnant politics, became a credible 'aggrieved party'. Sent to interview Harrington, I took a different tack – news as a positive intervention into an issue. Why did his opponents find him so obnoxious? What did he think of black students on campus? Had he himself been involved in race attacks? The viewer was suddenly treated to a very different political animal. Black people were not citizens and therefore had no right to be educated at the poly. They should be repatriated as quickly as possible. Harrington finally snapped and ran off. The response from the authorities was equivocal. They would have to see a transcript before they could comment. The miscreant might be 'warned'.

The second incident involved the occupation of Camden Town Hall by Bengali families following a fatal fire at a local hostel. One of my crew members declined to operate his sound mike when I selected a Bengali woman for interview. He said she would not be able to speak English. I protested and the interview eventually went ahead. But the matter did not rest there. Community relations workers were within earshot and officially complained to Thames.

The incident was part of a condition which is endemic in the British news media – unthinking and instinctive racism. Indeed, it was this condition which was behind the myopia of those otherwise caring and concerned professionals who made a controversial *TV Eye* film about racial harassment on an East End council estate. The focus of *Racial Outlaws* was a group of vociferous white people who objected to the arrival of Asian families in their midst. A sobbing Rose McDonnell is shown being evicted by Newham Council after a court case in which her sons were found to have persistently harassed Asian neighbours. Voice-over remarks about the brutality of that harassment lacked the visual impact of the eviction. Equally, racist council tenants were shown at length angrily discussing the legal action taken against them by the Commission for Racial Equality because they had signed a petition demanding an end to the placement of Asians on the estate. It was this controversy which sparked the *TV Eye* film – not the catalogue of monstrous racial attacks endured by Asians settled in the area. The implication was that the CRE was out to restrict the right of free speech and debate, however obnoxious the arguments. Critics of the screening of *Racial Outlaws*, including establishment figures like the Bishop of Stepney, failed to persuade the omnipotent programme-editors to explain more fully the context of their images and the damaging impact they might have.

History lecturer Sneh Shah, commenting about a BBC2 *Newsnight* item, points up the lack of sensitivity. The report was prompted by the publication of a special study which showed that black and Asian communities are still heavily disadvantaged when it comes to housing and employment despite 20 years of race relations legislation. Instead of probing why this is, *Newsnight* focused on Asian arranged marriages.

It was presented as if this was the problem in the Asian community. If you put the two [the report's findings and arranged marriages] together the viewer gets the impression that while the Asian community may be suffering, the main reason why is because they have created those problems themselves.'

Journalists cannot be coy about identifying racial discrimination. The NUJ is clear in its code on race reporting – though the guidelines cannot be found in most newsrooms.

Professor Bhikhu Parekh states:

Media must be more sensitive about what they present, become more self-critical of their assumptions. We are operating today within the larger historical context of the history of racism. Given that back-cloth one must be particularly careful to avoid those unconscious stereotypes that one is bound to have imbibed through language, through words, through comics, through literature.

Real progress will depend upon greater pressure being exerted internally and externally by black people. We must fully realize our industrial, political and economic muscle. In the Labour Party this is beginning to happen through the establishment of an autonomous voice – black sections, in trade unions through the establishment of black members' groups and in the broadcasting industry through the emergence of black workers' committees. The pressure without is being applied more and more effectively by a plethora of important single-issue campaigns like CAPA, Newham Seven and organized groups of black parents around the country lobbying on education. The growing confidence in Britain's black communities must result in black outfits winning from the Home Office franchises to run community radio stations. Demand suggests there must also be all-soul/funk stations run by black operators. At present, pirates cream off white profit from black music. There should also be a central black programme-making department, styled on the existing education and religious units, in BBC TV and Radio for network and local use. Critics like the Black Londoners' Action Committee, formed to defend the BBC's longest-running black radio programme, have highlighted the need for the mighty BBC to give a lead by radically reallocating black and white licence-payers' money.

5. Portraying the peace movement

Richard Keeble

In the *Daily Mail* of 16 May, just after the start of the 1983 general election campaign, Paul Johnson, a former editor of the *New Statesman* born again as a Tory, devoted a long feature to 'The sinister truth behind CND's election sham'. It was a mixture of smear, misinformation, insult and crude political propaganda.

CND was depicted as a secret, highly professional outfit determined to destroy all the values the *Mail* held dear. CND's election briefing document, which merely presented strategies for convincing parliamentary candidates of the unilateralist case, was described as a 'hard-nosed, highly professional and rather frightening document'. Johnson gives the impression of an authoritarian leadership issuing orders to its meekly dutiful followers. And he concludes that the briefing document 'reflects the skills of very experienced political activists and confirms my impression that CND has been penetrated and may now be effectively dominated by the professional left'.

Given the Conservative bias of Fleet Street, the Labour Party and supporters of unilateral nuclear disarmament could have expected rough handling during the election campaign – but the brutality of the attacks which finally came exceeded the worst fears. Johnson's attack then cannot be dismissed as the eccentric outburst of a right-wing extremist; its muckracking style was to be a typical feature of Fleet Street's coverage of the disarmament issue during the election campaign.

In his essay 'The Doomsday Consensus',[1] E.P. Thompson described how the media largely suppressed the issue of the nuclear weapons build-up during 1979. Months before the December NATO meeting, the planned deployment was presented as if it was already assumed. 'Viewers and readers were informed that "Britain" had decided and it was a matter of consensus.' Informed debate and protests could hardly have developed in this climate. Whereas in 1979 the media suppressed the real disarmament debate through exclusion, four years later they achieved the same result through distortion, stereotyping and Paul Johnson-style misinformation.

Media coverage of the Falklands War[2] a year earlier undoubtedly set the tone for the later treatment of the election campaign. Most of Fleet Street was again to indulge in hysterical adulation of Prime Minister Margaret Thatcher. Those who questioned the Thatcher line were to be smeared as traitors, communists and left-wing extremists. Fleet Street's earlier hatred of 'the Argies' was to be echoed in the coverage of the Labour Party programme, especially its call for unilateral nuclear disarmament. And the militaristic mentality of the *Sun* was to find its most appalling echo in the cry of the comedian Kenny Everett, to a gathering of Young Conservatives at Wembley just before the election, 'Let's bomb the Russians.' He drew loud cheers from the audience.

Even without the Falklands War, defence and disarmament would have featured as major issues in the election campaign. A few months after the 1979 election, the NATO council meeting in Brussels decided to deploy 572 cruise and Pershing ground-launched nuclear missiles throughout various countries in Western Europe, supposedly to counter the Soviet build-up of SS-20 missiles. The Soviet intervention in Afghanistan in December 1979, the Iranian hostage crisis and the election in the United States in November 1980 of Ronald Reagan, an outspoken supporter of massive rearmament, all helped change the political climate dramatically. The temperature of the cold war rose – and in response a massive movement for peace and disarmament developed in Britain, on the Continent and then in the US, Canada and Australia.[3]

By the time of the 1983 general election the biggest peace movement seen in this country had grown. CND was claiming 250,000 members; in December 1982 some 30,000 women had embraced the base at Greenham Common. Unilateral nuclear disarmament had been espoused by a large number of groups – the Labour Party, the Liberal Party, the Scots and Welsh Nationalist Parties, the Ecology and Communist Parties, certain Churches, the TUC and many individual trade unions. A consensus was growing in Britain, if not in favour of full-blooded unilateral nuclear disarmament, as least in opposition to the government's 'defence' posture. A Marplan poll published in the *Guardian* of 27 May showed that more than a third of intending Conservative voters opposed the deployment of cruise and fewer than half favoured the purchase of Trident.

Despite the enormous growth of the peace movement not one Fleet

Street daily or Sunday newspaper backed unilateral nuclear disarmament. The *Guardian*, since the re-emergence of the peace movement in 1979–80, had given the most detailed and sympathetic coverage to the disarmament issue and it might have been expected to stand somewhat aside from the anti-unilateralist stampede that overran Fleet Street during the election campaign. This was not to happen. It followed meekly in the wake of the Street's quest to blow to pieces the peace movement. E.P. Thompson, in a post-election analysis, wrote angrily:

> Despite the ability of many of its staff and despite the political opinions of some of its columns the *Guardian* is a newspaper conducted with a factional editorial zeal in pursuit of simon – pure Atlanticist ideology whose objective was to split the democratic and peace forces of the country down the middle.[4]

The *Observer* and the *Sunday Times* gave reasonable coverage to the disarmament debate – the first just couldn't make the leap into the SDP fold on the Sunday before the election while the *Sunday Times* hovered between the SDP and the Conservatives. The *Mirror* group, traditionally Labour's best bet, hovered for a while before settling for Labour – but it remained unconvinced about Labour's commitment to unilateral nuclear disarmament. The rest of Fleet Street differed only in the degree of fanaticism in their opposition to unilateralism.

The great Polaris conjuring trick

The most blatant case of distortion and misinformation by a united Fleet Street came over its handling of the dispute within the Labour Party over Polaris. For over a week this was to dominate the news from Fleet Street and from the (supposedly neutral) radio and television channels. Significantly the Polaris issue was very low down in the priorities of the peace movement during the run-up to the election. After all, the nuclear submarine was expected to become obsolete within a few years. On the other hand, cruise, Pershing and Trident were expected to transform the strategic balance between the superpowers if they were deployed and thus the European peace movement's protests were largely directed at these three targets. Fleet Street, in effect, performed an amazing conjuring trick. It extracted the Polaris controversy from the densely worded 'bag' of the Labour Party manifesto – pushing the major cruise and Trident issues from the stage

– slated both party and peace movement, and then cast Polaris back
into oblivion.

In prolonging the Great Polaris Split the media knew they were
picking at a sore within the Labour Party. Various factions within the
party had not settled their differences over the issue by the time the
general election was called. But then none of the other major parties
were without their divisions on defence issues. The gap between the
Liberal Party and its SDP allies was enormous: the former being firmly
opposed, since 1981, to cruise (though separated from its leadership on
the issue); the latter being equally firm in its support for cruise. Yet this
potential source of conflict was almost totally ignored by the media.
Only on the day before the election did the *Times* lead: 'Jenkins and
Steel split over future of nuclear deterrent'. Equally there were
divisions in the Conservative ranks on defence issues but the media
made not the slightest attempt to expose them. Opposition was
certainly growing within the party to the automatic reliance on the
nuclear 'deterrent' and various schools were emerging: one preferred
greater commitment to 'conventional' arms, particularly at sea;
another supported substantial investment in cruise missiles which
could be launched from the sea if required; a group called TACT
(Tories Against Cruise and Trident) had even emerged in CND and
was quite articulate at the campaign's 1982 annual conference in
Sheffield.

Certainly the media did a wonderful job for the Conservative Party.
By the end of the week in question all political commentators were
convinced that a Labour defeat was inevitable and discussions moved
on to whether the Alliance could prevent Thatcher from gaining her
landslide. The media men (and significantly all the protagonists in this
Fleet Street saga were male) could feel well satisfied. The *Mail*, the *Sun*
and the *Express* completed their efforts by inventing reports that
Michael Foot had been replaced as leader by Denis Healey – thus
presenting the image of a party wobbling at the top.

Controversy began in earnest on 18 May when Denis Healey was
reported as saying that a non-nuclear defence policy as outlined in the
Labour manifesto in fact meant the 'non-first' use of nuclear weapons
and could involve the maintenance of Polaris. This would only be
removed if Britain received 'adequate concessions from the Soviet
Union'. Thereafter the story ran and ran.

On Tuesday 24 May, the *Daily Telegraph* had its front page lead
story: 'Labour in disarray over Polaris'. There was little development

on the earlier report. Mr Healey had reiterated his commitment to Polaris and Mr Foot had offered a full statement on the issue later in the day. It never appeared.

On Wednesday 25 May, the *Times*'s front page lead was 'Healey wins battle on Polaris with Foot', while the *Guardian* led on 'Labour totters on the brink over nuclear policy'.

Above all Mr Foot had failed to offer a clear-cut statement on Polaris and had laid himself open to allegations of fudging. The *Guardian* reported: 'He answered a Channel 4 question on the subject by saying that he could not visualize circumstances in which the weapon would be kept. But he went on to add that any British government would have to judge such matters in the circumstances of the time.'

During the evening of 25 May, the former Labour Prime Minister James Callaghan joined Healey in challenging the unilateralist content of the manifesto, saying that Britain's 'deterrent' should not be abandoned before gaining concessions from the Soviet Union. The following day Fleet Street responded with evident glee. 'Callaghan bombshell' shrieked the *Mail*; 'Callaghan wrecks Polaris repairs,' said the *Guardian*. 'Keep the bomb, Labour urged by Big Jim' was the *Sun*'s headline. Thereafter Labour seemed doomed. The *Times* leader writer put it: 'It is too late to conceal the fact that the party at its highest level is incapable of reaching an agreement on one of the most important not to say dangerous issues of the day. That is not what the country should be able to expect of a party presenting itself as an alternative government.' The controversy continued. The following day the *Times* front page led with 'Labour defence split could cost election.'

It has to be stressed that it was not the Conservative Party which exposed the Polaris controversy; the media (and in particular Anthony Bevins, political commentator of the *Times*) did the Tories' work for them.[5] Fleet Street revelled in Labour's agony. It might have been expected to welcome the shifts towards its own views of multilateralism signalled by Healey and Callaghan. It might have portrayed the Labour Party as coming to its senses, becoming a broad church to answer the mindless arms-increase consensus in the Conservative Party. Instead Fleet Street suddenly appeared concerned about Labour Party unity and Healey and Callaghan were portrayed as dividing the ranks.

Mindless Marxists and lefty loonies

Most Fleet Street newspapers, by making a simplistic distinction between multilateralism and unilateralism, ignored the various complex shades to both policies. Most importantly this meant they ignored the fact that opposition to cruise and Trident had extended to many 'multilateralist' Alliance and even Tory voters and portrayed disarmament Paul Johnson-style as an 'obsession' of the far Left. In this way they encouraged its dismissal as a peripheral, dangerous and seditious cause.

In the *Daily Telegraph* of 7 June, Douglas Eden, senior lecturer in history and politics at Middlesex Polytechnic and a member of the SDP's Council for Social Democracy, gave an SDP gloss to Johnson's rabid smears: 'The Campaign for Nuclear Disarmament is dominated by an extraordinary amalgam of left-wing organizations . . . A strong element in CND is evidently Euro-Communist, but Trotskyist shades of communism and more pro-Soviet influences are also prominent.'

The Labour Party was, in fact, often described by the right-wing press as the 'Marxist party'. All its policies, in particular those on disarmament, were smeared with the same brush. Thus an expert in Labour Party politics becomes a kremlinologist – at least according to the *Mail* on 31 May: 'It was apparent to Labour kremlinologists that something sensational had happened in the hierarchy the moment Mr Healey took centre stage at a press conference yesterday.' On 5 June, the *Mail on Sunday* commented on the 'modern, Marxist Labour Party'. And on 1 June the *Sun* described the Labour Party as using Healey to put his 'beetle-browed acceptable countenance on Labour's ugly face of rampant, triumphant Marxism'. The *Sunday Express* of 15 May commented: 'The main elements of the Labour programme are either crazy or Communist inspired.' A leader in the *Guardian* of 20 May identified unilateralism with the far Left in the Labour Party. On 3 June, Andrew Alexander in the *Mail* castigated Healey for supporting the 'scurrilous methods of the far Left and its manic mythology'. Thus the left wing and with it unilateralism inevitably became associated with lunacy, eccentricity, abnormality and deviance.

Mischief from Moscow

If you are a peace campaigner and not a loony left or mindless militant then you are a misguided oaf, a dupe of the Kremlin – at least according to much of Fleet Street in the run-up to the election. In a leader on

11 May, under a headline 'Dupes for peace', the *Mail* derided the Quakers' Northern Friends Peace Board merely for inviting over some Russian women. The Quakers were described as 'innocent pacifists' who had 'swallowed the Kremlin propaganda line'. Attached to this 'dupes of the Kremlin' slur is the message that demands for disarmament can only be in the interests of the Soviet Union – the biggest smear of all.

In the *Sun* of 11 May, its resident 'intellectual' John Vincent, Professor of Modern History at Bristol University, indulged in some extraordinary logistical twisting and turning – all in order to slur the Soviet Union. Under a headline 'Mischief from Moscow' he described the Soviet disarmament proposals (though they were detailed) as 'obvious phoneys'. The secretive nature of the Soviet administration is usually the subject of condemnation. Here Vincent surprised everyone by arguing that Russian proposals were only to be valued if they were secret. 'If Andropov really wanted a deal with America he'd do it in the utmost secrecy instead of telling the world what he was up to.' One subtle way in which Fleet Street discredits the Soviet Union is by describing its peace proposals as 'propaganda' whilst the West's initiatives are presented as genuine. Thus Alex Brummer in the *Guardian* of 17 May wrote of the US 'hoping to bring life into the deadlocked Strategic Reduction Talks to counter Russian propaganda efforts among peace movements'.

On 18 May the *Guardian* carried a fascinating article on its front page which showed that Fleet Street, in its bias against the Soviet Union, was merely mirroring the attitude of the Conservative government. Richard Norton-Taylor reported that the Royal Navy had failed to substantiate to the Advertising Standards Authority statements attributed to Admiral Sergei Gorschkov, the Soviet Naval chief, in a two-page recruitment advertisement in the *Sunday Times*. Gorschkov was quoted as saying: 'Soviet sea power, merely a minor defensive arm in 1953, has become the optimum means by which to defeat the imperialist enemy and the most important element in the Soviet arsenal to prepare the way for a Communist world.' But as Norton-Taylor reported, it was all a figment of the navy's fevered imagination.

How non-nuclear came to mean defenceless

Enmeshed within this anti-Soviet bias on Fleet Street was its constant distortion of the defence debate – presenting unilateralism as total disarmament leaving the country defenceless against the invading Russian hordes. One of the most outrageous statements on this theme was given by George Gale in the *Daily Express* of 3 June:

> Were Labour to be elected and carry out its defence policy as maintained in its manifesto, Western Europe would be handed to the Warsaw Pact on a plate. The work of our Communist traitors stretching back into the thirties would be finally consummated by the treachery of an elected British government. The Popular Front Michael Foot once supported, the Communist Party Denis Healey joined in pre-war Oxford would be vindicated and would triumph. The defence of the realm no less requires a Conservative victory.

Similarly, in the *Sunday Telegraph* of 29 May, Gordon Brook-Shepherd argued that the Labour Party disarmament policy threatened not only the security of Britain but the whole of Western Europe as well. Foot's policies, he said, 'represent in themselves a heavy blow at our allies and a free gift to our opponents'. John Vincent in the *Sun* of 2 June kept up the theme that 'unilateral nuclear disarmament equalled total disarmament'. 'What is Labour's defence policy? It all depends who you ask. Ask Michael Foot and it is to leave us defenceless within five years. Ask Neil Kinnock and the left and it is to leave us defenceless at once. Ask Denis Healey and he would consider keeping our nuclear defence so long as it is not modernized.' In the *Guardian* of 10 May, Alex Brummer reported inaccurately that Labour was threatening to quit NATO; on 13 May Peter Jenkins wrote in the same paper: 'The public seems massively opposed to unilateral nuclear disarmament which has the ring of defenceless neutralism about it.'

The Falklands no-go area

The calling of the general election for June 1983, a year before the government had completed its full term is best seen as a supreme act of public opinion manipulation – a cunning exploitation by Mrs Thatcher of the glory Fleet Street had showered on her since the victorious Falklands campaign. And significantly the Falklands factor remained the great unnameable during the election campaign.

While local Conservative candidates, with the encouragement of Central Office, continued to harp on the victory during the election campaign, Tories nationally clearly decided to play down the issue.

The Falklands became a no-go area in large sections of Fleet Street. An all-party Commons foreign affairs committee report was published during the run-up to the election which questioned the government's 'fortress Falklands' policy and called for a leaseback arrangement with Argentina, possibly allowing compensation to enable those islanders who found the solution unacceptable to resettle. Even this did not manage to disturb the conspiracy of silence over the Falklands issue. However, when Mr Healey accused Mrs Thatcher of 'glorying in the slaughter' and 'at this very moment lending the military dictatorship in Buenos Aires millions of pounds to buy weapons, including weapons made in Britain' he felt the full weight of establishment outrage. This was one of the rare occasions when the vital issue of the arms trade was raised during the campaign – but it was immediately submerged beneath an avalanche of attacks on Healey.

The call by Mr Neil Kinnock, labour's education spokesperson, for an inquiry into the sinking of the *General Belgrano*, the Argentinian cruiser, was subjected to serious analysis in the *Guardian*, the *Sunday Times* and the *Observer*. But it drew a typical condemnation from the *Sun*: 'The fact is that the Argentines were not seriously interested in talks before their invasion, during the invasion or even after the invasion was repelled.'

The disarmament no-go area

Just as the vital debate over the Falklands factor lay suppressed, so the real debate over defence and disarmament never left the ground during the election campaign. Important areas largely ignored by Fleet Street included:

- the link between Third World poverty, the arms trade and the superpowers' investment in the nuclear industry;
- the links between nuclear power and the nuclear arms industry;
- the growing support of trade unions for CND (the Society of Civil and Public Servants, the Institute of Professional Civil Servants and the AUEW/TASS – all of them with substantial numbers of members in the defence industry – called for cuts in defence spending during the election campaign);
- the strategy of non-violent direct action (NVDA) against cruise and US bases being carried out at Greenham Common, Upper Heyford and other Ministry of Defence installations throughout the country. The Ecology Party raised the issue of NVDA at the press conference

to launch its manifesto but like other fringe parties (Welsh and Scots Nationalist, Communist, Workers Revolutionary Party etc.) it was virtually ignored by Fleet Street;

● the relationship between the growing militarization of Britain, the army's presence in Northern Ireland and the British collusion with the apartheid regime in South Africa.

In the end: silence

This inevitably selective analysis of a few weeks in the life of Fleet Street has attempted to throw light on the way in which the national newspapers deformed and distorted political debate on a crucial issue at a crucial time. Once Margaret Thatcher was returned to power with her huge majority the way was prepared (bar the hiccup of the *Guardian*/Sarah Tisdall affair) for the arrival of cruise missiles – and a new, terrifying stage in the ever escalating arms race had been reached.

Largely forgotten during the election campaign, the Greenham Common women[6] suddenly returned to the front pages of the patriotic pops. The freaks with their lesbian love-ins and man-hating militancy, funny faces and dirty dungarees became a threat again and exposé stories appeared in the *Sun*, *Mail on Sunday* and *Express*. The latter even managed to discover a Soviet mole in their midst. But then once the missiles were safely installed Fleet Street united to drop the Greenham groupies out of the news.

Indeed since the 1983 election the peace movement has been effectively ignored by the media. Its urgent priorities have been stamped on and cast aside. When, on 6 February 1985, then Defence Secretary Michael Heseltine, dressed for combat, witnessed the destruction of the Molesworth peace camp by 2,000 soldiers and police the *Sun* gloated: 'Tarzan army takes peace camp: surprise raid kicks out smellies.' Once again damaging stereotypes and militarist assumptions are being reinforced; once again peace campaigners are being dismissed as deviants and outsiders; once again the very crudity of the language[7] reflects the deformed Fleet Street culture.

Truth, it is said, is the first casualty of war. Indeed, as the cold war intensifies, as the military men perfect their scenarios of destruction and as the militarization of our culture advances, truth lies battered and bleeding today in Fleet Street's nuclear bunker.

References and further reading

1. Reprinted in E.P. Thompson, *Writings by Candlelight*, London: Merlin 1980.
2. See Robert Harris, *Gotcha! The Media, the Government and the Falklands Crisis*, London: Faber & Faber 1983; and Glasgow University Media Group, *War and Peace News*, Milton Keynes: Open University Press 1985.
3. For media coverage of the disarmament issue 1980–82 see Crispin Aubrey, *Nukespeak: the Media and the Bomb*, London: Comedia 1982.
4. *New Statesman*, 24 June 1983.
5. An analysis of Bevins's role in the Polaris controversy appeared in the *Sunday Times*, 29 May 1983.
6. For media coverage of the Greenham Common women see Henry Porter, *Lies, Damned Lies and Some Exclusives*, London: Chatto & Windus 1984; Glasgow University Media Group, *War and Peace News*; and Lucinda Broadbent, 'Greenham Common: the Media's Version' in *Peace News*, 21 January 1983.
7. For the militarization of language see Paul Chilton, 'Nukespeak: Nuclear Language, Culture and Propaganda', in C. Aubrey (ed.), *Nukespeak*, and Richard Keeble and Margaret Melicharova, *A Language of Silence*, Peace Pledge Union 1983.

6. British broadcasting and Ireland

Liz Curtis

The outcry in the summer of 1985 over the banning of the BBC's *Real Lives* programme, 'At the Edge of the Union', about two Derry politicians, republican Martin McGuinness and loyalist Gregory Campbell, highlighted in a particularly dramatic way the question of British media coverage (or non-coverage) of the political situation in the North of Ireland.

There was little new about the ban – it was just one more episode in a shameful and repetitive story. The reason it provoked journalists into an unprecedented nation-and-a-half-wide strike was that this time the censorship procedure was so swift, so surgical and above all so public. The film had been completed and had been publicized at length in the *Radio Times* when the *Sunday Times* alerted the politicians to it on 28 July. Next day the home secretary demanded that the BBC ban it, and the gutter press began howling for censorship. On the Tuesday the BBC's governors caved in. It all took just three days.

British government attitudes

Until British troops went onto the streets of Derry and Belfast in August 1969, unionist politicians policed the radio and television coverage of Ireland. Together with the usually compliant broadcasting chiefs, they ensured, till the end of 1968, that virtually no criticism of their unjust, anachronistic 'province' reached the airwaves.

Then for a few months British politicians tried to press the unionist regime towards reform, and the media praised the civil rights movement, treating people like Bernadette Devlin as celebrities. But when British strategy changed, pushing ever greater numbers of British troops into a highly aggressive role in nationalist areas, so the media, especially the right-wing press, became increasingly hostile to the nationalist community. The results were sometimes ludicrous, as in this *Daily Sketch* report in June 1970: 'Behind the swirling haze of CS gas, the croak of the frog summons Londonderry to riot . . . It moves from street battle to street battle pouring out a continuous stream of hate, vilification and obscenities.'

The big assaults by British politicians and newspapers (and the inevitable Mary Whitehouse) against radio and television coverage began in 1971. The introduction of internment without trial was accompanied by torture of detainees and widespread brutality by British soldiers on the streets – they killed 11 civilians on 9 August alone, the day internment was introduced. Reports of such atrocities on radio and television infuriated Tory MPs, who demanded 'patriotic censorship', and Home Secretary Reginald Maudling, who summoned the chairpersons of the BBC and Independent Television Authority (the body that oversaw the commercial stations, forerunner of the Independent Broadcasting Authority).

Christopher Chataway, the minister responsible for broadcasting, publicly lectured the broadcasters not to treat the 'soldier' and 'murderer' as moral equals. Lord Hill, chairperson of the BBC governors, agreed: 'The BBC and its staff abhor the terrorism of the IRA and report their campaign of murder with revulsion . . . as between the British army and the gunmen, the BBC is not and cannot be impartial.'

Since the start of internment, the BBC had censored numerous items including an in-depth programme on the IRA, an interview with released detainee Michael Farrell, and a report on the nationalist 'Alternative Parliament', as well as news of several incidents showing the British army in a bad light. Lord Hill's statement, which was soon echoed by the Independent Television Authority, formalized the situation, publicly committing the BBC to a biased and selective treatment of events in the North, in which the views and experiences of a large part of the nationalist community were taboo.

The Vietnam parallel

The particular fear of the British establishment at the time was that critical coverage of the British army would sap morale in the military and back home. Lieutenant-Colonel 'Mad Mitch' Mitchell, Tory MP and veteran of earlier colonial wars, for instance, accused the BBC of 'contributing towards IRA objectives by undermining the will of the home population to fight in Ulster'.

The fear was real. In September 1971 an opinion poll in the *Daily*

Mail showed that 59 per cent of British people wanted the troops brought home. Politicians and pundits invoked the alarming example of American television coverage of the war in Vietnam, which was being widely blamed (or credited, depending on your viewpoint) for the enormous growth of the anti-war movement.

The US authorities effectively spiked the anti-war movement not by censoring television coverage, but by 'Vietnamizing' the war, taking 'our boys' out of the front line (thus decreasing the number of coffins on the homeward-bound planes) and replacing them with locally recruited forces. In the mid-seventies, the British began to follow the same policy; 'Ulsterization', in the Six Counties, and the decline in the number of British troops was accompanied by a decline in British public interest. (The RUC and UDR, after all, are not considered by the British to be 'their boys', and their deaths have little impact in Britain.)

In effect, the Ulsterization of the 'security' situation, plus British governments' abandonment of the attempts at solution with an 'Irish dimension', helped to promote the Ulsterization of information. From about 1974, following the collapse of Sunningdale, Ireland dropped out of the British headlines. Since then, it has featured prominently only when British politicians wanted to promote a particular development – such as the 'peace people' of 1976 – or when the scale of republican resistance has made it impossible for the media to ignore the situation.

During the 1981 hunger strike, for instance, when Mrs Thatcher and others attacked the television companies for the amount of coverage given to the hunger strikers' funerals, the BBC's then Director General Sir Ian Trethowan defended his organization by saying, 'The irritation of many viewers at being shown so much about Sands was entirely understandable, but however much they disliked it, the Sands affair became a major international event which had to be reported to the British public.'

Within the North, however, there is an abundance of information from a variety of political perspectives. The radio and television companies look at events from a pro-British/Alliance Party/middle-class perspective. But they produce much more news and analysis of Six County politics, including statements from and interviews with Sinn Fein, and examinations of 'sensitive' issues such as plastic bullets, than do the British national media. Indeed, the Six County broadcasting companies have little alternative but to report fairly fully, because otherwise they would have no credibility with their audience, which is also receiving news from other sources, including local papers and, importantly, direct experience.

Internal censorship

The quality and quantity of television coverage of the North has also been reduced by the stringent internal censorship procedures operated by the television companies since at least 1971. These special rules for covering Ireland are laid down in the BBC's handbook for journalists, the *News and Current Affairs Index*, under the heading 'Coverage of Matters Affecting Northern Ireland', and in the Independent Broadcasting Authority's *Guidelines* handbook for the commercial broadcasting companies.

The system, which so far applies to no other political issue, is often called 'reference upwards' or 'managerial censorship'. Basically this means that top bureaucrats keep close control over all programmes dealing with Ireland. Reporters and producers, overwhelmingly white, male and middle-class (and, in the BBC, vetted by MI5 to weed out progressives), are normally trusted to make the 'right decisions'. But when it comes to Ireland no one is trusted.

Producers, editors and reporters have to 'refer up' all ideas for programmes on Ireland to top management, including, in the BBC, the Controller Northern Ireland, and have to continue to consult top management during the making of the programme. In ITV, programmes have to be referred to the management of the television company concerned, and then to the Independent Broadcasting Authority. In both BBC and ITV, programmes which are 'sensitive' – mainly those critical of the British authorities or giving time to republican politics – have to be viewed by top officials before transmission. The BBC's rules at the time of the *Real Lives* drama did not require reference to the Board of Governors, but the governors' action in banning that film raised the fear that reference to them would in future become the norm, with further stifling effects on the coverage.

In the course of this 'reference upwards' procedure, numerous programmes or items have been banned, cut, delayed or altered. From 1971 onwards, nearly 50 programmes are known to have been affected. They include current affairs programmes, plays and even pop music: in 1981 the BBC banned the Police rock group's video for their single *Invisible Sun*, which showed Six County street scenes of graffiti, youths, and British soldiers, from *Top of the Pops*. They include historical documentaries, such as Kenneth Griffith's film on Michael Collins banned by the commercial network in 1973; portraits of the lives of nationalist people, such as a film about the Short Strand district of Belfast banned by the BBC in 1977; plays and documentaries dealing with torture and other unsavoury British activities; and, perhaps not surprisingly, a projected programme for the BBC's 'access' slot, *Open Door*, which was to have examined British media coverage of Ireland!

The 'reference upwards' procedure, and the knowledge that Ireland spells trouble, also acts as a deterrent to career-conscious television journalists, many of whom are especially vulnerable because they are employed on short-term contracts. For every programme that gets banned, there are probably 20 that are never made in the first place.

Republican interviews

As well as the general 'reference up' rules, there are extra-tight rules for interviews with members of 'terrorist organizations' – which in practice means banned organizations – and with people 'who are or may be associated with such organizations'. Since the UDA, the largest loyalist paramilitary group, is legal (as is, of course, the paramilitary wing of the British government), these rules mainly restrict access to republican organizations. In the BBC, reporters wishing to interview members of the IRA or INLA have to ask the permission of the Director General both before doing the interview and before transmission. Reporters in the commercial companies have to consult their top management, who in turn have to ask permission of the Independent Broadcasting Authority.

Since 1979 there have been no interviews with spokespersons for the IRA and INLA, and no film of IRA or INLA members in action. (The only partial exception was a *Panorama* film about the issue of extradition, shown in 1982, which featured a number of people living in the 26 Counties who had escaped extradition by claiming membership of the IRA or INLA.)

This *de facto* total ban was the product of major rows over two BBC projects in 1979. In July an interview with an INLA spokesperson, transmitted by *Tonight*, provoked Mrs Thatcher (backed by Labour's Merlyn Rees) into 'lashing' and 'blasting' the BBC over its 'appalling error', as the papers put it. Then in November a planned film by *Panorama* on the IRA sank without trace after news leaked out that the team had filmed an IRA roadblock in the County Tyrone village of Carrickmore, sending Mrs Thatcher once more into apoplexy and reducing the BBC governors to 'giving their customary imitation of chickens running around with their heads cut off', as a BBC trade union journal put it. The police demanded – and got – the film from the BBC. The BBC management sacked the editor of *Panorama* from his post: he was reinstated after National Union of Journalists' branches threatened a strike. The Attorney General, Sir Michael Havers, investigated both the INLA interview and the Carrickmore film, and reported that there was enough evidence to prosecute the journalists under Section 11 of the Prevention of Terrorism Act for 'withholding information'. He refrained from doing so, probably because a furore about press freedom would have ensued, but the threat remained.

'Balance' and hostile interviews

In addition to the rules on procedures, there are conventions, which have been spelled out by BBC executives over the years, as to the content and character of programmes on Ireland. The first is that programmes featuring nationalist or republican views must also include the opposite view. So while British or unionist politicians, or pro-British figures such as Gerry Fitt, can appear unopposed, Sinn Fein representatives must be 'balanced' by people expressing the pro-British or unionist viewpoint.

The second convention is that all republican interviewees – whether members of military or political organizations – must be treated as 'hostile witnesses'. This means that the interviewee is questioned aggressively, often with frequent interruptions. The interviewer repeatedly challenges or even contradicts statements made by the interviewee. Where the interview is part of a film, it is often presented in a hostile context. Television films about Gerry Adams, for example, are usually done in this style.

These conventions, together with the 'reference up' procedures, are the way the BBC ensures that the coverage is moulded to fit its pro-unionist, anti-republican stance. In 1980 Richard Francis, a senior BBC executive, using words which were echoed time and again during the *Real Lives* uproar in 1985, wrote:

Nobody involved in the journalistic coverage of terrorism is other than sympathetic to the victims or repelled by the perpetrators of terrorist crimes . . . Not only do they get very much less coverage than those who pursue their aims legitimately, but the very manner and tone that our reporters adopt makes our moral position quite plain.

The BBC governors objected to the *Real Lives* film because in their view it was not sufficiently anti-republican. The *Times* reported on 3 August 1985:

They felt the portrayal of Mr Martin McGuinness, widely believed to be the Provisional IRA chief of staff, dandling a baby on his knee in his front room while being symapthetically interviewed, was disturbing.

The clinching factor was that there were no clips of the consequences of IRA violence cut into the interview to illustrate the background to Mr McGuinness's apparently moderately expressed views. The only violence depicted were scenes of Royal Ulster Constabulary policemen clubbing Republican demonstrators with batons.

In September 1985 the BBC announced that the film would, after all, be shown, but with alterations. These changes accommodated the governors' criticisms: a caption on Sinn Fein's recent election successes would be amended to state that they won 'only' 12 per cent of the votes cast, and the film would now include gruesome footage of the aftermath of the IRA's 'Bloody Friday' bombings in 1972. There was, of course, to be no additional material on killings by British forces or loyalists, who together have been responsible for some 38 per cent of the deaths since 1969, nor on the political and social violence suffered by nationalists under the present political set-up.

The British way of censorship

Way back in 1972, a broadcasting union official complained to the BBC that the 'checks and balances' on Irish coverage

were becoming as effective as censorship, probably more effective because they were not much known outside the circles immediately involved, were superficially merely an intensification of normal safeguards, and were too vague and distant a target for public criticism.

This hidden censorhip has been a classic British solution to the problem of how to censor without appearing to do so. Successive British governments have refrained from bringing in direct censorship along the lines of Section 31 in the 26 Counties. This option is available in existing British law, but the establishment fears – justifiably, as the international outcry over the *Real Lives* ban proved – the impact of such a step on Britain's reputation as a 'haven of free speech'.

When in 1971 rampant right-wingers proposed formal censorship, operated either by the state or by the broadcasting companies, BBC chiefs rejected this mainly on the grounds that it would undermine their credibility. Instead, they said, they were maintaining 'a scrupulous editorial watch' on programmes on Ireland. Sections of the military shared this view, as did the *Times*, which argued that censorship would help the IRA and 'would mean that no fact, no assessment offered by British television, radio or newspapers would be free of the taint that it had been presented under government supervision'.

At the start of 1972 Home Secretary Reginald Maudling tried to stop a BBC talk-in called *The Question of Ulster* by publicly telling the BBC that the show if transmitted 'could do serious harm'. The pressure was so blatant that the BBC felt obliged to go ahead with the programme since, as the *Financial Times* observed, 'as an independent public corporation it could not be seen to give in to political pressure'.

Since then, the politicians have kept the broadcasters under control by less direct pressure. Some have made private requests to senior executives to alter planned programmes (a method advocated by Merlyn Rees). Others, aided by the press, have created huge public uproars whenever the television companies overstepped the mark. Labour's former Northern Ireland Secretary Roy Mason was a leading proponent of this bullying approach, as is the present Prime Minister Mrs Thatcher.

Not surprisingly, both the BBC and the IBA have repeatedly responded to political pressure by tightening up their internal censorship procedures. Both the BBC and the commercial television network are very susceptible to government blandishments. The BBC's governors, who appoint the director-general, are government appointees, as are the members of the Independent Broadcasting Authority. The BBC's recently retired 'national governor for Northern Ireland', appointed by Merlyn Rees, was Lady Faulkner, Unionist and widow of Brian, who was replaced by Dr James Kincade, another unionist. The IBA's 'member for Northern Ireland' is Mrs Jill McIvor, wife of Basil, another former Unionist member of Stormont. (Jill McIvor is also a member, with special responsibility for Northern Ireland, of the panel appointed by Home Secretary Douglas Hurd to advise him on the selection of groups to be granted community radio licences.) Further, the government decides the size of the BBC licence fee – and the Tories are threatening to force the BBC to accept commercials – while the IBA awards the franchises to the 'independent' TV companies, which are therefore anxious to avoid trouble.

Real Lives

The *Real Lives* drama was caused in part because then Home Secretary Leon Brittan and the Chairman of the BBC governors', Thatcherite appointee Stuart Young, apparently did not understand the roles they were supposed to play in the charade. As a result, to put it bluntly, they blew it, causing consternation on every side. 'BBC World Service derided abroad as a state organ', announced the *Times*, while the *Financial Times* mourned: 'The next time an enterprising BBC team produces an exposure of slavery in the Middle East or gulags in the Soviet Union, foreign regimes will be able to tell their own people that the corporation is an instrument of the British government.'

Virtually all the protestors with access to the British media (that is, people from the centre of the Labour Party rightwards) lamented not that yet another film on Ireland was being suppressed, but that the actors had ignored the rules of the game. Neil Kinnock, and the National Council for Civil Liberties, complained that the ban had given more publicity to 'terrorists' than transmission would have done. (The NCCL made the extraordinary recommendation that, 'The government should rely on the BBC's usual high standards of impartiality to reveal terrorists for the violent men [*sic*] they are.' This might make an interesting starting point for a student essay!) National Union of Journalists spokespersons proclaimed their detestation of 'terrorism' and that they fully accepted the existing internal 'guidelines'. David Owen of the Social Democratic Party said the film should 'never have gone further than the cutting room'. Many of those who objected to the *Real Lives* ban will doubtless connive at censorship in the future, provided it is less obviously done.

What can we do?

The broadcasting chiefs of today are, with hardly an exception, timid guardians of the status quo rather than brave crusaders in the cause of truth. Until, therefore, there is a major shift in British government policy towards Ireland, we can expect no startling change in the broadcasters' approach.

It is still worth complaining and criticizing programme-makers – or on occasion encouraging and praising them – because this can sometimes stir a producer or reporter into action. But the main function of protests, if made publicly, is probably to help to develop among viewers a collective 'crap detector', so that we are better able to assess the coverage as we watch, and to some extent immunize ourselves against its habitual biases.

But developing an awareness of the shortcomings of the media does not of itself fill the gaps in the coverage. For that, it is necessary to turn to alternative sources of information. In the case of Ireland, there are plenty: newspapers and magazines from both parts of Ireland and from a variety of perspectives, publications from concerned organizations in Britain, as well as videos and films. You can even phone Belfast 8060 and listen to Downtown Radio, the Belfast commercial station, which broadcasts the news every hour.

Unlike many other territories in which British governments have waged war, Ireland is not distant either in language or in geography. The failures of the national media are not a sufficient reason for British people to say now, or in the future, that they 'don't know' what is being done there in their name. At the end of the day, they need only catch a boat and go and find out for themselves.

Further reading

Campaign for Free Speech on Ireland, *The British Media and Ireland: Truth, the First Casualty*, London: Information on Ireland 1979.

Rex Cathcart, *The Most Contrary Region: The BBC in Northern Ireland 1924–1984*, Belfast: The Blackstaff Press 1984.

Liz Curtis, *Ireland – The Propaganda War: The British Media and the 'Battle for Hearts and Minds'*, London: Pluto Press 1984.

A Resources Guide to the North of Ireland, London: Information on Ireland 1985.

Philip Schlesinger, Graham Murdock and Philip Elliott, *Televising 'Terrorism': Political Violence in Popular Culture*, London: Comedia 1983.

7. Living with the media – two views

A landscape of lies*
Bel Mooney

One of the surest signs of age is the recognition of change; suddenly the 'I remember when' is no longer the granny's prerogative, but the voice of your own experience. This melancholy reflection was occasioned by the odd sensation of publishing a collection of journalism and being interviewed by cordial fellow journalists, who asked, 'Have you seen many changes since you began your career?' Compared with the likes of James Cameron, Mary Stott and even Mr Levin-in-his-prime, I am as a presumptuous little Beaujolais Nouveau beside an excellent Château Latour 1973. Fact: I have lived but 37 years, and 15 of them have been spent plying my trade. I have had a good time – as the bishop said to the whore – but was it honestly worth the *strain*?

Only just. 'Yes,' I murmur, smoothing the Age-Zone Controller into my cheeks, 'journalism seems to have changed a lot since I was a gel, broaching the towers of Fleet Street with my ideas and a few ideals as well.' Then, I believed in the freedom of the press; now I recognize the slickness of the propaganda machine. The view has shifted. Journalism used to mirror a world of worried reality; now it paints a landscape of lies.

Do you recall the old colour supplement debate? It went like this: the magazines carried much of the finest writing and photo-journalism, often about uncomfortable subjects like war and poverty, but was it morally correct for such horrors to be shown in the context of glossy advertisements? The question would be irrelevant now. From my cupboard I pull a *Sunday Times Magazine*, dated October 1975. It contains five good, well-written features (including Clive James on

*This article first appeared in the *Listener*, 19 July 1984.

Monet), a magnificent set of anthropological photographs by Leni Riefenstahl, and a jolly guide to the pop business. The issue has a vitality which stems from the quality of the written word. Now the pre-eminence of the word in such magazines has gone; in both style and subject-matter, there is little difference between the editorial matter and the advertisements which pay for it.

The point is this: then, editors wanted writers like me to get out there with eyes and ears open, and tell it like it was. Now, they do not care a hoot. In November 1971 the great magazine *Nova* printed 10,000 glorious words of hard reportage by Peter Martin, called 'Brixton: the ghetto Britain built'. One of the strap headlines warned: 'By the year 2000, Britain will probably have a black helot class unless the education system is radically altered.' In 1980 I asked a quality Sunday newspaper to let me write an article about Brixton, to be called 'From the front line'. They did not want it. In April 1981 Brixton erupted, and then the reporters had to flock, to see the black men shout.

That *Nova* article was in the finest tradition of prescient reporting, and now it would not find a home. It was not that by writing about reality you thought you could cure its ills; simply that the journalist's job was to be the reader's source of information about the world. But now all the emphasis is on image and entertainment, and the sharpest comments come from the columnists who squawk in their cages like all-purpose parrots, safely barred from the real world. Style is the great seducer: faces, anecdotes, gossip, stars, products and leisure – all of which make our masters much money. The shift has happened in all journalism: in television it shows in the softer approach to documentaries, and the director's assumption of the reporter's role because (they say) it is the pictures that matter, not the words; the faces, not the ideas.

Beguiling all that may be, but it is a lie. The world is not like that, nor do most people want it to be. Yet newspapers assume that the 'punters' want entertainment, and treat them as suckers and dupes. Popular papers have lost all sense of what newspapers are for (like the reporting of news), and bamboozle their readers with bingo and cheap titillation – betraying them in the process. So when a pressure group, the Maternity Alliance, produces a disturbing report on the poor diet of low-income pregnant women and the danger to their unborn babies, *not one tabloid paper reports it*. I can see the eye-catching feature: Esther Ranzen, say, offering a quiz and advice on cheap good menus . . . But no. All those newspapermen are interested in is the private life of female tennis stars. Yet women go hungry in the Britain of the 1980s, and not to report that is a lie as bad as the terminological inexactitudes which regularly haul papers like the *Mail* and the *Sun* before the Press Council.

It is a sad experience to meet a group of the reading public (on *Any Questions?*, for example), and see their distaste for journalism. Papers do not tell the truth, they say, and all journalists are dishonest. In New York, just recently, the intelligentsia debated the Alastair Reid case: the *New Yorker* writer admitted he regularly made up quotes and fabricated stories. In 1981, a *New York Times* journalist was fired when it was discovered that he wrote a 'composite' (i.e. untrue) piece about Belfast, and, in the same year, the *Washington Post* had to return the Pulitzer prize it won for a fabricated story about drug addicts. So people no longer believe what they read in the papers, while newspaper editors justify their move away from responsible reporting towards mere entertainment by saying that the public 'doesn't want to know'. It is a pernicious circle of deception.

In an interesting piece in the *Guardian* recently (ironic, in the light of subsequent developments), Mike Molloy, the editor of the *Daily Mirror*, blamed the downward-spiralling of the tabloids on the ruthlessness of their proprietors, who want to destroy the opposition, not just compete with it. Maxwell has already made threatening noises against Murdoch; in such circulation wars, it is the readers' needs which are forgotten. Thus the men who own our newspapers are good, faithful servants of the prevailing political philosophy – if that is what we must call Mrs Thatcher's arid monetarism of the heart. The tantalizing promise that you, too, can Get Rich Quick (by crying 'bingo' or opening your Portfolio) is not just a distraction; it is a deception which mirrors the collective Cabinet belief that if you get on your bike and stand on your own two feet at the same time, all manner of things shall be well, and you need not ask for help, merely a medal. So the largely right-wing press, in giving up its responsibility to fairness and truth, shores up the establishment, and its lies are the pillars of the state.

H.G. Wells wrote: 'Lies are the mortar that binds the savage individual man into the social masonry.' But the masonry is crumbling, split by huge cracks. Mass unemployment, large-scale poverty, children barely educated, a heroin epidemic, terrible despair, apathy, and fear of the future . . . the 'individual man' is not savage, though he might well be, with his back to the wall. Mark Twain's three kinds of lies were 'lies, damned lies and statistics'. In the newspapers which reflect the punk conservatism of this England, the lies are those of complacency and ignorance; the damned lies twist words, so that inflexibility and ruthlessness are called statesmanship; and the statistics are manipulated daily to deceive the 'individual man' into thinking that it is getting better all the time – for someone.

Cash bonanzas and pretty pin-ups are just the icing on the cake, and would be tolerable (for, yes, let us sell newspapers) if the mixture beneath were rich, well made and nutritious. That is what the readers deserve. The person on the Clapham omnibus has a thirst (and this I believe with every fibre of my being, and when I stop believing it I want to be battered to death with my Smith-Corona) for information, for insight into this benighted world, and for access to his/her fellow human beings, even if only through the written word. People want to be told the truth, because they are much *better* than newspaper owners and executives (and television moguls) think they are.

You see – still crazy after all these years. But the night editor is hard at work on the back bench, and we must have some sex on the front page, and spike that story because it is too worthy and nobody wants to see pics of black babies any more, and there must be no hard-luck stories in the new *Sunday Times*, because the young professionals don't like it, and make up the quote from the grieving widow, and fill the spread with the bingo winner's picture . . .

No wonder this old lady wants to retire. No wonder she kneels each night, rephrasing Chesterton in a heartfelt prayer for journalists:

> From all the new fear teaches,
> From lies of tongue and pen,
> From all the easy speeches
> That comfort selfish men,
> From sale and profanation
> Of our most precious Word –
> Deliver us, good Lord.

Union world
Nell Myers

This contribution comes from the heart. Over a period of two years, the National Union of Mineworkers, and I as press officer, lived in constant confrontation with Britain's mass media, and discovered much in the process.

In the miners' strike of 1984–5, mining communities began the process of combining NUM experiences with those of families (and especially of women within families). The crucial intervention of women's experience (with its often muted history of knowing the personal as political) in industrial struggle where the parameters are set by men's experience, is vital to the development of trade unionism itself, as the NUM has begun to discover.

The collective experience of Britain's mining communities inevitably fuelled the intense anger which was levelled at the media during the strike.

What women and men actually experienced during that year was not, for the most part, reported – with all its causes and ramifications – by press or broadcasting. Worse than that, mining families observed day by day the ways in which broadcasting and press actually lied about the very nature of the struggle in which they were engaged.

Because their own experiences were also building a day-by-day framework of references and understanding, however, they knew the lies and distortions for what they were. No need to ask: 'What is real, what is the truth?' Their own circumstances gave them the answer.

Trade unions must equip themselves to participate in building those frameworks: constructions from which to launch campaigns that do not shut out real contradictions, but which instead draw strength from using those contradictions properly. Both the fight for the local authorities and the miners' strike have provided a reminder of this perspective.

Demonology is a device used by those who attempt hegemony; in societies such as ours it is used very effectively through the channels of mass communications. The National Union of Mineworkers and its president in particular have over the last few years been uniquely subjected to media-nurtured and propagated demonology, deployed in an unremitting attempt to discredit the NUM's fight to save the British coal industry.

What is bizarre is the extent to which the media's use of this instrument against the NUM is both admitted and acknowledged across the political spectrum. But few people, I believe, are truly aware of how far into the most active consciousness the toxin seeps. We know it's there of course. But our response is simplistic. We become protective – in some cases, even idolatrous – of those individuals who are particular objects of media attack; this protectiveness is understandable but it does not touch the essential problem. Arthur Scargill has often pointed out that he could become a hero of the tabloids tomorrow (well, maybe next week), if only he would from this moment suggest that the fight to save Britain's nationalized coal industry could not be won; if he were just to suggest that the miners' strike of 1984–5, heroic and admirable though it was, had not been either practical or winnable – that it had not been worth the hardships endured and the sacrifices made by mining families and communities.

It is Scargill's ferocious defence of principles on which history offers no example of honourable compromise which renders him so infuriating to those who have become his enemies (and because he is inseparable from the NUM, enemies of the union's struggle). Those enemies include, naturally, the present government and those who own and control the means of mass communication. Hence the inclusion of Arthur Scargill in the demonology.

I am not implying that there have been no decent interviews, features, etc., with radio and televison which, given the nature of electronic communications, perform much better than the press. But examples of honourable media treatment are essentially a by-product of demonology itself. They confirm the nature of a crusade against the NUM – which is to isolate an element (in this case, Arthur Scargill) important in one way or another to a particular struggle, concept or organization which challenges the hegemony of the state.

Demonology as a weapon to arouse fear, hostility and forms of hysteria is not of course confined to use against trade unionism nor against groups on the Left; ask the Women's Advisory Committee of the Greater London Council about it; or look at its deliberate use to create an amorphous panic in attacking heresies such as homosexuality. (For a chronicle of AIDS demonology, read '*J'Accuse*' by Andrew Lumsden, *New Statesman*, 19 July 1985.)

Journalists, printworkers, television and radio technicians are for the most part trade unionists, working (like other employed people) in even more insecure situations. During the miners' strike, media workers, through their unions, gave and gave to NUM branches and mining communities: food, money, holidays – provided by SOGAT, NGA and NUJ chapels as well as by ACTT and ABS members up and down the country. Their generosity was very impressive and deeply moving; it forged bonds of friendship and comradeship which have helped to transform people's lives.

But for generosity and moral support to cohere into solidarity there must be a two-way exchange. In the long term, the sympathy of media workers for the miners (overwhelming as it has been) will be wasted *unless* journalists, printers and broadcasting technicians come to terms as trade unionists with the way in which their waged labour is used to damage the movement of which they themselves are, consciously or potentially, a crucial part.

Since the autumn of 1983, the NUM has been involved with the media unions, NUPE and the Campaign for Press and Broadcasting Freedom among others in a project set up to combat media distortion by exploring common ground among trade unionists working in the media and those outside. It is a forum which has proved valuable on a number of occasions – but which needs to be *used* much more than at present.

During the miners' strike, the National Union of Journalists (NUJ) provided a key example of solidarity. The NUJ donated funds to NUM areas to be used as those areas saw fit in coping with media bias. In Durham, the NUM used that donation to employ a journalist whose skills and principles were put to use in the most practical and beneficial way possible: as a full-time press officer with responsibility for producing a regional coalfield newspaper.

It is true that the problems of media bias and distortion remain as great as ever in Durham. But the NUJ's act of solidarity has sparked off in that coalfield the organization of communications: something which is crucial to the NUM and to mining communities.

The NUJ's gesture to the miners during the strike was a particularly poignant one. The greatest difficulty trade unions face in terms of dealing with the media is with journalists themselves.

Media trade unions and their members at chapel level need support from other unions, and solidarity from the entire labour movement.

Trade unionists outside the media industry have only a general idea of how matters are inside it. But we know of the use of new technology to attack jobs and conditions; the right to strike is also under assault.

On a more esoteric but equally crucial level, we know that censorship is a matter of such grave concern to broadcasting journalists that they have been prepared to take industrial action in defence of civil liberties relating to the public's right to know. But these are also issues which affect the entire trade union movement, and trade unionists have a responsibility to bring them to the movement as a whole.

How else can common cause be made, solidarity built, and the world around us transformed?

8. The media and the state

Colin Sparks

There is no question but that the government influences the way in which the media reports events. However, the government is not the state, and the influence of the state is a slightly different question.

The government is a fairly small, although very influential, body of people. The state, on the other hand, is very large indeed. It is staffed by 'professional' people who owe their position not to any election, popular or otherwise, but to the allegedly rational internal bureaucratic norms of the sector of the state for which they happen to work. Although in theory the government is supposed to direct and control the state, the fact that they are two such different organizations, one small and transitory, the other large and permanent, means that any such direction will, in practice, be difficult. Indeed, there are substantial sections of the state machine, for example the judiciary, which are even formally independent of the government, and others, like the social services departments, whose first responsibility is to local rather than national government. There is plenty of scope for differences of strategy or opinion between the state and the government.

The row over the *Real Lives* programme illustrates that very clearly. The BBC is, on any rational account, a state broadcasting institution. The government has legal powers which enable it to direct the BBC, but much more important are the facts that they finance the institution and appoint its Board of Governors. However, the employees of the BBC have an integrated hierarchy (modelled on the civil service and vetted by the secret service) and a professional ideology which continue to operate whether the government is Tory, Labour or whatever. (It is worth noting in passing that the commercial television companies, and for that matter the cable companies, operate even more directly under state direction. The IBA has a legally defined control over the ITV companies and can determine the content of broadcasts. It has been said that the ITV network is a nationalized industry in everything except the destination of the profits.)

Nobody would wish to deny that governments do exercise some direction over the state (the example I have just cited clearly shows that they *can*), but it would be naive to imagine that this is either complete and permanent or entirely one-way. The state in this instance was able to stand up to the government and to defy its wishes.

The state and government acting either in unison or at cross-purposes can be said to influence the mass media in six roles: the patron; the censor; the actor; the masseur; the ideologue; and the conspirator. Let us look at each of them in turn.

The role of patron is one that is often overlooked. There are a number of important ways in which the state acts as the direct economic benefactor of the media. In the case of the BBC it simply hands over the cash to keep the institution running. In the case of the other cable and broadcasting activities it regulates the field to ensure that there is only limited competition, extracting some tax revenue in return. The functioning of this may be compared to the monopolistic corporations beloved of the early Stuarts, in that private individuals pay the state for the privilege of exploiting a resource. The state provides the press with negative economic patronage by exempting it from VAT, but it also provides some positive patronage through the placing of government advertising. This has, in general, been used as a selective instrument. The most notable victim has been the *Morning Star*, denied most state advertising for fairly obvious political reasons.

The role of censor is much better known. There are a number of ways in which the state can directly determine what does and does not appear in the media. The most obvious of these is positive censorship, in which the state intervenes to prevent the publication or transmission of a particular item. In modern Britain the exercise of this power is relatively rare in peacetime and causes a huge row when it is discovered. However, negative censorship is a much more important factor. The publication of a piece of information can most effectively be prevented if those likely to publish it never become aware of it. The state has a wide discretion over this, notably by means of the definition of something as an official secret. Since, in so far as these measures are effective, there is little prospect of there being any serious row over them until the state papers eventually get released perhaps a century later, this pre-emptive censorship is by far the most effective kind.

Negative censorship is silent and routine in its operation and it suggests that the major ways in which the state influences the media are not the ones which command the most obvious public odium. Perhaps the most effective avenues of influence open to the state are those which proceed by means of the normal functioning of the state machine itself.

The most sensitive area of censorship in the last 18 years has been the war in Northern Ireland. There we have seen both positive and negative censorship playing a prominent role and we can also observe the way in which informal agreements between the state and the media can lead to voluntary, or at least semi-voluntary, self-censorship by the media and thus act to obscure public knowledge and hence discussion of an important issue. So pervasive is this 'gentlemen's agreement' that a recent study argued that, in contrast with the legal bans operating in the South which forbid the television and radio services (RTE) to interview any supporter of the IRA or Sinn Fein, the British method of suppressing the truth works rather well.

> In Britain, the crudity of such direct government intervention has been avoided, and those who call for RTE rules have seriously missed the point of the present arrangements . . . The British way of censorship relies upon a mediated intervention which sustains the legitimacy and the credibility of the state and the broadcasting institutions. Naturally, this has its price for the state, which has managed to secure only indirect and partial control over broadcasting output. But it has nevertheless significantly defined the terms of reference under which the broadcasters operate.[1]

The influence of the state as actor is largely routine in its effect. The model of journalism dominant in Britain is one which stresses changes and sudden developments as the centre of news reporting rather than more gradual processes. Consequently the state is bound to provide a major source for the media. The more dramatic the development, the more likely it is to be reported; some of the activities of the state, for example wars, are very dramatic indeed. Thus there is a convergence between the actions of the state and the norms of modern journalism.

From the point of view of the journalist, the existence of a major bureaucracy as the source of a great deal of the news which forms the raw material of their daily working lives has important consequences. A journalist is forced to establish a working relationship with his or her sources and therefore builds up over time a relationship which is hardly likely to be adversarial. It requires no great credulity or venality on the part of a journalist to have a closer relationship with, say, the local police chief than with an unemployed youth who charges the police with brutality; indeed such a relationship is the condition for doing an effective job. Consequently, the official version of events is one which habit, let alone training, teaches the journalist to take seriously. Reviewing the relationship between the relatively feeble local state machine and the media, one commentator argued that there were structural factors which privileged the state as a provider of news:

> These factors are: the built-in dependence of the local press on the local authority as a source of regular news coverage which given individuals can cut off as a form of punishment; the need for speed in creating versions of events by local newspapers, which means that regular suppliers of information have power over the newspapermen [*sic*] that the supplier of one story or isolated piece of information does not have; the endemic secrecy of local government . . .; the commercial nature of the newspaper enterprise, with the consequent reluctance of the editor to touch 'risky' material; and the libel laws.[2]

All these factors apply even more strongly to the central state and the national media.

The fourth role of the state, that of masseur, follows directly from its role as provider of material for the media. Material can either be raw or, to alter the metaphor, it can be cooked. No doubt some of the material which appears in the media is the result of activities akin to the traditional fictional representation of journalistic practice, but a great deal of it emerges from the state itself in a form which has already been calculated to make it news of a certain sort. The state employs quite a large number of public relations officers. In the recent past the most publicly visible example of this was Ian MacDonald, whose delivery of government press statements on the Falklands/Malvinas War suggested that criteria other than a smooth media image are thought appropriate for the senior levels of this arcane activity. Normally, professional etiquette means that they are much less visible, since their job is to present the actions of the state in such a way as to make it appear that a journalist is the source of the material.

According to a recent account by Cockerell and others, the government information services issue 'over 10,000' press releases each year.[3] Obviously, a great deal of such work will be purely routine. However, it would be silly to assume that this process does not also involve what is termed 'news management'. The same study remarked that: 'All governments seek to manage the news: to trumpet the good, to suppress the bad and to polish up the image of the Prime Minister.' The most obvious example of this is the timing of particular press releases to ensure maximum exposure but there are numerous others of which the 'lobby system' is the best known. This is a system by which privileged journalists are treated to private chats by senior members of the government or state. They are allowed to use some of the material they get but not to reveal how they got it. Cockerell and his collaborators devote most of their book to examples of the lobby system in practice. They reveal, not surprisingly, that in this as in so much else that is manipulative and anti-democratic the Thatcher government has set new records. However, as in so much else, they also show that she was building upon solid foundations laid by others:

Despite the abolition of the regular briefings for the lobby by his press secretary, Sir Harold demonstrated during his second tenure at Downing Street that he had lost none of his old skills at media manipulation. While he was attending the 1975 Commonwealth Prime Ministers' Conference in Jamaica, he summoned the *Daily Telegraph* lobby correspondent, Mr Harry Boyne (later knighted on Sir Harold's recommendation) to see him. The Prime Minister told Boyne that he was intending to demote Mr Tony Benn in the Cabinet hierarchy. 'Mr Wilson gave me permission to write a story about it, which I duly did. I said: "Of course I won't put any by-line on this story. I think I'll just send it as *Daily Telegraph* reporter." "Well no," he says, "you can make it 'By our political staff'." This was typical of his knowledge, his quite intimate knowledge of how things worked in Fleet Street and in the lobby too.'

The suspension of lobby briefings by Mr Joe Haines had no lasting effect. On Sir Harold's resignation the machine cranked back into gear. Mr Callaghan's regime soon provided a notorious example of the lobby system being used through the non-attribution rule not merely to manipulate the news in the prime minister's favour but, in this case, to blacken the name of a diplomat. Mr Peter Jay, a *Times* journalist, was appointed British ambassador to the United States; Mr Jay was then married to Mr Callaghan's daughter. Mr Jay replaced an experienced and respected career diplomat, Sir Peter Ramsbotham, whose abrupt transfer was bound to cause controversy in Parliament and provoke cries of nepotism. Through the lobby a pre-emptive strike was organized on Mr Callaghan's behalf. Mr (later Sir) Tom McCaffrey, the Number Ten press secretary, briefed correspondents along the lines that Sir Peter was not entirely suited to the special needs of the *Washington Post*, and had to be replaced by a bright young man. Eventually the bottom line was revealed. Mr Christopher Moncrieff says, 'At the end of the meeting Tom McCaffrey privately ventured to one or two ears, accidentally I'm quite sure, that Ramsbotham, the man who was leaving the post, was a snob.' Within hours the *Evening Standard* and *Evening News* carried exactly the same story. 'SNOB ENVOY HAD TO GO' said the *Standard*; 'SNOB ENVOY HAD TO GO' said the *News*. No sources were given for these stories – picked up the next day in the daily papers – except 'the Callaghan camp' and 'governmental circles'.[4]

However, at this point we start to shade into a much more contentious area: that of the state as ideologue. It is commonly believed among academic students of the media that to give any weight to the notion that people, whether politicians, state officials or journalists, give conscious thought to what to present as news and how to present it in a light most favourable to their interests, is to hold to a crude and exploded set of ideas called 'conspiracy theory'.

Personally, I have always believed that such people give just as much thought to their actions and the consequences thereof as do the rest of us: we conspire to change the world and they conspire to keep us in our places. In this instance, there seems to me no reason to doubt that just as politicians employ people to package them so they, and the state as a whole, employ people to package their policies and actions.

Obviously a great deal of this activity takes place at the level of the unconscious or the semi-conscious. Those who people the state and those who people the media hold many of the same beliefs. This common ideology is an important part of the way in which the state influences the media. In modern society the state claims to represent the whole against the parts. It is the universal agency which permits, limits and controls the activities of partial sectoral interests. This 'universality' can be seen most clearly at the points when the state is threatened from outside. However, it also operates in other areas, for example industrial relations. Studying the media reporting of strikes in 1973, one writer observed that:

The unions are basically presented as being motivated by a narrow-minded concern for their own sectional interest, while the government is presented as being motivated, in a non-sectarian way, by concern for the 'national interest' . . . The state is presented as the representative of the 'majority of people' – not of any particular class interest.[5]

The notion, true or not, that the state speaks for all of us means that state definitions are often reproduced in the media, without any conscious process of 'conspiracy' taking place. This happens in two ways. The first is that the media adopt the definitions made by the state. At some point considerations of state policy, rather than media concerns, meant that Archbishop Makarios and Menachem Begin stopped being 'terrorists' and became 'statesmen'. No doubt a similar process will occur with Gerry Adams and Martin McGuinness. So, too, the 'Russians' became a 'threat' to the 'Free World': these are definitions dreamt up by ideologists in the service of the state, and by politicians, which are simply taken over by the mass media and repeated endlessly.

The second is more complex. It is an established part of the self-image of journalism that there is a strict separation of fact from opinion. No doubt every reader can think of a dozen recent instances in which that has not been the case, but the ideology does have some importance. It means, for instance, that the media rarely offer an independent interpretation of an event: rather they report the opinion of others, very often the spokespeople of the state or, more narrowly, the government. These people define the issues for the media and set the terms for all subsequent debate. Counter-opinions, which are often permitted in internal matters, are defined as sectional concerns which have to plead against the general interest as represented by the view of the state.

It is fair to point out that there is criticism of the state in some areas of media output. Policies believed to be mistaken are often criticized and there is a well-developed strain of populist criticism of individual state servants. However, at this point the identity between state and government starts to break down since much of the press, while supportive of the state, is hostile to non-Tory governments.

The final area is the one in which arguments about conscious belief and action are of the greatest importance. This is the area I have termed: the state as conspirator. The popular image of Macaulay's 'Fourth Estate' is of an institution suspicious of and hostile to state and government, but consider what they have in common. Both the state and the media are organized as hierarchies in which those at the top got there by proving their suitability to the people already at the top. Those at the top give orders which those lower down obey and enforce penalties of various kinds for non-obedience. In other words both are at their very roots deeply undemocratic organizations that are structured to ensure that the minority at the top controls the activities of the majority of those below them.

Further, those at the top of the media and of the state have a suprisingly high degree of shared experiences. They are likely to have had the same sort of education and they earn roughly the same sort of, very large, salaries. Their children go to the same schools. They often shift about between jobs at the same level. One study, looking at the people who own and run the press and comparing them with other groups of bosses, concluded that:

> If we take the chairmen and vice-chairmen of the ten leading press-owning concerns and their newspaper publishing subsidiaries the resulting group educational profile is remarkably similar to the known profile for other segments of contemporary capital. In all, 66 per cent of the press sample attended public school, compared with 71 per cent of the directors of the boards of Britain's top 200 companies and 70 per cent of John Wakeford's cross-section of industrial and other elites. Similarly, 62 per cent of the press sample went to Oxford or Cambridge, as against 60 per cent of the directors of clearing banks, and 61 per cent of those on the boards of merchant banks and discount houses. These educational communalities are further cemented by shared membership of exclusive social clubs.[6]

White's, apparently, was the top choice.

If we look at the governors of the BBC, we find exactly the same sort of people. Sir William Rees Mogg left the editorship of the *Times* to become chairman of the Arts Council and a governor of the BBC. (I am conscious that this is not entirely fair. There is an ex-trade unionist on that august body. His name is Sir John Boyd. I think it is fair to say that he was one of the most talented right-wingers during his time in the AUEW and he is a self-proclaimed Salvation Army trombonist. I would not wish to deny that outsiders get admitted to the class I am describing, but it seems that they have to do a great deal of hard work to prove their loyalty first.)

The people who call the shots in the state and the media are indistinguishable. Their relatives and friends people the boardrooms of industry and finance, both public and private. These people take all the important decisions about what is going to happen, how it is going to be reported and what will be done with anyone who objects. They are the ruling class.

We know from recent example that miners and their families fight hard to save their jobs, their communities and their way of life. It is not too difficult, then, to accept that the denizens of Mayfair and Guildford fight to defend their jobs, their communities and their way of life. The major differences appear to be that they are much more united, do it more consciously, more aggressively and, so far, with much more success than we.

The state and the media are two of the weapons that the people who rule us use to ensure their continuation in power. The state is an instrument of coercion, the media are instruments of persuasion. They influence each other as if they were the two arches of a bridge. (Of course the state also persuades, through, for example, the education system. The media also coerce: you get sacked if you get out of line.)

It is at this point that the differences between state and government become of some importance. If the state were the neutral and efficient servant of the government then it might be possible to improve the media by changing the government. The evidence suggests that changes of government leave unaltered the massive concentrations of unelected and irresponsible power concentrated in the hands of the various arms of the state. It is difficult to see how, if we believe that socialism has anything to do with people controlling their own lives, we can expect the judges who routinely jail the poor, the senior civil servant whose whole career has been free of popular criticism and direction, the generals who have been trained to regard expressions of dissent from the lower orders as mutiny, to suddenly change their ways, give up their servants and their luxuries and their exclusive privileges and live as the rest of us do. No more can we expect the Rupert Murdochs and the Lord Matthews, or those who ride high in their esteem and pen the filth that pleases their chiefs, to accept such a change.

Any government which seeks to get rid of poverty and inequality will come up against the opposition of those whose life has been built upon the fruits of poverty and inequality. Any government which seeks to establish democracy as the common norm for the conduct of human affairs will come up against the opposition of those whose whole life has been built upon the exercise of irresponsible and unaccountable power. The people who run the state, the media, industry and the banks will not just let us get on with changing the world because a temporary majority in the House of Commons tells them to. They will fight us with ideas and with weapons. It was, after all, that organ of ruling class opinion, the *Times*, then edited by the shameless Rees Mogg, that welcomed the bloody overthrow of Salvador Allende and the Chilean government with the words:

> The failure of the Presidency of Allende was also a tragedy for Chile herself, not because the coup put an end to a government which never had a majority either in the country or in congress, but because it marks the end of a long period during which Chile's peaceful and democratic political traditions were the envy of her neighbours. To apportion blame for this is no easy matter. Many Chileans will argue that the Unidad Popular government had itself made the coup inevitable by its hopeless mismanagement of the economy leading to a breakdown in public order, and at the same time had provided justification for it by its own unconstitutional acts. On the whole this would be our judgement; there is a limit to the ruin a country can be expected to tolerate . . .
>
> At this stage what a foreign commentator can say is that, whether or not the armed forces were right to do what they have done, the circumstances were such that a reasonable military man could in good faith have thought it his constitutional duty to intervene.[7]

No doubt Rees Mogg had discussed just such 'circumstances' with 'reasonable military men' at Pirbright and Aldershot. Fortunately, just as their armies are made up of the sons of the poor conscripted by unemployment into the service of the rich, so their media are written, filmed, printed and broadcast by working people. The evidence of all great social upheavals is that it is these people who can change the state and change the media, not the elite few who act on our behalf. Changing the state and changing the media have much in common: in both the only way it can and will be done is by the people whose labour makes these institutions work. A socialist society means a quite different state and quite different media.

References

1. P. Schlesinger, G. Murdock and P. Elliot, *Televising 'Terrorism'*, London: Comedia 1983, p. 129
2. David Murphy, *The Silent Watchdog*, London: Constable 1976, p. 62.
3. M. Cockerell, P. Hennessy and D. Walker, *Sources Close to the Prime Minister*, London: Macmillan 1984, p. 9
4. *Ibid.*, pp. 126–7.
5. D. Morley, 'Industrial Conflict and the Mass Media', in *The Sociological Review*, New Series May 1976, p. 250–51.
6. G. Murdock, 'Class, Power, and the Press: Problems of Conceptualization and Evidence' in H. Christian (ed.), *The Sociology of Journalism and the Press*, Keele University Press 1980, p. 48.
7. Editorial, *The Times*, 13 September 1973.

Part II: The Politics of the Media

9. The different approaches to media reform

James Curran

Our mass media are organized on contradictory principles. The press is based on free market competition, broadcasting on state regulation. One is justified by an ideology of capitalist competition, the other by a philosophy of public service opposed to the free market.

This makes the current consensus on media policy inherently unstable. The political values legitimizing the organization of the press can be invoked to overturn broadcasting policy. In theory, the same thing can be done in reverse, although this does not seem very likely in Thatcherite Britain.

The current consensus is made still more precarious by the fact that the buckle that once securely fastened broadcasting and press policy has loosened with age. It has long been argued that broadcasting has to be regulated because, unlike the press, it is constrained by the scarcity of wavelengths. This technical argument was once influential in reconciling enthusiastic advocates of the free market to extensive public regulation of broadcasting.

But this argument has now been decisively weakened by the development of new technology. Although conventional broadcasting continues to be limited by the scarcity of airwave frequencies, new cable TV and satellite broadcasting technology make it possible to have a multiplicity of channels. It is thus now technically possible to remodel broadcasting along the competitive, private enterprise lines of the press with a large number of pay-TV channels. This has already happened in the United States.

All the signs are that this is the direction in which we are heading. The government's decision to allow a major expansion of private enterprise cable TV, and from 1986 a wide extension of local commercial radio, will create a much larger private broadcasting sector. The short, sharp Peacock enquiry threatens to carry this process one stage further by undermining the public service basis of the BBC.

The New Right, aided by powerful commercial interests and a

sympathetic government, has so far made all the running in these developments. As we shall see, their arguments have struck a responsive chord even among part of the Left. Others on the Left, while not warming to a vision of a free market broadcasting system, have been reluctant to rally to the defence of what they see as a hierarchical, sclerotic BBC that is too closely linked to the state.

We are thus approaching an historic watershed in the evolution of the British media at a time when there is considerable uncertainty on the Left about where we should go from here. This seems to be a good moment, therefore, to stand back and take stock. This essay surveys the principal proposals for media reform and examines some of their strengths and weaknesses. It does this not by running through a shopping list of options but by examining how they fit into alternative strategies for reforming the media.

Surprisingly, this is the first survey of its kind.[1] To make things easier, the survey has been confined to the press, radio and television. Attention has also been focused mainly on traditional media, since this essay has been planned to complement that by Golding and Murdock, concerned with the new television industries.[2] At times, it has also been necessary to simplify by drawing clear theoretical distinctions between perspectives that sometimes overlap in practice, and by grouping together approaches which could be treated separately.

The aim of the essay is to assist a debate on the Left about how we should set about reforming the media. Unless our ideas crystallize in the form of concrete proposals, the New Right will continue to dominate – partly by default – the politics of the media.

Neo-liberal market approaches

Currently the most dynamic reform approach is inspired by classical neo-liberal perspectives of the 'free' market. It has attracted to its banner an extraordinarily diverse association of people – neo-liberal traditionalists, radical libertarians and those committed to a voluntaristic social responsibility approach. In terms of the political spectrum, they tend to come respectively from the New Right, New Left and paternalist centre. They represent a formidable – and possibly unstoppable – coalition.

Traditional neo-liberal approach
According to free market rhetoric, we have a free press because the

freedom to publish is not restricted by the state. This freedom ensures that all significant points of view – with a following large enough to sustain it in the free market – are aired in the press. Proponents of the free market approach point to the existence of a wide diversity of choice represented by 19 national newspapers ranging from the Communist *Morning Star* to the Thatcherite *Sun*, about 1,000 local newspapers (excluding freesheets), and more than 4,000 magazines catering for an enormous variety of minority interests, perspectives and tastes. Still more papers will mushroom, they argue, if trade union obstruction to cost-cutting new technology is overcome.

This wealth of choice allegedly makes the consumer the dominant influence over the press. Since publishers have to satisfy public demand in order to stay in business, they must respond to what people want. Thus the free market supposedly renders the press accountable.

Of course, this sometimes produces journalism that upsets self-appointed critics. But the journalistic defects that they discern are, according to free market apologists, really the defects of society writ – or rather printed – large. It is not really with the press that critics are dissatisfied. It is with people.

If reformers want to change the press, then they have to change people to their way of thinking. The alternative approach, imposing changes through the state or state-linked agencies, is an open invitation to political censorship. 'The state's capacity to do evil,' John Whale writes, for instance, 'is greater than the capacity of private citizens or bodies.'[3] Consequently, the dangers inherent in state 'reform' – even when well intentioned – usually far outweigh any possible benefits.

Indeed, the great strength of the British press is that it is free of pre-publication censorship. The press is able to champion the individual against Whitehall, the town hall or any source of authority which misuses its power. The press diverts and entertains, but there is also a serious side to what it does. It is the unchained watchdog and tribune of the people: its freedom is part of what makes Britain free.[4]

Neo-liberals have increasingly applied these same arguments to broadcasting. The root problem, they argue, is that 'a small elite with access to the control of the existing duopoly pass judgement on what is, and is not, a "good" programme, with the paying viewer having little or no say in what goes on'.[5] Broadcasting is also overregulated and too closely linked to the state. What is needed, therefore, are more channels, fewer controls and vigorous competition that will produce greater variety and greater consumer control in place of bureaucratic regulation.

One much-canvassed reform would lead to the privatization of the BBC into 'an association of independent and separately financed stations'; the reconstruction of the IBA as a 'more flexible and more commercially aware licensing body' interfering less with programmes and positively fostering competition; the transformation of local radio into a wholly commercial system, strengthened by numerous specialist stations as well as small highly localized stations, drawing upon voluntary staff; and, above all, the rapid development of cable and satellite television free of 'excessive' restrictions and controls. All this would be funded by a mixture of advertising, sponsorship and subscriptions, though what is currently BBC News would be funded by a levy on the companies that use its services. Controls against political bias in broadcasting would either be relaxed or removed altogether. In this way, the Adam Smith Institute argues, 'the newspaper industry's success in "informing, educating and entertaining" ' would be matched by a broadcasting system of equal quality.[6]

Variations on this set of proposals have been urged by neo-liberals closer to the central ground of British politics. David Graham, a distinguished ex-BBC producer, argues for instance that a small public service broadcasting organization, funded by a levy on the commercial channels, should be retained within the framework of an expanded, privatized broadcasting system. Christopher Dunkley, television critic of the *Financial Times*, argues that a major shift to a more deregulated, commercialized system should be deferred until cable and satellite TV have become fully established.[7] But despite these qualifications, they and others like them want to reorient broadcasting towards the free market model of the press.

Voluntaristic social responsibility approach

Social responsibility voluntarism is similar to the traditional neo-liberal approach but is much more critical of what it sees as the editorial shortcomings of the press and less fatalistic about the potential for reform. Its starting point is generally that much of the popular press is excessively irresponsible, trivial and sensationalist; the cure lies, according to this approach, in the exercise of better leadership and greater professionalism by those who control and work in the press.

In its most conservative and paternalist form, represented by the

Royal Commission on the Press (1947–9), appointed by the Attlee government, leadership is defined as protecting people from themselves. As the Commission put it, 'the failure of the press . . . is attributable largely to the plain fact that an industry that lives by the sale of its products must give the public what the public will buy'. However, 'the press does not do all it might to encourage its public to accept or demand material of higher quality'.[8]

In order that the press should give more of a lead to its readers, social responsibility voluntarists argue for a variety of strategies designed to strengthen the moral backbone of press controllers and awaken the idealism of journalists. These usually boil down to the following proposals: a vigorous Press Council that will 'encourage the growth of the sense of public responsibility and public service' through moral persuasion and public pronouncement; the recruitment into journalism of 'men and women of integrity, judgement and a sense of vocation'; better training and educational courses in which 'journalists learn about society' and are equipped 'to understand social institutions better'; well-informed research and regular public enquiries into the media; adherence to a voluntary press charter which will safeguard editorial standards and independence; or, more controversially, the enforcement by the National Union of Journalists of its professional Code of Conduct.[9]

Advocates of this voluntarist approach are usually deeply hostile to any form of state intervention in the media. Typical of this orientation is the last Royal Commission on the Press (1974–7) which stated its blanket opposition, in principle, to, one, any form of public intervention which might result in some publications becoming financially dependent on a state agency or, two, aid that would 'amount to censorship in the sense of preferring to support some publications and not others'.[10]

This anti-statist veto is significant because it would lead to a policy of counter-revolution if applied across the board to all media. The Independent Broadcasting Authority, Channel Four, The British Film Institute and the Arts Council would all have to go, since they 'censor' in the sense of supporting some applicants and not others. So too would the BBC, public libraries, and public sector education, the funding of which is determined by the state. This helps to underline the radical implications of our current, long-established consensus on press policy.

Radical anti-statist approaches

Ironically, the assumptions underlying this consensus have been accepted by many people who are bitterly critical of what the 'free market' produces. For instance, many Labour Party discussions of the press follow a set pattern. They begin with denunciations of Fleet Street's right-wing, anti-union bias; develop into criticism of the 'mindless' people who read 'comics' like the *Sun*; wander off into reminiscences about the long-defunct *Daily Herald* and *Reynolds' News*; and conclude with demands for the launch of a new Labour daily.

Generally underlying this familiar progression is a corporatist response to the reform of the press. It is tacitly assumed that the press really *does* give people what they want; and that the only way to change the press is for the Left to produce more readable publications that people want to buy. In effect, this approach accepts the existing organization of the press as 'given'; the prescription for change is limited to working more effectively within the press system.

Yet even among more fundamentalist critics of the press, there is often a strong reluctance to using the state as an instrument of reform. The only alternative to the free market press, in the political context of the 1980s, is some form of public intervention or regulation of the press by a state-linked agency. Yet all forms of public intervention that go beyond a legal right of reply and tightening of anti-monopoly laws have been robustly rejected by thoughtful Labour politicians in the mould of Roy Hattersley on the grounds it could open the way to government censorship of the press.[11] Ironically, the principal interventionist schemes on offer have also been rejected with equal vehemence by Socialist Workers' Party intellectuals like Colin Sparks on the rather different grounds that intervention by the state, as presently constituted, could lead to the incorporation of the revolutionary press, whereas an unrestricted market provides a space in which it can grow.[12] This is not the place to situate these different responses in relation to alternative theories of the state;[13] merely note that anti-statist strands within both socialism and social democracy lead paradoxically to conclusions about press policy very similar to those of libertarian strands within conservatism.

Suspicion of the state often goes hand in hand with an optimistic assessment of market processes in which it is assumed that changes in public consciousness will give rise to a corresponding change in the press. According to a conventional Leninist perspective, all discussion of limited public intervention in the press is merely a reformist diversion from the revolutionary class struggle in which a radical press will emerge linked to a revolutionary vanguard movement that will transform society. Ironically, there is also a strand in social democratic commentary which argues something not too dissimilar: public intervention in the press is unnecessary – as well as undesirable – because the revival of radicalism will take care of the need to revive a radical press.

This belief in the reciprocity between supply and demand has been influenced by the general, more positive reappraisal of market forces amongst the British Left. Commitment to the market has been further strengthened by the currently fashionable view that new cost-saving technology – notably computerized photocomposition enabling direct input of copy by journalists and facsimile transmission making possible decentralized production and distribution – is about to transform the structure of the press. According to Ian Aitken, political editor of the *Guardian*, for instance, 'only one serious obstacle stands in the way' of having 'entirely new newspapers representing all points of view' and that is 'the attitude of some print workers and their unions'. When union intransigence has been overcome, enabling production costs to be greatly reduced, new papers will allegedly mushroom in all the colours of the political rainbow. New technology now represents, in Aitken's view, 'an alternative solution' to all the proposals for subsidies and interventions, ranging from 'the ingenious to the frankly fanciful' that have been proposed for reform of the press. Whereas these threaten our liberties, new technology 'actually promises to extend them'.[14]

The extent to which pro-market, anti-statist views have permeated the British Left partly explains why New Right demands for the deregulation of broadcasting have caught the Left off balance. In effect, the New Right is building upon arguments that have been widely accepted in relation to the press, and are extending their logic to broadcasting.

New Right arguments also chime, to some extent, with a radical critique of public service broadcasting institutions that has gained increasing currency on the Left. As a leading radical producer, David Elstein, puts it, 'broadcasting habitually and unnecessarily accommodates the needs of politicians as the price of keeping the system'. This system enables, in his view, a small number of individuals at the top of the hierarchical broadcasting organizations, 'most of whom have been to Oxford, all of whom share a great number of assumptions', to filter out controversial programmes that trespass outside the safe consensus. These same custodians of our welfare, according to Elstein, also have a profoundly xenophobic notion of what is good for us, talking disdainfully of 'wall-to-wall Dallas' but never of 'wall-to-wall Coronation Street'.[15]

Radical libertarians like Elstein are now joining the New Right chorus for 'more channels and less regulation'. However, their detailed proposals, where these are available, sometimes deviate from the blueprints of the New Right. Elstein himself argues that the BBC should switch from the licence fee to private subcriptions funding. More broadly, he argues for the rapid extension of competitive broadcasting but within a framework in which revenue raising and programme making functions are separated. Similarly, Peter Lewis and other veterans of community media politics have long argued for the development of low-power community radio on the model of the radical community press, though with the significant rider that its growth would be financially assisted by a public agency.[16]

Culturalist approach

The culturalist neo-Marxist tradition sits awkwardly in relation to the free market tendencies that have been discussed. Its leading advocates do not endorse the free market case; they have also largely avoided becoming involved in the debates about media reform. Yet no survey can leave them out of account since they have exerted such a formative influence on the Left's thinking about the media. For reasons that will become clear, they are best discussed here.

The culturalist perspective, notably represented in the prolific writing of academics associated with the Birmingham Centre for Contemporary Cultural Studies, contests the central importance usually given to the influence of ownership and hierarchical authority within media organizations in conventional left-wing accounts of the media. These fail to recognize, according to Stuart Hall and his colleagues, 'the day-to-day "relative autonomy" of the journalist and news producers from direct economic control'.[17] Yet it is precisely economic control, in its broadest sense, that most radical media proposals are intended to modify. Implicit in culturalist analysis, therefore, is the uncomfortable thought that much of this reforming activity is largely misdirected or, at least, inflated in its expectations. Vanquishing the principal villains of left-wing demonology – the proprietors and senior managements of media organizations – would not achieve very much, according to the dominant culturalist perspective,[18] because they are not at the root of the problem.

Instead, culturalists offer an alternative view of how the media operate. Its 'bias' is rooted in bureaucratic newsgathering routines oriented around powerful institutions and groups, the reliance placed on them as sources, and the taken-for-granted assumption of the 'control culture' that colour journalists' thinking. The media are thus shaped more by the patterns of thought and power relationships outside the media to which journalists respond than by direct controls exerted within media organizations. As one influential, collectively written essay puts its, 'the media accurately reflect and represent the prevailing structure and mode of power. It is in politics and the state, not in the media, that power is *skewed*'.[19]

This view offers no very clear guideline to institutional reform of the media: indeed, the key to changing the media is seen paradoxically as lying outside the institutions of the media. The implications of this differ, according to which strand of culturalist analysis one plugs into. The dominant perspective within culturalist Marxism argues, however, that media institutions are highly 'permeable' in that they respond to changes in the balance of forces and climate of opinion in the country. Although the media tend to incorporate oppositional views within the terms set by the dominant spread of ideologies, sometimes radical counter-definitions of situations are not reconciled or reduced by their projection on to a more 'neutral' territory. 'Space *can* be gained, viewpoints expressed, contradictions emerge which are contradictory to the ones in dominance.'[20] The way to change the media, viewed from this perspective, is a strategic battle of position in which the Left influences the media by winning popular support for its ideas, skilfully intervening in debates by its timely and well-constructed counter-arguments, organizing strategically on all important fronts, and winning legitimacy within the system in a way that ensures that radical spokespersons cannot be automatically ignored or marginalized.

It is a powerful and persuasive set of arguments. But its effect has been to steer the Left away from a programmatic approach to the reform of the media. Culturalists have also helped to undermine support for the historic compromise represented by our mixed economy media by directing a well-aimed fusillade at public service broadcasting institutions. Culturalists thus leave us with a rather disarming legacy – a heightened awareness of the shortcomings of

Britain's broadcasting system, at a time when this is under sustained attack by Thatcherites, without offering any concrete alternative beyond a generalized espousal of political commitment.

Since free-market approaches dominate the current debate about the media and have a seductive appeal to part of the Left in the new prevailing climate of radical 'realism', they will be critically assessed in some detail in the latter part of this essay. But the three main alternative approaches – public service, radical market and socialist – will be discussed first.

Public service approaches

The central rationale of the public service approach is that broadcasting should be directed towards the public good rather than private gain. This results allegedly in both programme diversity and quality since public service broadcasting is not subservient to the commercial pressures that make for uniformity and low standards.

This conventional presentation of the public service case is now complicated in the case of British broadcasting by being applied not only to a non-profit-making, public corporation, the BBC, but also to its commercial competitors. Our commercial broadcasting system has been converted into a public service one, it is argued, because it is extensively regulated by a public service authority, the Independent Broadcasting Authority (IBA). The Authority insists that the commercial network provides a balanced schedule of programmes, and that it adheres broadly to public service standards and guidelines. And since commercial broadcasting companies need to have their franchises renewed at regular intervals by the IBA in order to stay in business, they internalize public service as well as private profit as company goals.

This hybrid system, according to official rhetoric, gives us the best of all possible worlds. The BBC is compelled to compete for audiences against ITV in order to justify its licence fee: it is thus forced to shed the paternalistic piety of a public service monopoly. Yet the quality of our commercial system is raised by being forced to compete with the public service standards of the BBC. The end result is, allegedly, the best broadcasting system in the world.

The cultural strengths of the system, according to its proponents, is that it encourages a greater willingness to take risks than would be the case in a purely commercial system; proper provision for minorities as well as mass audiences; and a flourishing television industry that reflects the cultural and social diversity of British society rather than a bland transatlantic culture.

Its political strengths are manifested in its allegedly balanced and high-quality coverage of current affairs. This offers universal access to news and analyses that helps to reduce, it is argued, the knowledge gap that traditionally exists between the powerful and powerless. It thus genuinely empowers people in the way that the press, split between quality and tabloid journalism, does not.[21]

A further merit of public service broadcasting is allegedly that it is fully accountable to the British public not only through competition for audience time but also through its relationship to parliament, which lays down guidelines for its conduct. This results in a service which conforms to public standards of decency and good taste, and which is not marred by sensationalism and the excesses of cheque-book journalism.[22]

Public service remodelling of the press

Public service broadcasting has inspired a number of proposals for reforming the press. What some radicals have sought to do is, in effect, to turn the New Right's argument on its head: 'the success' of broadcasting in informing, entertaining and educating the public justifies, in their view, transplanting the broadcasting model to the press.

Franchising the press

A proposal made by Stuart Holland that an Independent Press Authority (IPA) should be established with comparable powers to those of the IBA has been developed in greater detail by Michael Meacher and Chris Mullin in privately circulated papers.[23] Meacher proposes that 'publishing a newspaper would be subject to a franchise, offered by the IPA'. All existing newspaper owners would be franchised but their franchises would be renewed or revoked at regular intervals ('say, seven years') as in the case of ITV franchises. They would be required to conform to a code of standards, including a requirement to maintain 'a reasonable overall balance in the presentation of news and opinions between conflicting viewpoints'.

Chris Mullin's alternative scheme involves the IPA matchmaking profitable with loss-making papers and combining complementary papers to produce coherent, profitable group franchises. These would be tendered for competitive bids, with preference going a) to companies without vested commercial interests, b) to staff consortia and c) to forms of ownership in which the interests of all staff are represented. Mullin's proposal also differs from Meacher's in that the IPA would not require franchise holders to maintain a political balance. However, in awarding franchises the IPA would be required to provide outlets for a wide range of political views. It would also impose ethical safeguards and, as a kind of newspaper equivalent of the IBA's mixed scheduling policy, require newspapers to devote a specified percentage of editorial content to news and current affairs.

Mullin's proposal would be much more transformative since it would result in an immediate and wholesale change in press ownership. It also tackles head-on the problem of franchising individual loss-making papers, at least in the medium term, by franchising only profitable groups. Because it is the more radical of the two proposals, it would be politically more difficult to 'sell'.

Both schemes build on the precedent afforded by the IBA and are largely self-financing. However, one problem with both proposals is perhaps that the licensing of ITV companies is justified by the scarcity of airwaves, whereas there are no comparable physical constraints on the publication of newspapers. The political timing of these initiatives is now also less than ideal in that the application of new technology is likely to result, in the short term, in an unusually large number of new newspaper launches (though these presumably could be franchised individually or co-opted into franchise groups).

This said, the analogy with commercial broadcasting is not totally misleading. Every local morning and evening paper is, with one exception, a monopoly. Since their market dominance is currently as much a barrier to competition as are physical controls, there is a case for arguing that their unaccountable power should be subject to the same public service requirements as those which apply to ITV and local radio monopolies. However, there may be pragmatic grounds for not wishing to assume responsibility for franchising local daily monopolies, and all the problems that this would entail. Many local dailies are now in financial trouble with weekly freesheets eating like piranha fish into their advertising revenue.

Legal safeguards
The main alternative public service approach to the press is a *statutory* backed version of the social responsibility strategy discussed earlier. Its

principal objective is to eradicate unethical behaviour in the press, and to give the victims of press misrepresentation a chance to put the record straight.

A notable exponent of this approach is Geoffrey Robertson who chaired a committee of enquiry into the Press Council, set up by the Campaign for Press and Broadcasting Freedom.[24] His most important recommendation is for the establishment of a press ombudsman, with a statutory power to direct the publication of corrections and replies in newspapers which have failed to put right demonstrable errors of fact. This does not go as far as Frank Allaun's Private Member's Bill in 1983, which would have enabled replies to 'distortions' through exaggeration or argument where there was no demonstrable factual error.

The press ombudsman would be backed up by a reformed Press Council. The Council's rubber teeth would gain heavy metal fillings, in the Robertson plan, because newspapers would enter into a contractual obligation, enforceable in the courts, to publish its adjudications. The Council would also exercise a long-term influence on the press by promulgating proper codes of conduct, monitoring press output, advising the Monopolies Commission, and being involved in the formulation, teaching and examining of ethical courses for trainee journalists. It would also recommend publishers to incorporate into all contracts with employees a conscience clause to the effect that no journalist can be obliged to act in breach of a Press Council declaration of principle. This regulatory package would be sweetened with the introduction of a freedom of information act and relaxations of the laws of libel, contempt and breach of confidence.

Other proposals in the public service tradition have also been made. Tony Benn argued, at the time of Murdoch's takeover bid for the *Times*, that the paper should be established as a public corporation along the lines of the BBC. Major-General Clutterbuck, among others, has advocated setting up an institute for the mass media wih the same power as the General Medical Council to strike practitioners off its register who break its professional code.[25]

But perhaps the most significant public service plan to emerge is the legislative package recently proposed by Tom Baistow. Its most original features are proposals to shore up the independence of editors through legal safeguards against improper pressure on them by proprietors, advertisers and trade unions; the appointment to the boards of national newspapers of independent directors without whose approval editors cannot be engaged or dismissed; and the introduction of machinery for staff involvement or consultation in the appointment of editors. In the Baistow scheme, a reformed Press Council would also have a *statutory power* to enforce a code of conduct based on that of the NUJ and to impose fines; the more inclusive Allaun version of the right of reply law would also be introduced on the grounds that comparable laws in West Europe have not resulted in an avalanche of published counter-statements – the main grounds of Robertson's objection to it.[26]

Both the Baistow and Robertson plans would improve ethical standards (although Robertson's hope that proprietors will voluntarily give the Press Council teeth by entering into binding contractual relationships with it is, in the absence of the threat of legislation, highly unrealistic). Both schemes would also increase in a small way the opportunity to read alternative versions of events through facilitating a right to reply.

But the intention of the Baistow programme is to go further and significantly alter the character of the press by shoring up the independence of editors, and modifying the way in which they are selected. However, the trouble with this imaginative approach is that it is applying pressure at a sensitive but not vital spot. As Professor Jeremy Tunstall has rightly argued, editors are generally little more than 'departmental managers'.[27] Most major editorial initiatives involve spending money and, since editors do not determine their own budgets, their freedom of action and 'proper' authority is circumscribed. This is particularly the case when the editor is in conflict with the proprietor or senior management, as the celebrated feud in the early 1980s between the politically centrist editor of the *Times*, Harold Evans, and his right-wing proprietor, Rupert Murdoch, demonstrates. Although protected by Articles of Association and, in theory, independent directors, Evans had still to haggle over editorial decisions entailing expenditure. In the end, Evans resigned rather than suffer 'a thousand humiliations'.[28]

Indeed, Tom Baistow tacitly acknowledges the limited effectiveness of his plans by placing great emphasis on the future impact of new technology in bringing 'newspaper ownership within the means of all kinds of groups . . .'[29] This, he hopes, will 'bring about a gradual return to the diversity essential to an informed, socially balanced and politically literate democracy'. Whether he and others like him are right to place so much faith in the endogenous capacity of the free market to reform itself will be critically assessed later.

Reform of public service broadcasting

Although the public service tradition has been a source of inspiration for many radical press reformers, it has been increasingly criticized by radicals concerned with broadcasting. One response to a growing mood of disenchantment has been, as we have seen, to repudiate the public service tradition altogether. Another has been to find new ways of realizing the ideal of public service through a radical overhaul of the broadcasting system.

Redefining public service

One recurrent criticism of the public service tradition is that it results in a consensual style of broadcasting that excludes or marginalizes radical perspectives.

This consensual bias, according to one view, is inscribed in the concept of balance and impartiality that is at the heart of public service broadcasting. According to the Changing Television Group, 'the problem with the notion of balance and impartiality, as a suitable guideline for the broadcasting institutions, is that it is difficult to define *what* is to be balanced and to determine *where* the central balancing point is to be placed'.[30] Still more questionable, in their view, is 'the assumption that there is some balanced point from which society can be surveyed in a neutral fashion'. In practice, the problem of how to achieve a mythical balance is solved, they argue, by 'the homogeneous social, educational and economic background of the individuals who control and operate the BBC and ITV'. This results in a self-serving and self-deluding set of beliefs and practices that excludes important perspectives from being properly aired.

The Changing Television Group's solution is to abandon impartiality and balance as a goal of broadcasting institutions and to impose instead an obligation on them to 'represent fairly and accurately the differences within society, and . . . produce programmes from the different perspectives in society'. This can be best achieved, in their view, by having openly partisan, clearly authored programmes 'given always the requirement to report with accuracy'.

There is a danger in this approach that the range of views given airtime will reflect the rather narrow range of opinion and prejudice to be found among broadcasters. The Changing Television Group argue, however, that this problem could be overcome by recruiting broadcasters from a broader spectrum in society and making them accountable to democratic broadcasting authorities.

Another perspective argues for what is, in effect, a compromise proposal. It rejects the idea that programmes on controversial issues should normally be bi-partisan or impartial in their approach since this generally leads, in practice, to their being constructed around centrist perspectives. On the other hand, it is opposed to giving broadcasters a completely free rein to express their subjective opinions on the grounds they are always likely to be unrepresentative of the general public. This position proposes therefore that there should be an overall balance in the total spectrum of programmes that are transmitted by the broadcasting system, and that one role of democratic broadcasting authorities is to see that this is observed. In this way, the range of views on television and radio will reflect the range of opinion in the community rather than that of individual broadcasters.

An alternative recommendation surfaces from time to time, proposing 'enforceable guidelines . . . to combat racism, sexism and class bias in programming'.[31] This view is strongly contested on the grounds that there are already laws that lay down acceptable limits of racial intolerance, defamation and so on. To enshrine still stricter controls in broadcasting would be to negate the principle objective of libertarian radical reform – namely to make broadcasting more pluralistic and diverse. Liberty, as George Orwell once powerfully argued, means allowing people freely to say things you do not want to hear. It is a definition of freedom which, in the libertarian view, should be a foundation stone of the broadcasting system.

Democratic broadcasting authorities
The complaint that British broadcasting is dominated by narrowly consensual perspectives is often linked to criticism of the way in which broadcasting authorities are appointed. Members of the IBA and BBC board of governors are mainly recruited by government from the clubland world of 'the great and the good'.

Since they are government appointees, they are also not the best people to defend broadcasters from government pressure. This was brought home by the way in which the BBC board of governors attempted to suppress the controversial documentary about Ulster, *At the Edge of the Union*, in response to pressure from the Home Secretary, and only relented after an unprecedented strike by its staff.

The present system of unmediated government appointments is defended on three grounds: it supposedly produces representative public trustees who speak for the nation rather than act on behalf of vested interests; no one administration appoints all the members of broadcasting authorities since appointments are staggered over a number of years; and all the alternative schemes that have been proposed are worse than the system we now have.[32]

But in reality, members of broadcasting authorities are far from representative. Seven out of the twelve BBC governors were educated at Oxford or Cambridge university. Nine members of the IBA are graduates and, of the remaining three non-graduates, one is a university vice-chancellor.

The Thatcher government has also begun to pack the broadcasting authorities with its own supporters.[33] Thus the chairman of the BBC is the brother of a cabinet minister; his deputy is a former Conservative parliamentary candidate and ex-editor of an independent Conservative newspaper, the *Times*. And the feeble protection against abuse afforded by non-simultaneous appointments breaks down when a government is re-elected to office: all BBC governors currently owe their appointment to Mrs Thatcher.

Three alternatives have been proposed based variously on the principle of direct elections, nominations and an electoral college. The scheme favoured by members of the Glasgow University Media Group is direct election to newly created local and regional broadcasting authorities: these would send delegates, in turn, to a national conference which would act as the supreme authority in broadcasting.[33] The BBC Board of Governors and the IBA would be phased out under this scheme.

In practice, this would be a recipe for the direct politicization of broadcasting (although the Glasgow University Media Group may not be fully aware of this). Only political parties are fully geared to mobilizing large numbers of people to vote at elections, particularly at a regional level. The result would be not wholly dissimilar to the *proporz* system in Germany in which the regional broadcasting councils of the first and third television channels are composed mainly of political appointees, reflecting the political balance within the state parliaments. This has led to the politicization, in turn, of appointments within the broadcasting system. However, this builds political diversity of a sort into the system since programmes made by the regional broadcasting organizations are nationally networked.[34]

The alternative favoured by the Labour Party and, in a modified form, by the Standing Conference on Broadcasting is for broadcasting authorities to consist of both representatives democratically elected by workers in broadcasting organizations and persons nominated by the political parties, representative national organizations and local government.[35]

A third approach is a synthesis of these two proposals: representatives would be elected by an electoral college composed of representatives from national organizations and workers in the broadcasting industry. The representative organizations would include the major political parties, principal interest groups and large voluntary membership associations like the Women's Institute and the Campaign for Nuclear Disarmament. In addition, a small number of direct consumer delegates could perhaps be directly elected by a freepost write-in ballot in the *TV Times* and *Radio Times*, which would rightly give Mrs Whitehouse's National Viewers' and Listeners' Association an opportunity to secure representation.

The intention of this scheme is threefold: to secure broader representation than would be obtained solely through political parties; to have an elective system that symbolizes and establishes the role of authority members as public rather than corporate representatives; and to provide a chain of authority that makes broadcasters accountable to the community but not beholden to governments.[36]

However, the disadvantage of the last two schemes, it could be argued, is that they offer a corporatist framework of authority that would institutionalize a consensual style of broadcasting. The alternative to this approach, as we shall see, is to allocate control over different parts of the broadcasting system to different groups.

Who pays?

The present way of funding the broadcasting system has come under mounting attack not merely from free marketeers but also from those within the public service tradition. Although the BBC licence fee is supposed to symbolize the Corporation's independence, it has exposed it at a time of inflation to unhealthy political pressure. Governments, not the BBC, determine the level of the licence fee, and in the period 1975–85 the Corporation has been compelled to go cap in hand to ask for a licence increase (not always granted in full) no less than six times. This has made the Corporation more dependent on the goodwill of politicians than is good for it and partly accounts, in the view of some, for its partial loss of political courage and independence.

The licence fee system has also resulted in the BBC receiving much less in real terms than the commercial sector. The licence fee is also a regressive poll tax that does not discriminate between rich and poor.

Various ways of modifying the licence fee system have been suggested. It could be replaced by a rolling quinquennial grant awarded by parliament though this might increase, in practice, the BBC's dependence on government (the Corporation's own view). An intermediary body could be appointed to advise the government about licence fee increases. The licence fee could also be waived for old-age pensioners and those on long-term benefit, and the loss of income to the Corporation be met by a grand-in-aid from the Treasury.

An alternative much-canvassed proposal is for the licence fee to be supplemented by advertising. This would enhance the autonomy of the BBC and strengthen its finances. The defects of the proposal are that it would probably lead to a short-term reduction in the total revenue of the broadcasting system, and consequently in the quality of its programmes. It would also encourage both the BBC and ITV to maximize audience ratings at the expense of minority audiences.

A few voices are to be heard in favour of eliminating all advertising from broadcasting. This would drastically reduce the revenue base of British television unless there was a substantial increase in public funding. Without generous public provision, there would be a marked decline in the standards of British broadcasting and a significant loss of jobs.

This leaves the third option, favoured by the Labour Party, of pooling the revenue of broadcasting organizations, including both the public element and advertising revenue. But the structural reorganization implied in this proposal raises far wider questions than simply the ones posed by discussion of the licence fee.

The cultural dimensions of public service broadcasting

There has been mounting criticism of the cultural and entertainment performance of public service broadcasting on three counts. Allegedly, it has become too cautious; it has become too dominated by a metropolitan culture; and it has become too oriented towards audience ratings at the expense of cultural and minority provision. The complaint that the broadcasting system is too politically consensual is thus expressed at a cultural level as well.

In addition, there is a continuing debate about whether broadcasting should be oriented towards a universal audience (with a balanced diet of programmes on each channel) or towards differentiated audiences (with specialized channels). Those who stress the formative role of broadcasting in expanding the cultural horizons of audiences generally favour a universal approach and dominate television. The other approach that prevails on radio is geared to satisfying differentiated tastes within a socially stratified society.

In part, mounting cultural criticism of public service broadcasting is a response to the decline of Reithian commitment and cultural paternalism within the BBC.[37] But it also stems from a more general shift in cultural values and cultural strategy.[38] The BBC's monopoly position was once widely justified as a means of achieving regulated diversity and artistic excellence. Now, even its much reduced role in broadcasting is often said to be excessive, and the size and centralized structure of its organization to be an obstacle to realizing the very things that it was held to stand for. A similar process of disenchantment has developed in relation to ITV. It was originally conceived and promoted as a decentralized system. Yet because of its advance planning and networking arrangements organized through the Independent Television Companies Association, it has become in reality a highly centralized system.

A desire to inject new diversity into the broadcasting system led the Annan Committee to recommend the establishment of a fourth channel independent of both the BBC and ITV. A minority went further and argued for the subdivision of the BBC into separate TV and radio corporations.

A number of public service critics have carried this one stage further and argued for the complete disaggregation of the broadcasting system into smaller, competing units.[39] Thus the Labour Party has argued that programme making should be carried out 'by a wide variety of dispersed programme units reflecting the creative talent of all parts of the UK', organized through two television and radio corporations. A group of radical broadcasters have come up with a still more pluralistic blueprint in which television would be reorganized into four competing television networks and two independent news services, with a comparable reorganization of radio.

A common feature of these schemes is the central pooling of broadcasting revenue. This offers a number of advantages. It would prevent government from directly determining the finances of a major broadcasting organization (as now happens with the BBC). It could bring to an end the Cinderella treatment increasingly being accorded to the public sector in broadcasting. It could also insulate broadcasting from the cumulative pressure to satisfy the common denominator of mass demand and create new space in which to innovate and cater for the minorities that make up the majority.

But there are also dangers in concentrating so much economic power in one organization. These dangers are compounded by the form in which this new body has been proposed. It would have total discretionary freedom to allocate revenue to broadcasting organizations as it saw fit. In addition, it would have wide-ranging powers from overseeing schedules to commissioning special programmes. This prompted the Annan Committee to reject the proposal on the grounds that it would lead to overcentralized control over broadcasting.

However, the proposal could be reformulated in a more acceptable way. A central agency could be established whose function was limited to fixing advertising rates and gathering advertising and licence fee revenue. It would merely service competing independent broadcasting organizations under separate, democratically elected or nominated authorities. The key co-ordinating functions for the broadcasting system as a whole – allocating revenue, determining advertising quotas, programme import quotas and broadcasting hours etc. – would be carried out by a professionally serviced management board composed of representatives from the different broadcasting authorities.

Three other proposals are often advocated as a way of extending broadcasting diversity: better-funded access programmes over which minorities have full editorial control; regular public hearings or enquiries into broadcasting; and positive discrimination to make broadcasters more representative of the plurality of society as a whole. Thus, the Changing Television Group advocates the introduction of quotas for women and ethnic minorities, and the abandonment of formal educational and technical requirements in recruitment in favour of more intensive training programmes.

A brief reference should also be made to the new television industries. Satellite and cable TV could enormously extend the cultural range and diversity of British broadcasting if it is organized properly. On the other hand, it could potentially undermine what diversity there is now on British television. This is why all satellite broadcasting operations based in the United Kingdom should be licensed by a Satellite Broadcasting Authority and be made subject to controls covering, among other things, the amount of advertising and imported programmes they transmit. Non-British satellite operations reaching the UK should be brought under similar control through a negotiated pan-European agreement.

Radical market approaches

The radical market approach is a negotiated form of the free market approach. It takes at face value the way in which neo-liberals represent the free market, and seeks to translate their alluring picture into practice. Since the only way in which this can be done within a highly 'imperfect market' is through public intervention, it can lead ironically to a position not far removed from a radical public service perspective.

But there are various stopping points along this route. The 'radical' market approach is usually presented in a rather conservative form, and discussion of it has generally turned on technical arguments that seem far removed from the general issues raised by press reform. We will consider this approach in some detail since it represents the most developed and carefully considered reform strategy to have emerged in relation to the press and has enthusiastic adherents among some Labour politicians. However, it is arguably something of a cul-de-sac. From page 114 onwards, more radical versions of this approach and its possible applications to broadcasting, are discussed.

Anti-monopoly curbs

Concentration of ownership is recognized by free marketeers to be unhealthy. It insulates corporations from competition, and consequently undermines the dynamic process that is supposed to make the market responsive to public demand.

Partly for this reason, the Wilson government passed in 1965 an anti-monopoly press law which required large press corporations to gain ministerial consent before swallowing up further papers. Yet, although large groups have sought permission to buy over 80 newspaper companies since then, only one bid has been disallowed. The exception was a tiny minnow (West Somerset Free Press); yet Murdoch has been allowed during this period to create a press empire in Britain that now exceeds in circulation even that controlled by Lord Northcliffe in his prime.

This has prompted demands for the Fair Trading Act to be strengthened.[41] The onus should be placed, it is argued, on press groups to show that acquisition of new titles is *not* contrary to the public interest rather than the other way round. The Act could be extended to the smaller regional chains, which are currently exempted. Tougher criteria for referring acquisitions to the Monopolies Commission could also be adopted.

Although these reforms are desirable, they are not likely to make a great deal of difference: concentration of press ownership in Britain is now worse than in any other liberal democratic country in the western world. It is thus rather late in the day to be tightening curbs on press concentration: the damage to press freedom has already been done.

And even if the Act is strengthened, it is unlikely that the major groups will be prevented from taking over ailing papers. If the alternative appears to be closure, permission will generally be granted.

Freeze-frame approach

Over the years, a large number of proposals have been made for press subsidies and redistributive schemes on a newspaper industry-wide basis. The aim of these schemes has been to maintain a 'varied and competitive press' by preventing a further reduction in the number of newspapers. Most of these schemes operate on the basis of impersonal, automatically functioning criteria, irrespective of the editorial content of newspapers, and so are designed to prevent governments from allocating financial subsidies in return for political support.

A number of proposals involve bestowing general press subsidies in order to stave off newspaper bankruptcies.[42] But the trouble with blanket subsidies – such as the current VAT zero-rating concession on newspaper sales – is that they afford the greatest relief to the big and successful and least relief to the small and impoverished. Their lack of selectivity thus makes these subsidies an expensive and inefficient way of succouring the publications most in need of help.

This has prompted some reformers to propose discriminatory subsidies. A much-canvassed proposal, in various forms, is for the introduction of a selective newsprint subsidy that would diminish on a sliding scale in relation to the volume of newsprint published by papers.[43] This would help small-circulation and low-paging newspapers much more than large circulation and bulky ones. An alternative, self-financing variant of this proposal is for a newspaper levy to be imposed which would rise sharply with the level of tonnage. Its proceeds would then be redistributed on the basis of the total volume of editorial newsprint published. The net benefit of this scheme would be greatest for papers with little advertising, small circulation and most editorial.

Various ingenious attempts have also been made to devise schemes for redistributing the profits of advertising from strong to weak papers.[44] However, the central difficulty encountered by this approach is that it is very difficult to alter the relative advertising utility of rival media through fiscal means since advertising selection is not determined solely by price.

The reform most often proposed is a quota on the amount of advertising which each publication is allowed to carry with the intention of reducing advertising dependence and redistributing advertising receipts from strong to weak papers. But if this took the form of a fixed ceiling on the percentage of total space that could be devoted to advertising, newspapers could still increase their advertising by increasing their total paging. Even if an upper limit on advertising paging was imposed, newspapers in a strong advertising position would probably increase their rates to offset the effect of the scheme: this could well result in their attracting more advertising revenue at the expense of their weaker rivals.

The imposition of a limit on the percentage of revenue derived from advertising would be slightly more effective. But strong papers would probably increase their sales revenue through additional promotion in order to be free to increase their advertising. This would damage the papers the scheme was intended to help. The alternative approach of a flat-rate ceiling on the advertising receipts that any publication could earn would require constant official revisions of upper limits in different categories of publication, and would involve a public agency in directly determining the revenue of press friends and critics.

A preferable plan would be to impose a levy on net advertisement revenue, rising on a sliding scale, and redistribute the proceeds. But strong papers would probably seek to offset the effect of the duty by increasing their rates. This could prompt some advertisers to spend less within their available budgets on weaker papers the scheme was designed to assist. It could also lead to some advertising expenditure being diverted to other media or below-the-line promotion. This said, a progressive levy would in fact achieve a net redistributive effect – although this is contested – but it would be a leaky and imperfect way of doing it.

These difficulties led the Labour Party to favour, for a time, the nationalization of press advertising through the creation of an Advertising Revenue Board which would fix all advertising rates, sell advertising space and collect all advertising receipts. The revenue would be reallocated, under this plan, in the form of incentive payments to publishers (to persuade them to advertise in the first place), a newsprint subsidy fixed in relation to the volume of newsprint published by each publication, and finance for new launches. But in practice, this scheme would be immensely complicated to administer with separate arrangements for different categories of publication; it would result, in some cases, in revenue being redistributed from unprofitable to profitable papers since newsprint volume is an unreliable index of commercial success; and it would give the Advertising Revenue Board enormous discretionary power in determining the revenue of press publications since it would decide how much would be reallocated as incentive payments, newsprint subsidies and funding for new publications.

A simpler way of modifying the class bias of the advertising market would be to impose a levy, on a sliding scale, on all papers charging above-average rates per 1,000 readers, and to redistribute the proceeds to papers with below-average rates per 1,000. The scheme's intention would be to render more equal the advertising value of readers to publishers, and to overcome the advertising disadvantage of reaching a mainly working-class audience. But the scheme would have the effect of endangering the future of quality papers which derive the major part of their revenue from advertising because they deliver elite audiences. If the scheme was modified to apply separately to papers in the popular and quality category, this would undermine the egalitarian purpose of the scheme (unless new 'down-market' quality papers were to emerge). In this modified form it would also weaken the remaining middle-market, popular papers.

Probably the most effective way of redistributing advertising revenue between publications is a plan devised by Professors Kaldor and Neild (although this was ironically not the main intention of their proposal). Their formula is for a levy on advertising revenue to be imposed at a percentage rate which would rise with the newspaper's circulation. The proceeds would be distributed proportionately to circulation until a certain figure (say, 2 million copies) had been reached when no further payments would be made. This would cause advertising to be redistributed by influencing directly the market coverage offered by individual titles: high-circulation newspapers would become less attractive to advertisers because it would become uneconomic for publishers to have circulations above a certain point. The plan would also directly assist papers with high fixed costs and low circulations.

This plan at least has the merit of being technically effective. But it would cause mass circulation papers deliberately to shed sales, by for example, not delivering in high cost, outlying areas. A scheme that involves large numbers of *Sun* readers being denied copies of their favourite paper – with lengthy legal battles over whether, say, a Scottish edition of the *Sun* was really a different newspaper or not – is not politically feasible or indeed desirable.

There is a further more serious drawback to all these schemes. Their aim is to aid small-circulation and low-advertising papers, and so freeze and preserve what diversity there is left in the press. But it is not an appropriate strategy for the Left to adopt in Britain since there is no longer a significant socialist press to preserve or press diversity to conserve.

A complex system of press subsidiaries has been developed in most Western European countries designed essentially to preserve minority political papers against the onslaught of mass-circulation, entertainment-based papers.[45] Because this support system has been relatively successful and has confounded fears that it would lead to government control of the press, many radicals have been drawn to the idea of importing similar schemes to Britain.

But it is now too late to re-enact these schemes here (although it would not have been 25 years ago).[46] Within the framework of the radical market approach, there is no real alternative other than to devote resources to *generating* rather than conserving press diversity. This means, above all, funding new publications and scaling down some of the obstacles that lie in their path. One of the major obstacles that stand in their way is the market power of entrenched oligopoly.

Regulating the new information order

An effective anti-monopoly strategy needs to come to terms with the fact that media concentration is now a global rather than purely domestic problem. A small number of communications conglomerates have gained a dominant position in the production of information and cultural goods throughout the western world.[47] Typical of this new phenomenon is Murdoch's News Corporation which controls a world press empire with a total circulation of 20.5 million, a chain of television stations from Sydney to New York, a pan-European cable TV service, the movie major, Twentieth Century Fox, and the book publishers, Collins (Fontana) among other worldwide media interests.

Only action by national governments throughout the western world can make these sprawling media empires accountable. Among the countries to take a lead in this is, rather surprisingly, Reagan's America, where anti-monopoly curbs have prompted Murdoch to become an American citizen in order to retain full control of his American media interests. Even so, he may still be forced by the Federal Communications Commission to relinquish two prize newspapers in Chicago and New York.

The IBA has also taken an increasingly tough line in Britain. Ownership of ITV companies and commercial radio is now restricted to nationals of an EEC country and companies or organizations whose headquarters are registered in the EEC.

A similar set of rules should apply to the British press. Its effect would be to transform the pattern of newspaper ownership. Murdoch would be forced to relinquish the *Sun, News of the World*, the *Times* and *Sunday Times*; Conrad Black would no longer be eligible to control the *Telegraph* group; and Robert Maxwell would have to move his holding company out of Liechtenstein, if he wished to retain control of the *Mirror* group.

New diet plan

The American Federal Communications Commission's anti-monopoly policing has been mild by comparison with other precedents – the removal of the cinema chains from the Hollywood majors in 1947; the 1981 press anti-monopoly law passed in Italy forbidding any proprietor to control more than a 20 per cent market share; and the equivalent measure passed in France in 1984 setting the limit on 'national' daily sales at 15 per cent.

These measures should be reviewed in a British context. Just three men – Murdoch, Maxwell and Stephens – control 83 per cent of national Sunday and 75 per cent of national daily circulation. Beneath them is a further tier of regional chains which have a near local-press monopoly in many parts of the country.[48]

The stranglehold of these groups (or their successor organizations if a press nationality law was passed) could be weakened by introducing an anti-monopoly law specifying a limit on the market share or the number of papers that could be controlled by any publisher. A modest diet plan would be to limit overweight press corporations to owning no more than three national papers, 10 local dailies or 50 local weekly papers (paid and freesheet). This would force the Murdoch or successor group to shed one national paper, the Thomson group to lose two local dailies, and the Pearson group to sell off 23 local weeklies.

Joint ownership of voting shares in both press and broadcasting organizations could also be prohibited. In early 1985, press groups had voting shares in 12 out of 15 regional ITV companies, and 42 out of 48 local radio stations. In the case of ten radio stations and four ITV companies, the combined press share amounted to a 'controlling' interest. The effect of this measure would be to establish the press and broadcasting as wholly separate and genuinely competitive organizations.

Another way of establishing greater diversity of ownership in the press, advocated by Bruce Page, is to reconstitute the Press Association – the monopoly domestic news agency in Britain, collectively owned by the press groups – as an independent public trust.

Broadening access to capital

The freedom to publish is the cornerstone of the free market theory. If this theory is to be made to approximate to reality, new ways need to be found to facilitate this freedom.

At present, the high cost of launching and establishing a new paper in most sectors of the press amounts to a form of licensing more restrictive than the state licensing system abandoned in 1695 (not least because the latter was never made to work effectively).

Contrary to popular belief, new printing technology will not fundamentally change this situation. Although it will greatly reduce the production wages bill, this amounts – on the latest available figures – to only 21 per cent of total national newspaper costs.[49] This reduction in costs will help to restore profitability, in the short term, to flagging papers, and lower the circulation needed before a newspaper becomes viable. But it will not bring newspaper publishing within the reach of ordinary people.

This is borne out by the economics of Eddie Shah's new national paper which takes advantage of the latest cost-saving technology and flexible industrial practices. Its start-up and run-in costs are variously estimated at between £20 and £22 million. Another more modest project led by Whittam Smith for a national quality daily has been costed at £16–£17 million, assuming the use of a contract printer. Establishing a new local evening paper, with new technology, was estimated in 1977 to cost £2–£3 million.

The impact of the new technology in lowering costs reinforces rather than weakens the case for setting up a public agency which will help under-capitalized groups to launch new papers and magazines. It makes such ventures more possible: it does not make redundant the need for broadening access to capital.

One much-canvassed proposal is to set up a national printing corporation which would make available modern printing facilities at cheap rates.[50] However, this would not help prospective publishing groups to find the very substantial capital needed to research and develop a new publication and cover its initial trading losses. Nor would it answer the need to provide financial support for new ventures across the full spectrum of the media, including broadcasting, where high establishment costs are also a major obstacle to market entry.

Arguably, scarce resources could be put to better use by setting up a media enterprise board which would aid the launch of new media through development grants, low interest loans and management advice. The board would be required to support only those new ventures which appear, on the basis of professional assessment, to have a reasonable chance of succeeding. Its terms of reference could also specify that it give priority to projects mounted by groups a) without other media interests; b) with a demonstrable need for public venture capital; c) which have some form of democratic decision-making; d) which would significantly extend media diversity and e) create a significant number of new jobs.

The second role of the board would be to help finance alternative forms of ownership of media interests divested as a consequence of anti-monopoly measures. Thus, the board could help to finance, for example, a worker-management buy out of the *Times* or finance alternative groups – recruited from outside the magic circle of conglomerate capital – to take over the weeklies divested from the Pearson group. It could also intervene to ensure that not all the highly profitable media divested as a consequence of a media nationality act were bought up by other communications conglomerates.

The board's secondary role would be crucial to making anti-monopoly measures effective. One of the difficulties involved in divestment is that media groups will usually discard their least profitable media assets. Yet once some of these media are severed from their umbilical cord of corporate subsidy, they are immediately in danger of closing down.[51] The board should intervene, therefore, by backing consortia which it believes can turn around divested, loss-making media. Although the board would need to provide continuing financial support over the medium term for this purpose, this would merely amount, in most cases, to an alternative way of routing public money. The deficits of most loss-making media are currently being set against tax liability by their media combines. In the new situation, taxpayers' money would be directed not to serving the private interests of capital but to serving the public good of securing a more pluralistic press.

The media enterprise board would need to be composed of people from all political parties and be accountable to parliament. It would be funded directly by government, although its regional offices may obtain limited local government financial support. The cost of funding it could be met by the introduction of a levy on media advertising expenditure. If set at 3 per cent, this would generate an annual income of over £120 million.

Modifying market distortions

According to free market rhetoric, the market is merely the *neutral* mechanism that relates supply to demand. But, in reality, the market in the press industry is currently slanted towards the Right.

Economies of scale are particularly significant in the press due to the high proportion of costs that go into making the first copy. This generally gives publications with large sales a big advantage in terms of lower unit costs. Large sales also usually produce disproportionately high advertising receipts by comparison with publications with a similar readership profile. Size is thus a major advantage in the press industry:[52] this helps the Right since most large (as well as small) newspapers are right-wing.

Once newspapers gain a decisive lead, they are able to exert pressure on their smaller revenue rivals in a number of ways – undercutting on advertising rates, holding back on a cover-price increase, poaching their rivals' talent with higher salaries, spending more on editorial outlay, larger promotion budgets and so on. Again, most leading papers in Fleet Street and in the regional press are on the Centre Right.

Above all, advertising rigs the market in favour of the Right. Conservative publications generally attract more advertising revenue per reader than left-wing papers because they reach, on balance, a more affluent readership. A minority of advertisers also refuse, in principle, to advertise in left-wing publications. As a consequence, the advertising subsidy system favours, in general, the right-wing press. This has important consequences since all commercial newspapers and most commercial magazines charge a net retail price that does not cover costs and so depend on advertising for their profits.

It is difficult to neutralize these distortions across the whole industry except by taking the press into public ownership. However, it is technically possible and relatively inexpensive to identify certain key sectors of the press where these distortions can be offset in the interests of creating a more varied press.

Thus, it may be thought desirable to create a more varied quality press by making it possible for a middle-market or downmarket quality paper with a circulation as small as that of the *Guardian* or the *Sunday Telegraph* to be economically viable. This would certainly influence the political agenda of broadcasting and affect the quality of political debate.

To facilitate this, a subsidy scheme could be introduced which would confer a cash bounty for every additional 10,000 sales over the level of 50,000 copies up to 500,000 in the case of daily papers and up to 750,000 in the case of Sunday papers. Above these levels, the bounty would taper off and reduce to zero at a specified circulation point. To be eligible the newspaper would have to devote over 20 per cent of its editorial space to news and comment about public affairs and derive less than 40 per cent of its revenue from advertising. There is no newspaper that would currently qualify for this grant. But its introduction would help to encourage and sustain new quality-paper launches aimed at a downmarket or middle-market readership – something that the economics of the advertising-dominated quality press currently makes impossible at competitive retail prices.[53]

Another example of the way in which market opportunities could be increased is to intervene in order to assist the distribution of minority publications. The distributive trade is geared primarily towards selling large-scale publications. Some smaller newsagents also boycott socialist publications. As a consequence, it is sometimes difficult for minority publications to break out of the vicious circle of not being distributed, not being seen and not being bought.

Stuart Holland has proposed the setting up of a press distribution service, a publicly owned wholesale and retailing agency which would handle both minority and mainstream publications. But a more effective short-term strategy would be to impose a legal obligation on the distribution trade to handle and display publications as requested by publishers since this would give publishers guaranteed access to the whole distribution trade.[54] The commercial interests of wholesalers and retailers could be safeguarded by exempting them from liability for libel damages. They should also be entitled to charge a specified handling and administration charge for returning unsold copies.

In short, it is not enough simply to set up a media enterprise board.

Market distortions need to be modified and market opportunities maximized if it is not to be a convalescent home for lame ducks.

Industrial democracy

The first Royal Commission on the Press proclaimed in 1949 that 'it is undoubtedly a great merit of the British press that it is completely independent of outside financial interests . . .' This has long ceased to be true. Indeed, as the last Press Commission commented bluntly, 'Rather than saying that the press has other business interests, it would be truer to argue that the press has become a subsidiary of other industries.'

This has given rise to no-go areas where some newspapers are reluctant to probe for fear of damaging the corporate interests of their conglomerate parent company. As a paper owned by the Thomson Group frankly conceded to the last Press Commission, 'Coverage of Thomson organization activities (from North Sea oil to package holidays) tends, certainly, to be drily factual'.[55] It has also resulted in some papers being used to further their proprietors' commercial interests, as exemplified by Tiny Rowland's vendetta against the Al Fayed brothers in the *Observer*.

In these circumstances, industrial democracy should be seen not simply as a way of extending democracy to the work-place but as a way of defending the press against proprietors whose vested interests now compromise its editorial integrity. The diffusion of editorial power within newspapers and magazines would also be a way of safeguarding the independence of the press from government in the context of increased public intervention in the press industry.

A shift towards greater economic democracy in the press could involve any of the following (in ascending order of significance): guaranteed regular meetings with senior journalists and management; access to information about corporate decisions and advance plans; a code of conduct protected by contract; the right to participate in senior appointments; the election and reselection at regular intervals of senior editorial and managerial personnel; representation on an editorial committee, management committee and supervisory board; majority votes on all three.[56]

Workers' control can also be structured in different ways. It can involve exclusive control by the publication's entire workforce; shared control with public representatives and/or shareholders; and binary control (as in the Yugoslav press) in which intellectual labour controls the editorial side and predominantly manual labour controls the production and business side of a newspaper.

Industrial democracy in the press can be implemented directly by statute. Alternatively, it could be encouraged in new ventures through the terms of reference of the media enterprise board. The third option is to foster it gradually through fiscal means. The granting of VAT concessions to newspapers or the award of development grants to parent organizations controlling newspapers could be made conditional upon the introduction of some degree of industrial democracy.

Radical market approaches to broadcasting

One of the central problems in promoting the free market model for broadcasting is the high operating costs of television companies. So far only big business consortia have convinced the IBA that they have sufficient capital to assume responsibility for an ITV franchise. The costs of the new generation of television outlets are even greater. It currently costs over £30 million to set up a new cable TV station, and the capital required to develop a profitable satellite service will be very much more. However, radio costs are significantly lower than television costs. Groups with limited resources can establish a local radio station, though the IBA's decision in 1985 to require advance payment for new transmitters makes this more difficult.

A media enterprise board should thus be seen as a key institution in the context of a market economy for broadcasting. Only through its intervention will under-resourced groups, with different perspectives from those who control big business consortia, be able to bid for ITV, cable TV and indeed major local radio franchises.

To enhance the impact of the board, steps could also be taken to increase market opportunities for small independent companies. The television union, ACTT, has displayed its social concern by establishing cost-cutting workshop agreements for non-profit-making television organizations. The successful establishment of Channel Four on broadly the basis first brilliantly advocated by Anthony Smith has also helped to open up broadcasting since it acts as a publisher of programmes rather than a production centre. This could become a model for reforming the BBC: the Corporation could be required to commission and transmit a specified proportion of its programmes from independent, UK-registered companies. The IBA's and Cable TV Authority's terms of reference could also be modified so that they are encouraged to include non-profit-making local trusts in their franchise awards. Another way of helping the independent film-making and video sector would be to give production companies the same legal right of access to video shops as has been proposed for publishers in relation to newsagents.

All these reforms entail modifying existing broadcasting institutions so that they reflect a broader plurality of political views and cultural experiences. An alternative approach would be to institutionalize consumer representation – rather than monopoly franchises – as the basis of the broadcasting system. The Dutch broadcasting system points to one way in which this could be done. Both airtime and the use of publicly owned production facilities, with technical staff, is allocated in the Netherlands to different groups on the basis of the size of their membership usually linked to the sales of their programme guides. This results in a plurality of organizations from commercial groups like TROS to VARA (with close links to the Labour Party) and the NCVR (a conservative, protestant organization) each providing a comprehensive package of services. None of these groups, unlike the central news service, are required to adopt a bi-partisan approach. The result is a broadcasting system that reflects a much wider spectrum of political opinion and cultural values than that in Britain.[57]

The Dutch broadcasting system is not without its problems. It has a smaller revenue base than that in Britain; the rise of TROS, with a heavy diet of American programmes, was not anticipated by the original architects of the broadcasting system; and Dutch broadcasting is now seriously threatened by the development of satellite broadcasting. But its strengths also suggest that the current lack of interest on the Left in broadcasting experience overseas – rooted in the conventional wisdom that we have the best broadcasting system in the world and, consequently, nothing to learn – is misplaced.

Socialist approaches

When the means of communication are so expensive that they are beyond the reach of most people, then the public must hold the means of communication in its own hands in trust. This is the basic, underlying rationale of the libertarian socialist perspective. It is a liberating, emancipatory approach in which common ownership is conceived as a way of opening up and extending the means of communication rather than shrinking and curtailing it.[58]

There is another socialist tradition in which the media, under public ownership, are conceived of as instruments for promoting the public good as defined by the state and the party which embody the collective interest of the masses. This gives rise to media systems such as that in the USSR which – though deviating in some respects from cold-war stereotypes – seriously restrict freedom of expression.

Surprisingly little detailed consideration has been given to how the British media might be reorganized along libertarian socialist lines. An exception is a blueprint offered by Militant, based on the nationalization of all press and broadcasting facilities.[59] The Militant plan distinguishes between editorial control over media content and control over the means of media production. They propose that the production sphere would be under the control of a management committee of which a third would be elected by the relevant trade union, a third by the TUC and a third by government. Management committee representatives would be subject to recall, paid average wages and be exposed to democratic checks through trade unions.

But editorial control over both newspapers and broadcasting would be vested in political parties in proportion to the votes they received at elections. This is a pluralistic formula which would probably give the Conservative Party in socialist Britain a larger press than the Labour Party and trade union movement have now. In addition, specialist publications would be controlled by scientific, technical and professional groups and organizations.

The Militant plan is only quasi-libertarian. It explicitly excludes fascist political parties and all specialist groups which do not have democratic structures from having a stake in the media. While it provides community access to media production facilities, it makes no provision for the financing of operating costs. What happens when media outlets operate at a loss, and what role the market plays is also less than clear. But perhaps the general aspect of the plan that is most questionable is whether political parties, which would become pivotal controllers of the media, can be really thought to adequately reflect and represent the full range of diversity within British society.

The Militant proposal is valuable, however, in signifying what an alternative to the Soviet model might look like. Various ways of revising and reworking it suggest themselves. But this is not the place to debate alternative plans for a distant future.

If a socialist media system emerges in Britain, it will be determined by the social and political configurations that have transformed British society as a whole. It will also be shaped by the accumulated lessons and experience of reforming media institutions. The long and arduous business of amendment and revision is part of the process of achieving something that does not exist in the world – a genuinely libertarian, democratic media system.

The free market seduction of the Left

The press
Little progress will be made towards reform so long as a substantial body of opinion, including many on the Left, believe that the press can be transformed without modifying the free market basis of its organization.

This is not to disagree with those who argue that the Left should develop more entrepreneurial, managerial and editorial skills in building up a radical press,[60] and that trade unions should give greater priority to financing and aiding this rebirth.

But the limits to what can be achieved within the existing system also need to be assessed realistically. Many trade unions are currently going through a financial crisis because their fixed costs have not declined in line with their fall in membership caused by the sharp rise in unemployment. Furthermore, new publishing ventures in the main commercial sectors of the press will continue to require an enormous capital outlay despite the introduction of new, labour-saving technology. Even to launch just one national daily using new technical processes will cost the equivalent of five times the total annual income produced by the Labour Party's entire individual membership.

Of course, Stuart Hall and others are also right to argue that a systematic effort needs to be made to 'permeate' the press by seeking to change the ideological and political environment in which journalists operate. But again the limits of what can be achieved need to be recognized. The relatively bi-partisan press of the 1960s has been superseded by a much more overtly right-wing, propagandist press dominated by more interventionist proprietors and a more hierarchical style of management. The task of 'permeating' the press is now much more difficult than it was.

The belief that a major revival of radicalism will produce a *corresponding* change in the press is also misplaced. There is not now and never has been in the last 100 years – save significantly during the 1940s when the press was subject to extensive economic controls – anything like a match between public opinion and the editorial opinions expressed in the press. Thus in the 1983 general election, the Conservative press accounted for 74 per cent of national daily circulation: yet the Conservative Party only secured 44 per cent of the poll – and even less (32 per cent) of the total registered vote.

A marked discrepancy between press opinion and public opinion has not been confined to general elections. Every single national newspaper, save one, supported trade union 'reform' in 1969, backed Britain's membership of the EEC in the 1975 referendum, opposed the TUC's day of action in 1980, supported Denis Healey in the Labour Party's watershed 1981 deputy leadership contest[61] and applauded Kinnock's attack on his party's 'hard Left' in 1985. The one exception has been the *Morning Star*, seldom running to more than six pages, with less than 0.1 per cent of national daily circulation. Yet there was clearly not 99.9 per cent agreement amongst the British public on all these issues.

Underlying this disjunction between press and public opinion has been a number of distorting prisms – the high cost of publishing, the personal commitments of proprietors, hierarchical authority within press organizations, journalists' own values, heavy reliance on elite sources, the 'structuring' effect of advertising finance, the brute force of oligopoly – that cause the press to refract rather than reflect public opinion.[62] In the absence of public intervention, many of these distortions will persist.

Furthermore, the press as it is presently constituted is a significant obstacle to rebuilding the popular base of the Left. The issues of lack of genuine pluralism in the press and lack of popular support for the Left are not separate issues. If the Left is to regain support by communicating its ideas more effectively, channels of mass communication need to be unblocked.

Similarly, there are strict limits to the degree to which the social responsibility, voluntaristic approach can be successful. Any move towards strengthening the professional consciousness of journalists, whether through better training courses or a more energetic Press Council, is to be welcomed. But the weakness of this voluntaristic approach stems from its idealistic belief that the quality of the press is determined by the qualities of individual journalists. This fails to take account of the way in which the organization of the press constrains what journalists do and shapes even their perceptions of what constitutes professionalism. Unless organizational structures are changed or modified, well-meaning reforms based on admonition or uplift will accomplish relatively little.

The second bedrock against radical reform is the fear that public intervention will lead to political censorship. This is usually rooted in the mistaken assumption that the market guarantees press independence from government whereas public intervention automatically threatens this independence. In fact, Britain's overwhelmingly conservative press is closely linked to conservative governments through a shared commitment to broadly the same political philosophy, close working ties and informal social contacts at many levels. However, public intervention even in a highly regulatory form, with too few safeguards against government manipulation, still produces a broadcasting system that has a real degree of autonomy from government. Proof of this is demonstrated every day: broadcasting current affairs output contains a higher proportion of material critical of this government, because of the obligation on broadcasters to be bipartisan, than that of the overwhelmingly conservative national newspaper press. Nor do the substantive examples of public intervention in the press in liberal democratic countries – from the economic controls imposed on the British press in the period 1940–56 to the highly complex press intervention system developed in Sweden – justify the inflated fears about the threat to press freedom posed by statutory reform.

State power is the only means by which the interests of the community can be established as paramount above those of monopoly press capital. The question at issue – as far as radicals are concerned – should be not *whether* but *how* the enabling power of the state should be harnessed to the general good.

Broadcasting

Ironically, the claim implicit in the word 'deregulation' – the emancipation of broadcasting from state control – turns out, on close examination, to be highly misleading. Conventional broadcasting will continue to be regulated by the state due to the need to allocate airwave frequencies; cable TV is being developed (at the request of 'deregulators') in the form of state-licensed monopolies; and satellite broadcasting will not be developed as a free for all.

What deregulation means, in practice, is not the removal of all state controls but their relaxation in ways that will assist the leading communications conglomerates to expand at the expense of broadcasting diversity.

The only obstacle to the leading leisure conglomerates dominating the broadcasting industry in the same way that they now dominate the press, record, film and publishing industries in Britain[63] is the existence of a large public sector in broadcasting and the IBA. The rising volume of criticism directed against the BBC and in favour of 'reform' of the IBA is no coincidence: they have both been targeted partly because they are obstacles in the path of the leisure conglomerates' expansion.

If 'balance' requirements on broadcasters are lifted *in the context of big business control of both television and radio*, the result will be a general, overall shift of broadcasting towards the Right of the political spectrum. The relaxation of schedule controls will also lead, on the main channels, to the reduction of minority programmes in favour of common-denominator material.

What the long-term effects would be of extending advertising across an expanded, multi-channel broadcasting system is more difficult to predict. All the indications are that it would contribute, as it has done in the press, to a polarization between mass market and quality, elite provision. The lifting of the current prohibition on advertising sponsorship would also lead to direct advertising influence on programme content, as it has done in the United States.[64]

A move towards deregulation would also destabilize the economic foundations of the British TV industry. Market research shows that American imports tend to be among the more popular programmes screened on British television. They are also much cheaper than domestically made programmes because it costs much less to replicate than to make programmes: the US television majors, enjoying worldwide sales, can also afford to heavily discount. The enormous disparity of prices involved was graphically underlined by the Hunt Committee which found that, while ITV spent on average £40,000 and the BBC £30,000 per hour of programming, the same one-hour time slot could be filled by a popular American programme for as little as £2,000.[65]

At present, British television is protected by the import quota imposed by the BBC and IBA which restricts the screening of non-EEC programmes to about 15 per cent of transmission time. The abrupt removal of this protection would shrivel the British industry, and bring Britain into line with the growing number of countries which rely on US imports rather than domestically made productions for the majority of their drama programmes.

This is not to imply support for xenophobic opposition to increased imports of American and other foreign programmes. The issue is not a simple one of being for or against 'wall-to-wall Dallas'. Rather the question is how to achieve a balance in which foreign imports are encouraged as an extension of consumer choice, while a British television industry is also maintained which reflects the cultural and social diversity of British society. It is impossible to achieve this balance without controls.

In short, the siren voices calling for deregulation need to be treated with caution. This is not to suggest that the Left should be corralled into unthinking support of the status quo. On the contrary, the best way to defend our present broadcasting system is to improve it through the adoption of some of the reforms that have been discussed. But when attacking the defects of the existing system, we also need to be aware of what could be lost – and the penalties of keeping poor company.

The way ahead

The potential exists for mounting a successful, popular campaign for reforming the mass media. Newspaper excesses, like the invention of a fictitious interview with Mrs Marica McKay, the widow of the 'Falklands VC hero' (*Sun*), the touching up of a photograph of Lady Di to give a hint of nipples showing through a low-cut dress (*Sun*), and the offering of 'blood money' to friends and relative of the mass murderer, Peter Sutcliffe (*Daily Mail, News of the World, Daily Star* and *Daily Express*),[66] have given rise to a groundswell of popular criticism of the press that extends right across the political spectrum. This is reflected in the relatively high level of dissatisfaction expressed with the press in the SCPR 1985 survey.[67] The BBC was also shown in the survey to command below-average satisfaction by comparison with other service institutions.

The key constituencies that should be targeted in a reform campaign are those groups that are regularly portrayed in the media in a negative way – women, ethnic minorities, trade unionists and gays.

Disaffected media workers are the second group important in constructing a popular campaign. Technological change has radicalized print and distribution workers. Significant signs of opposition to proprietorial political intervention have surfaced among journalists on some Fleet Street papers. Above all, a growing number of broadcasters have been alienated by the press campaign against the BBC.

The other important target is the Labour Party and, given the changed political landscape, the Alliance. After over 50 years of immobility, the Labour Party is showing the first real indications of wanting to put into effect some kind of media reform programme. In 1974, it published its first-ever policy document on the mass media. In 1983, it committed itself for the first time in a general election manifesto to radical-sounding media reforms (although, admittedly, some of these were imprecise and, in the case of broadcasting, totally opaque). At a local level, the Labour-controlled GLC took practical steps to promote media diversity by setting up the Greater London Enterprise Board.

But the key to sustaining a successful media campaign is to formulate an effective programme around which popular dissatisfaction with the media can gel. A draft programme is set out in the Appendix that follows this essay. It may well be that an alternative selection or reworking of the policies that have been discussed in this chapter will be preferred. But what is now clearly desirable is for some kind of consensus to be reached around a reform package that the largest possible number of campaigning activists can support and promote.

If this does not happen, the prospects for reform look decidedly bleak. A formidable coalition of commercial and political interests has taken shape which is opposed to all press reforms, and which is committed to reconstituting broadcasting on free market lines. The quickening pace of technical change will facilitate their project. They command the high ground now because they have the ear of a sympathetic government. But they are also so well entrenched in the media hierarchies that they could well determine the future shape of media policy, even if the next election produces a change of administration. Only a formidable counter-coalition, organized around an alternative programme, is capable of stopping them.

References

1. The nearest equivalent is an American survey: F.S. Siebert, T. Peterson and W. Schramm, *Four Theories of the Press*, Urbana: University of Illinois Press 1956.
2. See below, pp. 175–191.
3. John Whale, *The Politics of the Media*, London: Fontana 1980 (revised edition).
4. These arguments are constantly reiterated in press editorials. But for a particularly eloquent presentation of them, see Lord

Shawcross (former Chairman of the Royal Commission on the Press, 1961–2 and former Chairman of the Press Council) in *The Twelfth Commonwealth Press Conference*, London: Commonwealth Press Union 1975.

5. Adam Smith Institute, *Funding the BBC*, London: 1985, p. 40.
6. *Ibid.*, p. 39.
7. Christopher Dunkley, *Television Today and Tomorrow*, Harmondsworth: Penguin 1985.
8. Royal Commission on the Press 1947–9, London: HMSO 1949, p. 177.
9. *Ibid.*, Royal Commission on the Press 1961–2, London: HMSO 1962; Royal Commission on the Press 1974–7, London: HMSO 1977.
10. Royal Commission on the Press 1974–7, p. 126.
11. Roy Hattersley, speech at Blackpool, 1 October 1978; *Parliamentary Debates*, London: HMSO 18 February 1983, col. 598 ff.
12. Colin Sparks, 'The Working Class Press: Radical and Revolutionary Alternatives', *Media, Culture and Society*, 7, 2, 1985.
13. For further discussion of this, see in particular G. McLennan, S. Hall and D. Held, *State and Society in Contemporary Britain*, Cambridge: Polity 1984.
14. Ian Aitken, 'Whose Back Against the Wall?', the *Guardian*, 25 November 1985; cf. Robert Taylor and Steve Vines, 'Farewell to Fleet Street', the *Observer*, 5 January 1985.
15. All quotations taken from transcripts of speeches given by David Elstein in 1985.
16. For instance, Peter Lewis, 'Neighbourhood Set to Drive Out Pirates', *New Statesman*, 23 August 1985.
17. S. Hall, C. Critcher, T. Jefferson, J. Clarke and B. Roberts, *Policing the Crisis*, London: Macmillan 1978.
18. However, greater emphasis is placed on the influence of ownership and managerial control in some culturalist accounts, including Stuart Hall's opening essay in this volume.
19. S. Hall, I. Connell and L. Curti, 'The "Unity" of Current Affairs Television', *Working Papers in Cultural Studies*, 9, 1976, p. 92.
20. *Ibid.*, p. 93.
21. This is a more sophisticated version of the classical liberal argument that broadcasting provides balanced information enabling citizens to participate responsibly in a liberal democracy. This variant comes from an unpublished paper by Paddy Scannell.

22. For a fuller discussion of the public service concept, see *The Public Service Idea in British Broadcasting*, Broadcasting Research Unit pamphlet, London: 1985.

23. Stuart Holland, 'Countervailing Press Power' in James Curran (ed.), *The British Press: A Manifesto*, London: Macmillan 1978; Michael Meacher, 'Reform of the Press', March 1982; Chris Mullin, 'The Case for an Independent Press Authority', January 1981.

24. Geoffrey Robertson, *People Against the Press*, London: Quartet 1983.

25. Richard Clutterbuck, *The Media and Political Violence*, London: Macmillan 1981; cf. unpublished evidence of the Institute of Journalists to the Royal Commission on the Press 1974-7.

26. Tom Baistow, *Fourth-Rate Estate*, London: Comedia 1985. Baistow also proposes in passing a press nationality bill without drawing out the radical implications of this admirable proposal, which is discussed later in this chapter.

27. Jeremy Tunstall, ' "Editorial Sovereignty" in the British Press' in O. Boyd-Barrett, C. Seymour-Ure and J. Tunstall, *Studies on the Press*, Royal Commission on the Press Working Paper No. 3, London: HMSO 1977.

28. Harold Evans, *Good Times, Bad Times*, London: Weidenfeld & Nicolson 1983.

29. Tom Baistow, letter to the *Guardian*, 9 December 1985; cf. T. Baistow, *Fourth-Rate Estate*, 1985, p. 108.

30. *Changing Television* (mimeo), 1981.

31. 'Broadcasting: Draft Proposals' (mimeo), 1981.

32. Annan Committee, *Report of the Committee on the Future of Broadcasting*, London: HMSO 1977.

33. Glasgow University Media Group, *Really Bad News*, London: Writers and Readers 1982.

34. John Sandford, *The Mass Media of the German-Speaking Countries*, London: Wolff 1976; Arthur Williams, 'West Germany: The Search for the Way Forward' in R. Kuhn (ed.), *The Politics of Broadcasting*, Beckenham: Croom Helm 1985.

35. Labour Party, *People and the Media*, 1974; evidence of the Standing Conference on Broadcasting to the Annan Committee.

36. James Curran, 'Hands Up for New Governors', *New Statesman*, 16 August 1985.

37. Tom Burns, *The BBC, Public Institutions and Private World*,

London: Macmillan 1977.

38. James Curran and Jean Seaton, *Power Without Responsibility: The Press and Broadcasting in Britain*, London: Methuen 1985 (revised edition).

39. Labour Party, *People and the Media*; 'Broadcasting: Draft Proposals'; Raymond Williams, *Communications*, London: Chatto & Windus 1966 (revised edition).

40. James Curran, 'Reconstructing the Mass Media' in J. Curran (ed.), *The Future of the Left*, Cambridge: Polity 1984.

41. Royal Commission on the Press 1974–7; Geoffrey Robertson, *People Against the Press*.

42. Royal Commission on the Press 1947–9, 1961–2, 1974–7.

43. George Matthews, 'Freedom for Whom?' in E. Moonman (ed.), *The Press: A Case for Commitment*, London: Fabian Society Tract 391; the *Guardian* in unpublished proposal to the Wilson government in the mid-1960s.

44. John Ryan, 'The Role of Advertising' in E. Moonman (ed.), *The Press*; Young Fabian Group, *Royal Commission on the Press*, vol. 5 and vol. 6, London: HMSO 1962; R. Kaldor and R. Neild, *Royal Commission on the Press*, vol. 6, London: HMSO 1962; Labour Party, *People and the Media*, 1974; Labour Party, *Labour's Programme*, London 1982.

45. Anthony Smith, *Subsidies and the Press in Europe*, London: Political and Economic Planning 1977.

46. The one exception to this is the Press Subsidies Council in Sweden which helped to finance the launch of 17 newspapers between 1976 and 1983 – with only two failures. It is a model, in some ways, for the media enterprise board discussed later.

47. Tapio Varis, 'The International Flow of Television Programmes', *Journal of Communication*, 34, 1984; M.-L. Kalkkinen and R. Sarkkinen, 'The International Entertainment Industry and the New Media', *Nordicom Review*, 1, 1985; J. Tunstall, *The Media Are American*, London: Constable 1977.

48. *The Press and People 1984*, London: Press Council 1985; N. Hartley, P. Gudgeon and R. Crafts, *Concentration of Ownership in the Provincial Press*, Royal Commission on the Press Research Series 5, London: HMSO 1977.

49. *Royal Commission on the Press Interim Report*, London: HMSO 1976.

50. *The British Press*, London: Political and Economic Planning 1938;

the minority report of the *Royal Commission on the Press 1974–7*; Peter Golding and Graham Murdock, 'Confronting the Market: Public Intervention and Press Diversity' in J. Curran (ed.), *The British Press*.

51. The effect of the Labour Party's general election manifesto (1983) proposal to impose an upper limit on the number of publications any publishing group could control would probably have been to close papers down since no provision was made to aid papers after divestment. See Labour Party, *The New Hope for Britain*, 1983, p. 26.

52. However, there can also be significant diseconomies of scale. See N. Hartley *et al*, *Concentration of Ownership*.

53. This is a variant of a scheme proposed by Fred Hirsch and David Gordon, designed in their case to remove the advertising penalties inhibiting quality papers from attracting a larger, less elite readership. See their *Newspaper Money*, London: Hutchinson 1975.

54. D. Berry, L. Cooper and C. Landry, *Where is the Other News?*, London: Comedia 1980; L. Cooper, C. Landry and D. Berry, *The Other Secret Service*, London: Comedia 1980.

55. The clause in parenthesis has been added by me.

56. For further discussion of this issue, see Harold Frayman (*Labour Weekly* journalist), 'Democracy and the Press', unpublished paper, 1980; and Neal Ascherson, 'Newspapers and Internal Democracy', in J. Curran (ed.), *The British Press*.

57. Kees van der Haak, *Broadcasting in the Netherlands*, London: Routledge & Kegan Paul 1977; Jan Wieten, 'Media Pluralism: The Policy of the Dutch Government', *Media, Culture and Society*, 2, 1979.

58. Raymond Williams, 'A Socialist Commentary' in E. Moonman (ed.), *The Press*; S. Hall, R. Williams and E. Thompson (eds), *New Left Manifesto*, London, 1967.

59. *What We Stand For*, London: Militant 1985; *A Fighting Programme for Print Workers*, London: Militant 1976.

60. Charles Landry, David Morley, Russell Southwood and Patrick Wright, *What A Way to Run a Railroad*, London: Comedia 1985.

61. Support for Healey relates only to those papers which expressed an editorial opinion.

62. For a full presentation of this argument, see J. Curran and J. Seaton, *Power Without Responsibility*, London: Methuen 1985, Chapter 7.

63. *Ibid.*
64. Erik Barnouw, *The Sponsor*, New York: Oxford University Press 1978.
65. *Report of the Enquiry into Cable Expansion and Broadcasting Policy*, London: HMSO 1982.
66. Henry Porter, *Lies, Damned Lies*, London: Chatto & Windus 1984.
67. R. Jowell and S. Witherspoon (eds), *British Social Attitudes: The 1985 Report*, Gower 1985.

Appendix: A programme of media reform

1. Press and Broadcasting
- Establish a ministry of arts, communications and entertainments, headed by a minister of cabinet rank, to oversee co-ordinated media reform.
- Introduce a freedom of information act and relax laws of libel, contempt and breach of privilege.
- Introduce a levy on all media advertising.

2. Press
- Impose an upper limit of three national newspapers, ten local dailies or fifty local weekly papers (paid and freesheet) that can be controlled by any one proprietor or group.
- Restrict ownership of British newspapers to nationals of all EEC country and companies whose headquarters are registered in the EEC

ting shares in the press, commercial radio and television.
   radio and television.
- Strengthen the Fair Trading Act to curb future acquisitions of newspapers by the large press groups.
- Establish a media enterprise board to aid the launch of new media ventures, fund alternative ownership of divested media, and recommend the introduction of selective press subsidies.
- Introduce a 'conscience' clause in the contracts of journalists; create new machinery for staff participation in the appointment of editors; and establish legal safeguards for the editorial independence of editors.
- Ensure that the distribution trade handles any lawful publication at the request of the publisher, subject to a handling charge.

- Establish a statutory Ombudsperson to enforce the legal right of reply for victims of factual misrepresentation, and give the Press Council the power to enforce publication of its adjudications in offending publications.

3. Broadcasting
- Establish six competing television corporations covering four channels, cable TV and satellite TV.
- Create five competing radio corporations covering the four nationally networked radio channels and local radio.
- Redefine the terms of reference of broadcasting organizations to include a commitment to 'represent the differences within society, and to produce programmes from the different perspectives in society'.
- Establish a central agency to collect both the license fee and commercial revenues of broadcasting organizations.
- Establish a central co-ordinating board composed of representatives from each of the broadcasting corporations.
- Elect members of all broadcasting authorities through an electoral college.
- Introduce positive discrimination in the recruitment of broadcasting staff so that they are more representative of the public they serve.
- Negotiate a European agreement for regulating satellite television.

10. Selling the paper? Socialism and cultural diversity

Geoff Mulgan and Ken Worpole

There is a widespread belief that the media of the Left are in a crisis. It is not hard to paint a picture of decline, comparing 1985 with the heyday of the *Daily Worker* or *Daily Herald*. Equally, there is little doubt that the radical community and alternative newspapers and magazines of the 1960s and 1970s have experienced a painful decline along with the 'underground', voluntarist culture that sustained them. Interestingly many of their stalwarts have moved into the very positions they used to attack: the guerrilla journalists of the Hackney and Islington self-styled 'gutter presses' of the early 1970s now enjoy leading positions on their respective local councils.

But to see the question solely in terms of the organs of socialism is misleading. Political and ideological battles are now fought on very different terrain.

We believe that left and oppositional culture in Britain is now sustained as much through forms such as popular music, video, television and film as it is through the printed word to which so many socialists understandably have a deep historical attachment. Many of the most powerful and profound movements for change have come from forms with which the left media are quite unfamiliar. One example of this is the experience of the women's movement which has grown and sustained itself through narrative forms and the reappropriation of popular genres such as the fictional epic rather than through the close political reporting and argument of the organizationally based newspaper. Equally there is little doubt that the movements of radical black politics have found their most powerful articulation and expression not so much in theory and polemical journalism as in poetry, music, film and the theatre.

Television, a form which is often (and correctly) attacked for its complicity with the state or international capitalism, and for its role in generating political passivity and apathy, has nevertheless generated the most powerful and enduring images and slogans of dole-queue

Britain in programmes such as *Tucker's Lot* and *The Boys from the Blackstuff* with its ubiquitous slogan 'Giz a Job'. (One might ask how many slogans from *Socialist Worker* or *Militant* are actually chanted from the Kop). Similarly, it was the culture of capitalistic and ephemeral popular music which lifted the Specials 'Ghost Town' to No. 1 in the month of the 1981 riots and the Royal Wedding, or 'Anarchy in the UK' to No. 1 in the month of the Queen's Jubilee.

To argue that media like television, music and fiction play an important role in ideological struggle is not to deny that, as industries, they are dominated by massive multinational or quasi-state organizations, or that they operate within the constraints of the market-place. The important point to recognize is that any serious materialist analysis of how socialist ideas are communicated must start from the realities of how representations are consumed – from the fact that 80 per cent of adults in Britain watch not less than two hours of television daily, and that 4.5 million video tapes are rented in Britain each week, or, from another perspective, from the fact that the UK circulation of the *Morning Star* or *Socialist Worker* is less than 0.5 per cent that of the *Mirror*.

The symptoms are those of the gulf that separates the organizations of socialist opposition – the Labour and Communist Parties, the far left sects and the trade unions – and the cultural expressions of that opposition. The sheer scale of the Thatcher government's onslaught has obscured this fundamental fact. Despair continues to drive people towards organizations whose language and goals often seem archaic and inappropriate to the crisis they are living. So much of the work of sustaining popular opposition to the organized conservative consensus, so assiduously developed since the mid-1970s, has been done by those involved in popular culture. So, too, in the long-term battles of ideas and ideals – the Gramscian 'wars of position' that shape popular perceptions of what is possible and desirable – such struggles have often been fought from outside the traditional politics of a Left which has often seemed inward-looking and unwilling to take up new challenges or develop new forms of organization.

The growth of many of the new movements – in black and women's politics, around issues such as ecology, food, health and the Third World – has no doubt been aided by an increasing impatience and frustration with the generalities of a socialist project which seemed to claim to have an incontrovertible answer to every problem under the sun. It is in these areas that the traditional left politics of having 'the correct programme' and 'selling the paper' – a paper and behind it a programme that expects to have a correct and coherent line on every subject – has come unstuck. For the new currents reflect more than the awakening of political consciousness in new areas. They can also be seen as part of a more profound process of ideological fragmentation, where political views and lifestyles are increasingly chosen as if from the supermarket shelf, thrown into inconsistent bundles and discarded if they don't fit. We are all familiar with this from everyday life – with anti-statist socialists who are addicts of *Dynasty*, with black trade unionists who read the *Sun*, with working-class Labour voters who believe in the 'short, sharp shock', with members of Tory CND who believe in the welfare state, and with unemployed men who would say that Mrs Thatcher is 'the only man in British politics'. The left media have found it hard to adapt to these new configurations and complexities.

What this means is that the terrain of ideological struggle has changed, probably irreversibly. The nature of the Right's strategy during the 1970s, focusing as it did on a politics of 'personal values', of home, family and security, is highly significant. For Mrs Thatcher, the pages of *Woman* or an appearance on the *Jimmy Young Show* count for more than the approbation of the political elite. The projection of a set of images and values counts for more than (an apparent) ideological consistency.

Their success has pointed up the problem of the limited repertoire of imagery and iconography made available through the traditional left media – cartoons and photographs of demonstrations and mass meetings, picket-line violence, or head and shoulder photographs of individual cadres taken from below to give them that 'upwards and onwards' look so beloved of early constructivist photography. Socialists have let the vision of a world of peace and plenty, of self-organized forms of mutual support and good humoured everyday solidarity, be appropriated by the advertising agencies and the glossy magazines.

So the politics of representation is immensely important. This is what feminists and cultural workers, particularly in the field of photography and other forms of visual imagery, have been telling us with a degree of urgency for the past decade. We need to listen. And of course the politics of representation (cultural) is not exactly unconnected with the politics of representation (political).

These problems tie in closely with popular perceptions of what the role of culture and the media might look like in a socialist Britain.

Whether we like it or not, it is likely that people have a greater distrust of the Left than of the Right when it comes to the editorial control of magazines and newspapers. The Right 'give people what they want', so they say, whereas the Left 'give people what they think is good for them'. Popular socialist journalism is a rare animal, though it is true that for some periods of its embattled editorial life *Socialist Worker* has been a highly readable weekly socialist paper with a wide appeal and influence. But in general socialist journalism is not very convincing. Let us take two traditions, one old and one new. The old one is the trade union press itself, the union journals that head offices produce for their membership, a press that reaches millions of people each month – but with how much effect?

Tony Grace recently undertook a general survey of the trade union press, and a series of interviews with some of the editors revealed that the most important function of this sector of the monthly press was seen by its editorial staff as 'communicating from the leadership to the membership'.[1] As Grace says, 'Despite the fact that material generated by the membership is included in every issue, it is always ranked lower in importance than *the downward movement of messages from leadership to membership*.' (our italics) The iconography of these magazines is equally conservative, consisting largely of photographs of the general secretary (we counted 13 in just one issue) complemented by lots of small passport-size photographs of full-time officials like a Special Branch internal bulletin or house magazine. One's general impression is that such magazines are amongst the most unread of publications and many of them are never even unpacked from the bundles in which they are sent to workplaces. Happily this is changing, and some unions are endeavouring to find out how to make their journals – potentially a very important vehicle for the discussion of political and cultural issues – into genuinely popular forms of reading. Some, though, will clearly never let any form of editorial independence interrupt the downward flow of approved exhortations and self-publicity. This does not encourage people to think warmly about approving the handover of media editorial control from right-wing populist businessmen to committees which include political and trade union apparatchiks.

A more recent tradition of socialist journalism is only slightly more encouraging. This comes from the growing number of local council freesheets issued by many Labour local authorities in order to win public opinion to the policies they are pursuing. Very few of them manage to break out of the straitjacket of 'municipalism', which exhorts electors to be grateful to Labour politicians for what they are doing for them (with their money). For many older readers this attitude will remind them of one of the most controversial (because politically ambivalent) exhortatory posters of the Second World War – '*Your* courage, *your* determination and *your* strength will give *us* Victory!' Once again many of the photographic images consist of councillors wearing construction hats emerging from manhole covers, or opening old people's homes, and are complemented by block graphs showing how much money is being spent on meals on wheels. It is all very laudable but it is also all highly self-congratulatory and is based on one of the most politically disabling concepts of all – that people as electors are a different category of human being from people as politicians (just as readers are from writers). There is little sense of belonging to a common political project, possibly because the political base of so many constituency parties has been allowed to atrophy into a rump of tireless activists. (The problem with socialism, Oscar Wilde is alleged to have said, is that there aren't enough evenings in the week.) A local newspaper could be a part of developing such a wider base, but mostly are used to the opposite effect – to consolidate (and celebrate) the difference between electors and elected.

It is worth noting how energetic the popular press is in promoting the idea that the readership actually dictates the content of the papers it buys – See what's in YOUR *Sun* today! The paper you buy because it gives you what you want! Competitions, puzzles, prizes for readers' letters, special offers, even readers' holidays and other forms of merchandizing, are part of the tradition of comics and the popular press to win the readers into a sense of personal involvement in the fortunes of the press it buys. That is the name of the game in the open market. (Surprisingly, many of these were pioneered by the *Sun*'s forerunner, the *Daily Herald* during the 1930s; unsurprisingly, many of the left intelligentsia viewed its 'lightness' and unashamed populism with horror.) In contrast, nothing could be further from such a close (though totally false) sense of identity than that of the first four decades of BBC wireless, the first nationalized broadcasting system in Britain and allegedly a flagship for the notion of the public control of the media as a form of public service. As D.G. Bridson noted in his invaluable account of the early days of BBC radio, *Prospero and Ariel*: 'It seemed to me that since its inception, broadcasting by the BBC had been the exclusive concern of "us", and listening the lucky privilege of "them".'[2] The BBC has not proved a model of cultural democracy.

Socialist traditions in the medium of journalism and publishing, and
public ownership traditions in broadcasting, have directly followed
from centralized, leadership-based, mainstream political traditions.

There is of course a place for 'party literature', for close and rigorous
political argument. But to argue for a programme of popular
democracy involving readers, trade unions, journalistic and editorial
workers themselves is another project altogether. This is the project we
are interested in, one that must go well beyond newspapers and
magazines, to come to terms with the new technologies of video, cable,
low-powered TV and radio and with the languages of narrative,
experience, humour – even of doubt – as well as those of the party
programme.

There are many signs that the Labour movement *is* learning to use
new techniques. There is no doubt that the six *Miners' Video Tapes*
produced by a consortium of radical film-makers played a crucially
important role in the national campaign to win popular support for the
NUM during 1984–5. There were literally thousands of showings of the
tapes up and down the country at meetings and other fund-raising
events. At the 1984 History Workshop conference it was reported that,
just to take one example, one activist in the Danish dock-workers'
union had personally raised tens of thousands of pounds by showing
the tapes at meetings throughout Denmark. The six short films were
very convenient to use at meetings and in classrooms, and because each
film took a different theme, it was possible to match a particular tape to
a particular audience. Many on the Left had pointed to the success of
the GLC's advertising campaigns – based on the close and perceptive
analysis of market research – as providing lessons for the future. But in
many ways the anti-abolition campaign was just a more sophisticated
version of the familiar top-down methods of the media, while its
politics had much more to do with the values of liberal democracy than
those of socialism. The miners' tapes, on the other hand, showed how
new media and techniques could be used within a genuinely participative context of dialogue, while the way they were geared to distribution
– and to the needs of an audience – provides a much more useful model
for communicating socialist ideas.

At the Greater London Enterprise Board (GLEB), one of the aims of
intervention in the cultural industries, beyond the primary one of
creating secure jobs in a city with 400,000 on the dole, has been to show
what one kind of socialist cultural strategy might look like in practice.
Our aim has been to avoid the pitfalls of the elitist paternalism of public

institutions like the Arts Council and the BBC and the crude, left, mirror image of this which argues that 'we' must take over the same institutions and use them in our ideological battles in the same way as the present ruling class uses them for its own goals.

This strategy has involved above all a commitment to diversity and to the value of the many different, often conflicting, voices that rise up from the realities of oppression and change in Britain today. For the state-funding body it requires a degree of conscious cultural and political abstinence and the guarantee of editorial independence for those receiving funds. We believe strongly in state intervention in the modern forms of cultural production – in broadcasting, newspapers, magazines, books, records, tapes, videos, film and video production – because to leave the financial control of these forms in the hands of 'the market-place' is simply to leave them in the hands of a small number of international oligopolies, geared solely to the cultural needs of small, wealthy minorities and undifferentiated 'mass' audiences. But we believe that state intervention needs to take new forms – forms which involve very large degrees of independence at the levels of production and distribution and which ensure that the producers' first concern is to meet the needs of their real audience rather than the demands of the bureaucrats and politicians who administer state funds.

The Cultural Industries Unit at GLEB was set up in 1984 in order to develop a strategic policy for investment in the cultural sector, and as a way of consolidating the effects of four years of massive GLC funding of the arts in London. A large proportion of this GLC funding was given to a wide range of cultural production in theatre, film and video, photography, publishing and music, particularly that produced from new constituencies and 'communities of interest': young people, the unemployed, black people, women, gay men and lesbians, as well as in priority geographical communities. After four years of rapidly expanding, subsidized production, it was felt necessary to take stock and look at ways in which some elements of this production could be put on a self-financing basis, or economically strengthened through new promotion and marketing resources. For as the threat of the abolition of the GLC came closer to realization it became necessary to see how cultural producers could be encouraged to become more economically self-sufficient and less heavily dependent on subsidy.

What emerged from a study of this variety and prolixity of production was how little thought many groups and projects had given to marketing, promotion and distribution of what it was they had spent so much time producing, whether it was books, films, videos, plays or records. A hundred flowers had bloomed but nobody had been invited to visit the garden. (Or rather only those who knew where the garden was could find it.) It became clear that what was needed was a greater sense of audience, readership, viewing public, call it what you will, by radical workers in the media and in other cultural forms, a more developed sense of targeted audiences and some degree of shaping the products towards such audiences.

Therefore the criteria for investment by GLEB in media projects started by prioritizing companies or co-ops that offered a 'common service' to a range of producers within a particular sector of production, whether this took the form of marketing, promotion or distribution. GLEB saw the main problem not as production but as distribution; not the needs of producers but those of potential consumers. In this respect it was seen that such techniques as market research, readership surveys, advertising and promotion campaigns, developing the concept of target audiences, were not inherently tools of capitalist rationalization, but could be developed for socialist purposes too. For there is nothing inherently anti-socialist in finding out what people are interested in, or want, and going half way towards addressing those interests or meeting those needs. Nor is it difficult to see that informing people of the availability of a new product, creating publicity around the launching of a new magazine, or the performance of a play, or the publication of a book, has socialist implications too.

One example of GLEB Cultural Industries Unit investment is in independent record distribution, a substantial investment in Rough Trade and the computerization of the network it set up (which links the most imaginative distributors around the country) has been linked to unionization and turning the company over to a workers' trust. Other investments, or recommendations for GLC grants, have been in radical book distribution (Turnaround), Afro-Caribbean book distribution (where Bladestock, a new distributor, is now providing a common service for the many small black publishers which have sprung up over the last decade), and in Asian book distribution, where support was given to the Independent Publishing Holding Company, which links a library supply service, a book shop (Soma, based at the Commonwealth Institute) and a distribution service.

A video distribution service for public libraries has been set up (now supplying around a third of all library authorities in the country) and a forum of independent distributors covering feminist work (Circles and the Cinema of Women), trade-union based video (Team Video/Video at Work), and the community and workshop sector (through Albany Video) has been established under the aegis of the Independent Film and Video Makers' Association. The aim has been to enable each distributor to concentrate on material that comes through the forum of their own specialist markets, to take advantage of economies of scale in areas such as bulk purchase of tapes, and to use common computer systems (which are being developed by GLEB's New Technology Network) to that they can keep up with how different audiences are using different kinds of material. The IFVA will also regularly bring producers and distributors together to discuss the tensions between what viewers want to watch and what producers want to make.

Support has also been given to marketing, promotion and distribution services for fringe theatre, feminist publishing, and independent video producers. By concentrating skills in one servicing organization, such as ArtsAdmin which provides administration, promotion and touring work for performing arts companies, the creative workers can focus on their own area of expertise.

Individual projects have also been funded – including several radical publishers, notably Pluto, Sheba and Zed Press, recording studios and record labels such as Firehouse and Shuttle (the aim being to link commercial activity with community access), a new radical national newspaper project (*News on Sunday*), several new magazines ranging from Afro-Caribbean sport (*Sportscene*), to women's culture (*Women's Review*).

The main aim has been to get the work to larger audiences. The hope is that within time much of this hitherto highly subsidized work (subsidized either by the state, by political organizations, or more often by massive self-exploitation) will begin to generate more of its revenue through larger audiences, bigger readerships and so on.

Given limited financial resources, and the need to develop fairly hard criteria for rejecting applications for funds, GLEB has prioritized distribution projects for funding, earning in some quarters a reputation of being 'the enemy of production', to use Brecht's phrase. The emphasis on distribution, we would assert, is not at the expense of production because *distribution is part of production too*.

Cultural products without audiences are not cultural products at all. It is the audience, or readership, or viewing public, which gives any form of communication its meaning and sense of purpose. The piles of old pamphlets and newspapers which gather dust in the backrooms (the average length of membership of some left sects is directly related to the number of unsold papers it takes to fill a wardrobe), the boxes of unsold books which sit in the warehouse, the records and videos that took so much effort to product but which nobody ever heard about and therefore never ordered, all testify to past forms of cultural production which were never realized and therefore cannot be said to fully deserve the name of production at all. For it is distribution which effects the link between production and its audience and which is, therefore, the key element in any definition of radical cultural practice. An exemplary study of the key part distribution plays in cultural production is given by Jane Root in her account of distributing the controversial feminist film *A Question of Silence*.[3] As she demonstrates, it was the effectiveness of Cinema of Women's promotion and distribution strategy of *A Question of Silence* which turned what might well have been a marginalized film into a national cause célèbre, turned a film which had been peremptorily dismissed by mainstream (largely male) film critics into the subject of a national debate.

Part of the problem lies, perhaps, in the continuing role of the labour theory of value in the collective subconscious of the Left. There remains a deeply rooted view that real value derives only from the point of production (preferably some form of manufacturing) and that anything else – be it marketing, distribution, retailing or even design – is at best less real and at worst parasitic (the old bogey of the 'middleman'). It is a perspective that is particularly confused when applied to culture. Where does the value in a book or record 'come from'? From the writer or musician, the typesetter or producer, the printer or the presser? Phrased like this there is of course no answer. One needs only to think of value in the context of piles of remaindered books or unsold newspapers to realize how intimately it is bound to the process of distribution and an active relationship with the demands of an audience. It is significant, too, that many of the most profoundly radical and democratic analyses of culture in recent years have focused on use – on the ways in which meanings and values are created in reading, in watching (or throwing bricks at) television screens and in listening to music in the disco, sound system or living room – rather than, as in the past, on the 'art' (or class position) of the author or artist.

Perhaps part of the problem lies in the word 'consumption'. Its implication of passivity goes against our deepest understanding of a participative, socialist society. One of the most fertile areas of cultural study over the last few years has been to look at the ways in which cultural products are used. The picture they reveal is very different from the one accepted by many on the Left and Right (though of course it never applies to them) of atomized, passive dupes, uncritically consuming whatever the television companies or multinationals throw at them. In the cultural sphere consumption – or use – is an active and highly critical process. Audience participation isn't limited to embarrassing interludes in alternative theatre.

A concern with the relationship between politics and everyday life, and between cultural or political forms and experience has been one of the great strengths of the women's movement. It has helped feminist writers to come to terms with, and more recently to play a leading role in, popular literary forms. For rather than using narrative and fiction to illustrate an ideological position, women's writing (to the extent that any generalization is valid) has been less concerned with establishing ideological position than with exploration, whether of utopias or of experiences of oppression. For us this has important implications for the relationship between socialist strategy and content.

Many of the plays, books, films and videos, records and cassettes, magazines, distributed by GLC/GLEB-backed projects are not, in themselves, explicitly socialist. Does that mean that the GLC/GLEB strategy is not a socialist strategy? We don't think so. Socialist cultural practice is defined as much by the social relations of production and use as it is by its content. We believe that it is socialist to argue for cultural diversity, and for the right of all people who so wish to become involved in making culture. We are aware that this may err too much on the side of libertarianism, for what if the only people who wish to make records, write histories and novels, produce their own television programmes and so on are racists and members of the National Front? This has been put to us on a number of occasions. There is no simple answer to that (although we are worried that it is the first question that everybody thinks of), except to say that a programme of cultural democracy only makes sense if it is developed alongside a programme of economic and political democracy too. And since so many of the ideologies of the far Right are directed at people's sense of powerlessness and exclusion, the Left will have to address those issues as well. There should not be too many preemptive criticisms of cultural libertarianism. A highly sophisticated degree of political foresight has often meant in the past that nothing actually got started! Conditions are never quite right for most things. It's bound to rain.

Of course there will have to be editorial decisions as part of these devolutionary processes. Not everything that people write, sing, film, photograph, record and act could possibly warrant large-scale public distribution at public cost. Those painful rejections and subsequent exclusions from wider distribution are part of the price to be paid for cultural democracy. The roles of editor, commissioning editor or A&R (Artists and Repertoire) executive will remain in any system in which resources are scarce.

The important point to make is that a socialist strategy based simply on appropriating these roles will be doomed to a failure both political and cultural. It will always be in danger of undermining a democratic culture's crucial role of communicating the needs and demands of the powerless (socialist leaders are by no means immune from the fatal trap of the powerful – that of believing their own propaganda). And it will always be in danger of allowing liberal capitalism to play one of its most powerful ideological cards – the assertion that it alone can guarantee choice and cultural freedom.

The models of socialist planning cannot easily be extended to the cultural sphere. Instead, we would argue that a socialist strategy should be committed to the principle that editorial decisions must always be made at arm's length from the state (a state that may well, of course, be taken over by our ideological enemies). In the appropriate spheres of cultural production, existing initiatives and projects have learned by bitter experience how best to match editorial and critical selectivity with a commitment to access. The argument for cultural diversity is likely to win more public support for the socialist project than the argument for the more detailed development of a 'party' culture that puts politics in command and aesthetics and popular democracy on a subsidiary agenda.

Political loyalties are now much more diffuse – and also much more volatile – than they have been for many decades. The old routines have lost the audience. The arguments have to be made in new ways and using new forms. Simply replacing a dowdy image with a glamourized, televisual cult of personality (Kinnock-style) – a revitalization of the 'head and shoulders' style of communication in new clothes – is no answer either.

There is no longer *one* argument for socialism, but many; not one broad highway but rather a complicated network of different (and often contradictory) paths and byways linked less by leaders, parties or programmes than by fundamental convictions and understandings of right and wrong. A socialist cultural policy is both about finding similarities, and also about recognizing and respecting the dignity of differences. The forms of cultural expression and argument it uses should reflect this.

References

1. Tony Grace, 'The Trade Union Press in Britain', *Media, Culture and Society*, April 1985.
2. D.G. Bridson, *Prospero and Ariel*, London: Gollancz 1971.
3. Jane Root, 'Distributing *A Question of Silence*', *Screen*, Vol. 26, No. 6, November–December 1985.

11. Reconstructing broadcasting

Phillip Whitehead

It takes no more than a smidgen of sense to see that the Peacock enquiry into the practicability of advertising on the BBC was not really about the better financing of the Corporation at all. It was about the way in which a public corporation, of a type now offensive to those who rule us, can be thrown open to the discipline of the market, with knock-on effects for the commercial half of the broadcasting duopoly. At the moment of writing, it is uncertain whether the advertising lobby can prevail, so ragged was their case as presented to Peacock. But changes to the financing structure of broadcasting will be proposed. And this will be at a time when the really important decisions about broadcasting, taken elsewhere in the international game of space invaders now developing in satellite communications, may obliterate our whole public service tradition. Nor is it ours alone. If one thing differentiates the European from the American system, it has been the idea of the public service system, publicly financed, regulated at arm's length by the delegated institutions of the state.

Such institutions have everywhere been thrown on the defensive by rising costs and the clamour for unrestricted choice. These problems came relatively late to Britain, by virtue of the long established reputation and favoured international status within English-language broadcasting, of our duopoly. Securely protected from each other by their mutually exclusive sources of revenue, the BBC and ITV/ILR could go their own way. The British imported less than most European countries, and exported more to the key markets, though far behind the vast continental-scale output of the USA. The duopoly had advantages of size, and comparative security of revenue. Only slowly was it seen as the 'strait-jacket' described by the Annan Committee. Since the BBC laid claim to the whole territory of public service broadcasting, all alternatives to it were clamped into the commercial system. Whatever emerged therein the BBC felt it had to match, on the principle of the universality of its service. Successive generations of administrators asserted their claims as though the whole broadcasting spectrum was some new Antarctica, to be won for the flag lest others get there first.

When pirate radio came over the horizon, the BBC discovered virtues in local radio to which it had long been indifferent. When the IBA tried to test the market for breakfast television, the BBC diverted all necessary resources to destroy the new station, and forced it downmarket into the territory of Roland Rat. When Roland nibbled into the BBC's lead the answer was simple; buy him up, to re-emerge as ratus corporationus, the authentic public service rodent. A commercial bid for *Dallas* produced so much BBC hysteria that you would have thought Broadcasting House had been compulsorily purchased for use as a bordello. Sweeping changes of policy and principle could be made almost overnight. The Corporation high-flier stayed aloft by the ability to predict and advocate subtle changes of policy five minutes ahead of the rest. Short of funds? Disastrous, old boy. Elstree on the market at last, symbol of much of the waste and folly of ITV . . . snap it up. The licence fee? It is universally levied for a universally available service. . . Except when satellite broadcasting would need a special subscription; this form of Pay-TV being unblushingly accepted if it was the price of the BBC staying in the DBS (direct broadcasting by satellite) game. Cable? A snare and a delusion. Unless the BBC were able to to be dominant within it, when, as one now fallen executive put it 'the important thing is to get your name on as many channels as possible'.

The examples proliferate. They have had two consequences. Firstly, the BBC has not been taken seriously when it protested that it was short of funds. Secondly, its sheer size, its claim to be in on everything as the dominant force, helped to make enemies. In financial terms it would in any event now face a crisis. Its expansion in the 1950s and early 1960s was financed by the growth of revenue, as more and more households invested in black-and-white television sets. There followed a second sustained boom with the expansion of personal investment in colour sets. This has now reached saturation. Yet personal investment in the new artefacts of the 1980s, turning the household into a leisure centre, has never been higher. The second television in the bedroom, the VCR downstairs, relay and record BBC programmes. So does the tranny in the kitchen. But they bring no extra income to the BBC. VCR-ownership and rental, now up to nearly half of all households, is to the mid-1980s what the colour set was to the late 1960s. Whilst there may be some VCRs used purely for movies from the high street hire shop, all the evidence is that their first use, 85 per cent of the time, is as a scheduling device, to record programmes for later use, or (in the case of movies) for retention. The viewer becomes the time-lord of the schedules. Unlike the decision to purchase the first television set, all this new investment does not accrue in licence revenue for the BBC.

Thus, each new triennial application for an increase in the licence fee now appears more burdensome than the last. The fee, like all poll taxes, is regressive. Less and less does it reflect the differential ability to pay. There are no exemptions for the old, the sick or the unwaged. The cost of collection is high, especially when combined with the revenue lost in evasion. The licence payer does not quantify the cost of the 'free' television provided by ITV. Such public pressure as there is on the Home Office through Members of Parliament is therefore hostile to increases of the scale demanded. With new patterns of viewing, 'universality' is harder to assert, even with Wogan, *Dallas* and *East Enders*. Simultaneously, the Home Office, which is more and more becoming a Ministry of the Interior, is the instrument for pressure on broadcasters; not just the blundering attempts at political pressure by Leon Brittan, but his successor's flirtation with the lobby for increased moral censorship. There is no buffer body between the applicant and the bestower. The former has all the weaknesses of its apparent strength. Its size makes its needs greater, but gives it enemies on every front. Press lords who covet the only part of the real estate of communications to be outside their direct control give the BBC a hard time. And the Corporation does not always help itself.

The casual observer of the BBC in the year 1985 would be hard put to vote it a Hit rather than a Miss. The revelations of persistent and continuous security vetting; the bizarre Christmas tree symbol on the closed files; the pathetic initial collapse of the governors to direct government pressure and the feeling that some of them, like William Rees-Mogg, were avid for more; the eagerness to placate the critics of *Rough Justice*; the alternation between consummate arrogance and craven terror with which the BBC faced its critics: all showed a severe crisis of identity. So do some of the other problems which sheer size brings in its train. There is the endless overlap and duplication of middle management, the lengthening chains of command. In one instructive recent case which came to the NUJ, a BBC employee was fired after two successive bad annual reports. Previously his conduct had been exemplary. The documents bore the counter-signatures of six separate functionaries in the personnel departure. None had bothered to delve into the exceptional personal circumstances which had led to the man's temporary collapse. Too often BBC staff in the outlying part of its domains feel that their activities are not weighed in the scales when the major decisions of investment and competition are being taken by the limo-borne hierarchs of Television Centre. And yet, in the sense of the public service ethic, they are the BBC. The studio manager in the bowels of Bush House or BH, aching for an attachment to creative work elsewhere, the producer in exile in Bristol or under fire in Belfast – they are the Corporation as in its finer moments it sees itself. At the height of the *Real Lives* controversy they were a rediscovered strength, able to take action to express outrage which stiffened the resolve of their seniors, properly rebuffed the craven governors, and ultimately helped to demote the Home Secretary himself.

The problems of the past year have demonstrated that the BBC is too big for some things, too small for others. In terms of traditional British broadcasting it seems too big to cover too much of the field. Therefore, it attracts cupidity and malice as much as legitimate criticism. It has assets that others could use for private gain. Its size and occasional arrogance make it open to claims that it should pay its own way, or live more modestly. The whole Peacock enquiry seems to have been set in train by a combination of such diverse motives. Yet at the same time, the BBC is too small to do other things which a national public service operation seeks to do to remain in the Superbowl of international broadcasting. It has had to pull out of a self-financed DBS system. It seeks co-production money for an ever wider range of products, increased threefold in 1985, with the consequent change of market and audience orientation that such operations demand. The need to bid for foreign cash alters the nature of programme proposals just as surely as imported programming alters a schedule. Meanwhile the international entrepreneurs, free of restraint, flush with cash, seek to penetrate the British market through the cable networks and the domestic dish aerial.

The response of the BBC has been to try to join those whom it feels it cannot beat. As the sky grows dark with DBS satellites the Corporation has flirted with all the new boys. The SuperChannel would draw it in with ITV and other communications giants in beaming a mix of British programmes to the cable systems of Europe. Rupert Murdoch's Sky Channel is only one of the satellite operations up there already, saturating every field and fjord with its canny mix of TV entertainment. At the moment it loses £15 millions annually, because advertisers have been slow to take to an international medium, but its programmes are already forcing tactical re-scheduling in some of the smaller European countries where it is widely viewed. How will the SuperChannel break in past competitors like this? In the United States, the BBC may see its best hope in a link-up with the Turner international 24-hour news service, using the expertise of the World Service. Wherever you see the international Turner newscasts, at whatever hour, they are unmistakably the voice of Atlanta. Should the BBC get involved with such operations? Would it ever have considered, and would governments have continued to fund, a World Service transmitted by international private news services? What is left of the public service, once it is entwined in deals like this in order to stay in the international big league?

Those who defend the new strategies will say that they have no choice. As long as they are the only broadcasting outlet not financed directly or indirectly by advertising they have to raise money how they can. They must demonstrate business acumen, be seen to slim down staff and strike international deals, or become just another medium destructively competing for advertising revenue. The case presented to Peacock by the advertisers never rose above the level of blatant self-interest. It is hard to see it being taken seriously, even by the carefully selected members of the committee. Behind the agencies who would happily accept a massive BBC, provided they could sell on it, are other, covert interests: those who as competitors would wish to see the BBC weakened, or the unrivalled assets which its production portfolio gives it used to satiate their demand for visual wallpaper to furnish the new cable and satellite outlets. To resist them, one line of argument runs, the BBC should embrace any friend, confront any foe. If its own programmes have to be altered for greater popular appeal, with soap, chat and games shows extended, so be it. The quality will still be there too. And it is. *Yes, Prime Minister* has fans around the world wherever it is safe to laugh at the eternal bureaucrat. *Comrades, Edge of Darkness* and many more offer a thoughtful alternative to the Rambo-style outlook of most American cinema and television. Why worry about a possible adulteration? The answer is that the authentic note which the BBC at its best can still strike will be made uncertain by the kind of programmes it must increasingly provide for the multinational strategy. If the alternative to £100 million provided by advertising on the popular channels is £100 million (instead of the current £15 million) raised in co-production finance, will the end product look all that different?

The answer to the current dilemma of the BBC, I believe, is to make the public sector of broadcasting bigger, but the role within it of the exposed and top heavy corporation smaller. There needs to be a larger sector which has some insulation from the market, asserting the best of the national tradition which has made us a broadcasting power. It does not need to be a single agency which claims a unique status and attracts odium, fear, jealousy, and greed as a result of its size. We have made the mistake for too long of thinking that we can have only one monolithic type of public service.

There are other similar public agencies, which operate at one remove from the market although prepared to benefit from its earnings through philanthropy as well as redistribution or general taxation. The BFI is one such, as was the NFFC. Channel 4 is another kind of public service broadcasting, funded by the direct transfer of revenue from the ITV companies as monopoly sellers of advertising. Because of its remit, and the limits within which it operates, Channel 4 and its small Welsh sibling S4C are thought of quite differently. Channel 4 attracts far less odium than does the BBC for its controversial programming. Partly this is because of the difference of size and therefore exposure, but partly too because the commissioning procedure allows a certain perceived license.

The BBC has begun to adapt to the new world of pluralists. Some co-productions now involve outside British talent as well as overseas finance. A gesture to accept 100 hours of programming from the independent sector, and set aside £10 millions for it, may be no more than a strategy to shed staff and to rely heavily on underpaid incomers on short contracts or no contracts at all. Equally it may be a gesture just large enough to persuade the post-Peacock debate that the BBC is changing. But there is as yet no sign that the Corporation sees any areas of its dominion which are now ready for commonwealth status. Radio retains a 29 per cent share of the television licence fee, without any independent funding of its own. Local radio remains in the fastness of the reorganized regional management structure. BBC Enterprises, the great oxymoron, continues in its gentle way to make far less out of the treasure chest which it guards than its principal commercial rivals. No doubt its efforts at overseas sales will continue to be frustrated if it clashes with the BBC's other face – provider of programming to SuperStations and SuperChannels in the skies.

The possibilities for devolution are there. Why is it that the nation's 99 per cent radio listeners get their BBC services without direct payment, so that ads on Radio 1 can now be advanced as a plausible alternative? A radio sales tax, combined with a household radio licence from which exemption had to be claimed, would rapidly become practicable if a public sector radio system had to look to its own funding. So would some attempt to increase the diversity of local and community radio under a Local Radio Authority. Public service stations, independent of the BBC, could be funded by a combination of levy from the large quasi-regional commercial stations and subscription for news and local services paid by the BBC. Such steps would increase the range and variety of public sector radio in Britain, rather than leaving the beleaguered BBC fighting on all fronts to preserve a single view of 'public service' against the admen.

In television too the notion of a variety of public agencies makes better sense than attempting to group everything around the Corporation laager. That does not mean the break-up of BBC Television. For all the self-satisfaction of its Cleese commercial, it is right to take the case to the public that what it gets is still a lot for what it pays. Proper financing of BBC Television means more, not less, public money, whether from a licence fee made less regressive and buttressed by contributions from the VCR-users who have now replaced colour-set owners as the great new source of consumer buoyancy, or from general taxation. In either event, the needs should be assessed by an independent review body, able to recommend to government what the level of funding should be. Any such calculation cannot avoid the earning potential worldwide of one of the few British products to win almost universal acclaim. Subscription through some system of decoding, advanced as a plausible way of allowing the BBC independently to charge what the market will bear, runs into all the old difficulties about markets from which the notion of the public service was to advance. Since fewer would pay, the cost would rise; so would the charges, until the 'market level' for BBC subscriptions was reached numerically well below that of the present number of licence payers.

Such a public service BBC would still be vulnerable in a communications system dominated in every other respect by the multinational market leaders. Great opportunities have already been lost there. Cable TV never looked like being the entertainment-led investment boom predicted with fatuous optimism by Kenneth Baker. As subscriptions fall away and the day of domestic dish aerial comes closer the satellite operators will drop any pretence that they are there to service cable systems under effective (or in the British case ineffective) national regulation. The BBC cannot overstretch itself to attempt to be the public service presence in both cable and satellite. The effort would lead to financial overload infinitely worse than the sudden switches of reserves to occupy new areas of off-air time.

In cable that would be better done by making the various systems part of a national cable grid in which the public once more has the largest holding. (That in turn awaits the day when the public once more has the largest stake in British Telecom.) The vicissitudes of the cable enterprises will leave most small operators not unwilling to accept such a body as the common carrier of a multitude of franchised channels, loosely regulated and with an obligatory element of community programming. The carrier would automatically relay off-air television. It would do more. Linked with its interactive and business services, built up through time, it could carry services bought directly from other public agencies. When, eventually, parliament gets around to televising itself, the output of a parliamentary broadcasting unit could go to cable as well as being available in exchange for seconded personnel and expertise from the big broadcasters. So could local government, educational and ethnic organizations. There is no reason why these and many more should either depend for their portion entirely on the existing public service BBC, or be a 'market' served up only if advertising-linked.

Every prediction made in the last five years about cable has been wrong. How quickly the figures and the dramatis personae have been changed can be seen from a reading of the final chapter of Timothy Hollins's 1984 BRU survey, 'Beyond Broadcasting: Into the Cable Age.' A prediction of railways written in the age of Hudson would have had the same difficulty. A national cable grid, not dominated by the international satellite bosses, offers greater public service plurality. An increase in the number of such outlets off-air, utilizing redistribution of funds, adds to that plurality. It cannot by itself ensure that public service bradcasting remains strong enough to maintain the international quality in the face of satellite competition which British broadcasting needs. For that we have to face the funding issue direct. Is a major national asset worth support which, however equitably arranged, averages out at £100 per annum for every viewer and listener? If we want the end, we must will the means and not flinch from the persuasion: not just for the BBC, but for the power of the wider public service ideal.

12. Pornography annoys

Jean Seaton

Who wants to defend pornography? Who favours video nasties? Who sympathizes with the profit-takers in an industry that manufactures degrading images of women? Who views without disquiet a trend in popular taste which makes obscenity the staple commodity in every newsagent?

Not, to be sure, the major political parties which have united, with few dissentient or even questioning voices, in support of a bill limiting the sale and distribution of videos. Not the Police Federation, the Roman Catholic Church nor the National Viewers' and Listeners' Association. And not – perhaps most emphatically not of all – those who are currently in the vanguard of the movement for women's rights, equality, liberty and protection.

The literature of pornography has, indeed, inspired a feminist counter-literature, angry and purposeful rather than merely appalled, describing the economics of pornography, pointing out its ubiquity, studying its themes, analysing and indicting its imagery. Much of this counter-literature presents pornography as a kind of psychic napalm in the sex war, the 'essence of anti-female propaganda'.[1] On the one hand it is seen as a secret weapon, cunningly hidden from the gender enemy, on the other as a violent affront to the sensibilities of women who react with justifiably instinctive revulsion when they encounter it. 'This book will shock, appal and hurt,' Susan Griffin promises of her own *Pornography and Silence*. 'Women do not know how much men hate them.'[2]

An important aspect of the feminist anti-pornography writings is that they are a reaction: a radical attack on what the most recent generation of feminists sees as the false radicalism of the supposedly pioneering 1960s, when many feminists, in common with campaigners for homosexual rights, opponents of divorce and abortion laws, and other opponents of the moral despotism of the state, regarded obscenity laws as one aspect of the system they hoped to destroy. What the old feminists saw as a campaign for freedom, the new feminists regard, in retrospect, as a dangerous moral slippage, at worst decadent, at best naïve. Brownmiller, one of the most fervent and articulate of the revisionist campaigners, writes:

> Pornography has been so thickly glossed over in the name of verbal freedom and sophistication, that the important distinction between freedom of political expression (a democratic necessity), honest sex education (a societal good) and highly suggestive pornography (the deliberate devaluation of the role of women through obscene and disgusting depictions) have been hopelessly confused.[3]

The so-called 'sexual liberation' movement of the permissive decade thus becomes, at least in this respect, paradoxically repressive: inhibiting in the name of currently fashionable ideology a natural, even primordial, female response. Where, in the 1960s, 'disgust' became something educated women were supposed to be ashamed of – evidence of irrational feelings of sexual fear or guilt – in the 1980s it becomes a sensitive instrument, unique and precious monitor of good or ill.

To be effective, however, disgust must not be passive. It needs to be aroused, inflamed, excited. Fortunately for the new campaigners, arousal and excitement have not been hard to achieve. It has been one of the headiest discoveries of the modern movement that on this issue, the demands of the avant garde find ready listeners among the oppressed masses. Where earlier generations had to struggle, not just against the hostility of men, but also against the indifference or even derision of most women, feminist campaigners against pornography have been received with a heart-warming enthusiasm on all sides. Divided on other matters, radical feminist, socialist feminist and apolitical woman worker can find common cause in opposing the pictorial humiliation of their kind. Thus, when Susan Lurie, in an influential essay, urged sisters to 'anger, bitterness and action' on the matter of pornography ('Women will not have this put upon them'),[4] there was really little need. Once the spell of the earlier 'freedom of expression' movement had been broken, it was not difficult, in the face of the booming degradation industry, to evoke a mood of widespread outrage. The muted nature of left-wing opposition to the video nasties bill (which was proposed from the Right) is one result.

No sensible or public-spirited person will cry over a reduced right of access to films like *Driller Killer*. Most people will therefore applaud the recent legislation and most will have some sympathy for the feminist campaign. And yet, perhaps, thinking people – especially thinking feminists – would do well before claiming too readily the video nasties law and other similar measures as victories. For the change of public, and establishment, mood on pornography, partly feminist-induced, has wide social implications which go far beyond the issue itself, and affect feminism in particular. New feminists see the issue in terms of vicarious violence and moral corruption. But what may also be at stake are civil liberties, public toleration of sexual difference, and the freedom to say and depict things which others find objectionable – a freedom which, it should not be forgotten, once enabled feminism to take root. Who is to decide what is to be allowed, and what forbidden? That is at the centre of all debates about censorship, as of debates about other freedoms to which freedom of expression is organically linked. At the core is the concept of moral outrage: the instinctive evaluation of the behaviour, ideas, tastes or interests of others that determines taboo and the basis of law in every society.

Sexuality and subversion

Almost all serious violations of national laws and conventional standards have been seen, from time to time, as dangerous to the existing social order. In advanced western capitalist countries, however, none – since the mid-nineteenth century – has seemed so threatening as sexual variation. Sexual variation existed independently of radical or revolutionary politics, but the link was seen, not only by upholders of the status quo, but also by radicals, or at any rate by radical men who, as one modern feminist puts it derisively, believed that 'sex, more sex and sex the powers didn't like would bring the house down'.[5] The relationship between 'deviant' – or just plain excessive – sex and subversion certainly continued well into the post-Second World War period, and provided the background to the humanitarian or moral reforms of the mid-1960s. As late as 1968, Samuel Brittan was writing in his essay, *Left or Right: The Bogus Dilemma*, that being in favour of pornography was one of the characteristic attributes of being on the Left.[6] Brittan's argument was that the causes that made up left-wingness (or right-wingness) were a pot pourri, with no connecting thread. Contemporary feminists implicitly agree, arguing that the supposed 'subversive' power of obscene writing, or imagery has never been more than a male-inspired, and man-serving, myth.

There is no doubt, however, that it has not only been male homosexuals, libertines and the like who have linked the sexual to the political. The political and juridical establishment – always, of course, almost exclusively male in composition – has traditionally seen in any kind of extension of sexual or, indeed, marital freedom grave dangers to existing, natural hierarchy. To the legal or political conservative, morality was the underpinning of society, society determined the nature of morality, and without a socially determined morality, society would collapse. It was necessary, therefore, for parliament and the courts to uphold the values which most people (or at least those who could reasonably speak on behalf of most people) held dear. It was this view of morality in relation to sexual matters that the famous Wolfenden Report, published in 1959, sought to challenge. It succeeded to a remarkable degree, and the decriminalization of 'deviant' sexual acts became part of a package or reforms, preceded by the change in the anomalous law on suicide, affecting the regulating of divorce, abortion and prostitution.

The new, age-of-affluence liberalism – based on what Beverley Brown has called 'the Wolfenden strategy', namely the principle that private behaviour should be free from public control –[7] prompted a heated debate between the liberal legal philosopher Herbert Hart and the conservative jurist Patrick Devlin. Wolfenden had argued that 'there must remain a realm of private morality and immorality which is, in brief and crude terms, not the law's business.'[8] This argument, and the implication that 'morality' could exist in a domain quite separate from the law, was fundamental to moves for greater liberalization. Opposing it, Devlin argued that the law was, or should be, inseparable from moral feelings. 'The suppression of vice is as much the law's business as the suppression of subversive activities,' he maintained. 'It is no more possible to define the spheres of private morality than it is to define one of private subversive activity.'[9] The position appeared simple: if behaviour which undermined generally accepted moral codes was legally permitted, then both the authority of the law and the very basis of society was placed in jeopardy:

> The pressure of opinion that in the end makes and unmakes laws is not to be found in the mouths of those who talk most about morality and reform, but in the hearts of those who continue, without

reflection, to believe most of what they learnt from their fathers.[10]

For Devlin, the Wolfenden concept of a publicly harmless, private immorality was a contradiction. In less sophisticated terms, this is also the position of Mrs Mary Whitehouse. Less obviously – and in some ways ironically – it came close to the attitude of one important section of the 1960s radicals who by 1968, were arguing that 'to fuck . . . was to fuck the system'.[11]

Hart argued the liberal, not the revolutionary, case. The issue for him was not smashing bourgeois morality but upholding a higher morality which provided for the freedom of the individual to make moral choices. The essence of private immorality was that it was private, and had no public consequences. 'Private subversive activity is of course a contradiction in terms,' he declared, 'because "subversive" means the overthrow of government which is a public not a private thing.'[12] Other liberals saw an implicit totalitarianism in Devlin's logic. If harmless immoralities were to be punished, argued Joel Feinberg, then 'morality would have to be enforced with a fearsome efficiency which would show no respect for anyone's privacy'.[13] The most sacred freedom of all, to the liberals, was freedom of expression. Invoking J.S. Mill, they maintained that this vital liberty could only be justifiably infringed in order to prevent manifest harms to the individual – such as physical violence, libel, slander, and possibly (with an eye on the moral conservatives) invasions of privacy. It was absurd to regard harmless immoralities as a form of treason.

During the 1970s, the permissive revolution largely won; the debate lost some of its power to enrage either side. In the 1980s it has been revived – with a convergence of forces attacking the 'old' liberalism or radicalism from Left and Right. Yet, in re-entering the fray more or less on the opposite side from before, feminists have opened a Pandora's box of political and philosophical problems, with consequences which they may be unable to control.

The essence of the new feminist argument is a critique of the assumptions of the old liberalism. Hart has been concerned to defend what might be called 'moral innovation'. He pointed out that people who wished to challenge current morality might be seeking to refine, rather than undermine or destroy, moral standards. Instead of seeing proposals for moral change as a threat to society, he was anxious to protect such proposals from the lynch law of public opinion. He stressed the importance of a distinction between the democratic principle that 'power should be in the hands of the people' and the notion that 'the majority with power in their hands should respect no limits'. In their appeal to the instinctive reactions of the majority of women, this is the argument that the new feminists are concerned to challenge. And yet, as has already been indicated, the triumph, 20 years ago, of precisely this argument had been one of the most important factors in creating an environment in which feminism has been able to flourish. Devlinite in their moral prescriptions, the new feminists have been – and remain – Hartite in their insistent demand for toleration of themselves, in a still largely hostile world.

To put it more basically, the new feminists want to have their cake and eat it. Feminists have seen their past campaigns as part of a struggle against majority opinions – not, until recently, in support of them. Feminists have always sought to challenge and reshape existing moral structures. It is easy to forget – it should not be so easy, in view of attitudes still prevailing in western society, still-oppressive laws in many countries including this one, and the crushing prohibitions in many parts of the Third World – it is easy to forget how recently basic feminist demands over contraception, abortion, marriage, work and property were not only resisted by law, but were also greeted by the incomprehension, anger, hatred and revulsion of the overwhelming majority, including or especially the majority of women. What alarmed Devlin was that 'private' breaches of existing public mores would have 'public' effects, corrupting the populace. This was precisely what earlier feminist campaigners intended. They aimed to change the climate of opinion, and to change what society found acceptable.

But the feminist campaign has not simply been a liberal, rationalist, enlightened appeal for the rights of half the human species. It has also been fundamentally sexual, and much of its influence has derived from that. Feminists have used, and it is important in the context of pornography to recognize it, the enormous subversive power of sexual unease to disturb established social assumptions.

Sexual offensiveness and feminism

'This awful, sad, terrible women-hating at the centre of all our cities,' writes Andrea Dworkin on the subject of pornography, 'at the centre of all men, cannot, will not, be tolerated.'[14]

We need not doubt the sincerity of this dislike and alarm with which the new feminists regard pornography, nor dispute the seriousness of the thinking that accompanies it. We may feel that some of it is a bit over the top. ('I am particularly grateful to the women who told me about the use of pornography by their husbands, fathers, sons, brothers and lovers,' writes Dworkin in one passage, 'and about the use of pornography in the acts of sexual abuse these women suffered.') But we may sympathize with much of it. A great deal of mass-market sexual obscenity, when it is not simply absurd, is lifeless, aesthetically displeasing and insulting to women (also, not infrequently, to men). We may feel sick, even morally incensed. But we need to distinguish these common and natural reactions from the quite separate question of whether the marketed images do public damage, and whether there is an imperative to suppress them.

Should we regard moral indignation, *even when it is our own*, as sufficient grounds for restricting the private behaviour of others? Is our contempt and fury, even if shared by the majority, reason enough for limiting the range of liberty? Patrick Devlin evidently believed so. 'Not everything is to be tolerated,' he wrote. 'No society can do without intolerance, indignation and disgust.'[15] What mattered to Devlin was the intensity, and the generality, of public emotion: in his view, anything over which public feeling reached 'a concert pitch' of disgust required some form of legal action.

It should be obvious, however, that this 'moral conservative' argument ignores grave difficulties. Clearly there has to be some relationship, if the law is not to fall into disrepute, between public feeling and the law. Too close a relationship, however, fails to allow for the fickleness (and not infrequent psychotic convulsions) of public opinion. At best, it is a recipe for conformity; at worst, for the terrible oppression of minorities. Public feeling moves very quickly, often following in the wake of changes in the law. Today, though homosexuality is feared and even hated, majority opinion does not support the legal punishment of privately conducted homosexual acts. The same was not true when Devlin wrote in condemnation of the Wolfenden Report. Then, his contention was that the indignation and disgust which most people felt, 'the general abhorrence', as he put it, of the populace for homosexual acts, precluded any liberalization of laws which, today, the very feminists who make their appeal to the general disgust felt towards pornography regard – rightly – as barbarous and unjust.

Popular disgust can act as a brake to legislative reform. It can also, as Devlin implied, act as a spur to radical innovation. In the past, this has produced horrifying results. In the sixteenth century, what Devlin calls, with approval, 'the final appalled and sincere intolerance that leads to action' helped to produce one of the fiercest and most protracted persecutions of women in recorded history. Why were witches killed and tortured? The reasons were complex, but Trevor-Roper suggests that a major factor was social, and sees a similarity between witches and Jews, two scapegoated minorities. 'The witch and the Jew both represented social nonconformity,' he writes. 'That their persecutors felt them to be intolerable agents of the Devil is not disputed.'[16] In Germany in the 1930s (as throughout Europe during the Reformation), feelings against Jews – even among moderate, gentle supporters of pre-Nazi democratic parties – could be marked by 'genuine' and sincere repugnance, as Christa Wolfe, in her autobiographical novel, *Model Childhood*, has described.[17] Equally, in Johannesburg or parts of Alabama today, 'miscegenation' between persons of different races causes a deep, and righteous, feeling of revulsion, among decent, law-abiding citizens.

Of course, moral instincts can be right as well as wrong. So can moral indignation, and one would not wish to argue that those who feel indignant should not be at liberty to express their opinions or seek to influence the views of others. The difficulty arises when the anger of one human being is directed against the (arguably private, and publicly harmless) freedom of another. As Jeffrey Weeks has put it, on the subject of nineteenth-century moral purity campaigns, 'the problem we have to grapple with in trying to understand the significance of the events is the contradiction between the ostensibly humanitarian instincts of those who campaigned for legal change, and the controlling impact they had on people's lives'.[18] With all kinds of puritanism – religious, conservative, feminist – there is the danger that one kind of infringement of freedom may lead to another, in ways that the moral crusader may not be able to dictate.

Moral instincts can be right: but they can also be oppressively wrong. Those who appeal for judgement to a majoritarian jury should be wary lest they fall into a trap. Devlin need not worry: most of his values are those of what Richard Nixon called, in a North American context, the silent majority. Feminists, however, need to pause. For feminism offends, and many of their causes frequently disgust.

Pornography and public harm

Is it correct to see pornography as publicly harmless? According to the tenets of classical liberalism, no kind of expression should be prohibited or censored unless it was likely to lead to certain, clearly identifiable, types of injury. J.S. Mill was quite clear that 'mere offence to tender sensibilities' was an insufficient ground for censorship, for the harm caused to the principle of the free expression of opinion took precedence. Modern liberal opinion does not go all the way with Mill. Thus, the Williams Report on Obscenity and Film Censorship extends the category of harm requiring censorship to that of 'offence'. It recommends the removal of pornographic materials from public display and the restriction of public access to films and publications which might offend the casual viewer or observer.[19] Feminists might regard this erosion of liberal principle as a minor victory. Yet it may have been a very doubtful one – as Beverley Brown has pointed out. For – from the campaign for votes for women to the struggle against nuclear weapons – public offensiveness has been one of the mainstays of the feminist movement.

The new feminists, however, see pornography as much more than a mere nuisance. They argue that it has a direct effect on behaviour. According to Dworkin, men murder, rape and abuse their wives, sisters and daughters under the influence of pornography. Once it was the demon drink: today it is the demon obscenity. Under its baleful sway, the home becomes a brothel, torture chamber, abattoir. 'In pornography I saw so many photographs of common household objects being used as sexual weapons against women,' reveals Dworkin, 'that I despaired of ever returning to my simple ideas of function.'[20] That social research should fail to provide any statistical correlation whatsoever between acts of violence against and the consumption of pornography is dismissed as irrelevant. The harmful effects seen by the feminist campaigners are not – so they would argue – empirically analysable. They relate, rather, to a deep psychosocial malaise – both as symptom and as cause.

The new feminist attack springs from a deeply held conviction that the most outlandish or violent of pornographic images do not merely cater for the fantasies of a small number of individuals: they reveal, tellingly, what *all* men would actually like to do to women. In other words, pornography encapsulates the essential misogyny of the male-dominated world – what Griffin calls the 'women-hating nature' of every existing society.[21] In this view of social dynamics, particular acts of crazed violence become symbols – made more powerful through pornography – reflecting and stimulating all violent behaviour that characterizes male relations with women, and with other men. Pornography, in this view, is a visible aspect of the appalling evil that exists in malekind.

What can be said of this approach? There is its metaphysical nature – its reliance on literary or emotional impact rather than on rational argument. There is its remarkably simple view of male sexuality (constant, unchanging, non-socially determined). And there is its highly traditional view of female nature – suffering, static, martyred, victimized, throughout history.

Conclusion

'Outrage' is a two-edged weapon. On the whole, feminists have gained from being the subject of it – shocking press, politicians and public into taking notice of their demands. To side, therefore, with the outraged – however tempting the cause – is to risk being taken captive.

One reason why the women's movement has been 'outrageous' is that it has been disquietingly innovative in sexual matters – challenging, above all, established notions of male and female sexuality. It has invited scorn and contempt by questioning assumptions about the allocation, by gender, of talents and capacities. It has disgusted and revolted in order to place on the agenda of public discussion female organs, bodily functions and ailments that were previously regarded as unmentionable.

In helping to shift the remnants of nineteenth-century sexual taboos, the feminist movement has – hitherto – eschewed sexual puritanism. On the contrary, at a time when any non-medical discussion of sexuality – particularly discussion by women – was still regarded as indecent, feminism became the centre for advanced debate. So fast has been the shift to public mores precipitated by women, that it is hard to conjure up the frisson of horrified amazement – with echoes of the *Lady Chatterley* scandal – that greeted the publication of Germain Greer's *The Female Eunuch*, or to remember that, to some at least, its frank, no-nonsense approach to certain issues appeared pornographic.

Against this progressive background, it is both sad and perturbing to see the emergence, among a new generation of feminists that has little memory of the old, of a dangerously repressive dogmatism. The old feminists fought a long battle for sex for pleasure. Now, once again, we find that only some kind of sex with some kinds of people is to be regarded as morally proper. All men are now wicked: how long before we return to a world of good girls and bad?

Fashions change. A clear sky becomes overcast: from contraception for the under-16s, to promiscuous male homosexuality, newly won areas of sexual freedom are encountering public disapproval, with others increasingly at risk. Even some of the old feminists, like St Augustine and Don Juan, are repenting of their youthful ways. Most notoriously of all, Germaine Greer, in her latest book, repudiates almost everything she wrote in her first one. As more and more jump on the ship, the age of permissiveness is giving way to the age of positive celibacy – with an impetus which comes by no means solely from the feminist movement. If, indeed, a new puritanism does take hold, past experience suggests that it may go much further than its originators would like; and the beneficiaries are most unlikely to be of the feminist movement – or women.

References

1. Andrea Dworkin, *Pornography: Men Possessing Women*, London: The Women's Press 1982, p. 225.
2. Susan Griffin, *Pornography and Silence*, London: The Women's Press 1980, p. 37.
3. S. Brownmiller, *Against Our Will: Men, Women and Rape*, London: Secker & Warburg 1974, p. 7.
4. Susan Lurie, 'Pornography and the Dread of Women', in Laura Lederer (ed.), *Take Back the Night*, London: The Women's Press 1979, p. 242.
5. Laura Lederer, introduction, *Take Back the Night*, p. 23.
6. Samuel Brittan, *Left or Right: The Bogus Dilemma*, London: Secker & Warburg 1968, p. 20.
7. Beverley Brown, 'In Defence of Pornography', *Ideology and Consciousness*, No. 7, 1979, pp. 3–14.
8. The Wolfenden Report, *Report of the Committee on Homosexual Acts*, Cmnd 7031, Para. 61.
9. Patrick Devlin, *The Enforcement of Morals*, London: Oxford University Press 1965, p. 175.
10. *Ibid.*, p. 125.

11. Germaine Greer, *Sex and Destiny*, London: Chatto 1984, p. 48.
12. H.L.A. Hart, 'Immorality and Treason', in L. Blom-Cooper (ed.), *The Law as Literature*, London: The Bodley Head 1961, p. 221. Hart's case was put in H.L.A. Hart, *The Law and Liberty*, London: Oxford University Press 1959.
13. Joel Feinberg, *Rights, Justice and the Bounds of Liberty*, Princeton, NJ: Princeton University Press 1980, p. 82.
14. Andrea Dworkin, *Pornography: Men Possessing Women*, p. 253.
15. Patrick Devlin, *The Enforcement of Morals*, p. 17.
16. Hugh Trevor-Roper, *The European Witch Craze*, Harmondsworth: Peregrine Books 1978, p. 33.
17. Crista Wolfe, *A Model Childhood*, London: Virago 1981.
18. Jeffrey Weeks, *Sex Politics and Society*, London: Longmans 1981, p. 87.
19. The Williams Report, *Report of the Committee on Obscenity and Film Censorship*, Cmnd 8801.
20. Andrea Dworkin, *Pornography: Men Possessing Women*, p. 303.
21. Susan Griffin, *Women and Nature: the Roaring Inside Her*, London: The Women's Press 1984, p. 5.

13. Campaigning against pornography

Melissa Benn

The debate among British feminists about pornography seems to have
died down recently. But it may surface again, and this time with a very
specific focus, if things develop here in the same way as they have in the
United States. A debate is currently raging in the American women's
movement about whether pornography should be banned by legislation. Some anti-pornography feminists (like Andrea Dworkin, author
of probably the best known feminist polemic against pornography[1])
have drafted civil rights legislation to directly outlaw pornography. In
the process, they have made some uneasy, if expected, political
alliances with the right wing. This legal initiative raises questions of
principle that need to be addressed by feminists here. Is legislation the
right way to deal with pornography? If it is, what kind? And if it isn't,
what else should be done?

The anti-pornography movement in Britain was intimately connected
with, and emerged from, the anti-sexual violence campaigns of the
1970s. Those campaigns, supported by most sections of the women's
liberation movement, were successful in arousing awareness about the
extent of violence against women, and in creating lasting institutions –
rape crisis centres, women's aid refuges – to combat it. Not so the
movement against pornography. This movement has chiefly found
institutional expression in Women Against Violence Against Women
(WAVAW), and 'Angry Women' actions like attacking sex shops. The
women behind these actions – whom for the sake of clarity I shall call
'anti-porn feminists' – have set much of the terms of debate on
pornography. They don't bother so much with a definition of
pornography. Their line is 'she who feels it knows it'. But they do have
a strong line on what it *means*. To them, pornography equals violence
against women; it both reflects and causes it. Hence, the slogan 'porn is
the theory, rape is the practice' which blurs a time-honoured liberal
distinction between fantasy and reality, freedom of expression and
action.[2]

What was good about the feminist anti-porn campaigns was their gut-level anger and action to match. Once again, radical and revolutionary feminists stole the initiative from socialist feminists in their capacity to directly address women's experience on key issues. Most women do believe that pornography humiliates, irritates and dehumanizes both the women depicted in it and the women who 'see' it. And here, at least, was a distinctly feminist attack on pornography which distinguished itself from the existing positions of liberalism and libertarianism. This approach says: pornography is not merely, or even mainly, a series of representations of a variety of sexual acts. Pornography is not so much about sex, as it is about images of women produced for male consumption. Isn't the chief characteristic of pornographic images their constant suggestion of women's availability? Whether as dominated or dominatrix, women are always open, accessible, ever-present-spread-before-you ready. And waiting . . .

It is therefore too simple to argue as someone like Jean Seaton[3] has done that because feminists have an interest in making sexuality 'public' they must make common cause with pornographers in defending pornographic material: 'the pornographers' freedom to play games on the margins of social revulsion, and the need of women to be heard, are inextricably linked.' She may not be wrong (ultimately) about the kind of alliances feminists should, or shouldn't make, and the dangers inherent in them. Yet having to make alliances – or avoid them – is different from the formation of an analysis which underpins a given political perspective. Pornography is about a great deal more than sex, and feminists are right to oppose it, while maintaining a distinct right to the discussion of sexuality, and the expression of different and various sexualities 'in a safe context'.

Anti-porn feminists also rightly picked up on the connections many women feel exist between the images in pornography, and elsewhere, and their own bodily safety. It may not be the case, as anti-porn feminists claim, that there is a *direct* relationship between pornography and violence against women, such as that men look at a pornographic depiction of rape and then go out and do it.[4] But in a more diffuse way, women know that the existence, and display, of such images is bound to shape men's view of women. How could it not? It may sound obvious to us now, but at the time (the 1970s) such questions were just beginning to be explored.

But ultimately the politics of anti-porn feminism was, and remains, 'bad politics'. Much of it borders on the counterproductive, to say the least. It is too simple to say that pornography *is* violence against women. Anti-porn feminists ignore the myriad of sexist images in society, in advertising, on television and in films, which echo the 'meanings' of pornography and contribute to men's views of women. This argument has been one of the most significant contributions of socialist feminists to the debate.[5] For instance, I find it more directly threatening to sit on a tube platform opposite a blown up image of a single female leg, sheathed in the sheerest of stockings, curved provocatively, cut off from a body, than I do to go into a newsagent and see copies of Playboy and Penthouse lounging on the top shelf. Soft porn magazines are now heavily outnumbered by computer magazines, I notice.

Anti-porn feminists also have a fixed, trans-historical view of male sexuality which amounts to a belief that 'men never change' and that porn shows what men are '*really*' like'. Anti-porn feminists often illustrate this argument in reference to the worst kind of hard core pornography, involving the brutal degradation of women. In common with the moral Right, anti-porn feminism holds a view on the innately aggressive character of male sexuality. Male sexuality is full of drive, domination and danger to women. It's just that the Right thinks that's fine as long as it remains within private, heterosexual, married relationships. In 1981 Andrea Dworkin went on a tour of Soho sexshops, soon after Mary Whitehouse had done the same. She distinguished herself from the latter by saying: 'The difference between us is, I want women to *see* it'[6] – meaning that women should confront pornography and see in it the hatred and contempt men hold for women. And attack them back. But whom else might anti-porn feminists be, inadvertently, attacking?

Some 'Reclaim the Night' marches – which linked up the existence of sex shops and the sale of pornography with women's lack of safety on the streets – were accused by black women of being insidiously racist. Women were often marching through areas with a high black population, and thereby potentially fuelling racist links that exist in the public mind between black crime, black male sexuality and 'white' victims. And women who worked in the sex industry were angry at their jobs being attacked, and at the failure of some anti-porn feminists to see that if pornography was driven underground, the women working in it would simply go 'underground' too.

Arguments like this are surfacing in the current American furore over anti-pornography legislation. At its heart is the Dworkin–

McKinnon ordinance (local legislation) against pornography. This ordinance, first passed in Minneapolis, declares pornography to be a violation of civil rights. It holds that pornography promotes violence against women, keeps women subordinate and inhibits access to equal employment, education and opportunity. It does not create new criminal offences: women claiming under the ordinances can only bring an action for damages. Similar anti-pornography ordinances have been considered by other city councils. In each place the political alliances for and against have differed somewhat. However, in general there has been the alliance, so often predicted, between anti-porn feminists and the Right, with sexual and civil libertarians opposing it.[7]

What would be the legislative equivalent in Britain? It would probably look something like the Sex Discrimination or Race Relations Act, only it would make the production and sale of pornography a civil wrong on the grounds of sex discrimination. This would distinguish it from obscenity and indecency laws which seek to ban material on grounds of 'taste' or the test of how a 'reasonable' person would be affected by it. There could also be an 'incitement to sexual hatred' clause, similar to the clause on racial hatred, introduced under the Race Relations Act, which would carry a criminal penalty.

The main danger in bringing the law into the realm of sex and sexual representation, even on grounds of sex discrimination, is the counter-productive ways in which it could be used. Recent Custom and Excise swoops on Gay's the Word bookshop, and the blasphemy case a few years ago against *Gay News* are just two examples of how just about any law can be turned against any sexual radicals. Further, whatever the feminist intention behind such a law, its interpretation by politicians, magistrates and judges could yield alarming results. In the debate in the States, Kate Millett and others have said: 'I hate this racist and sexist shit [pornography] but I'm against this law.' I think they're right.

One alternative possibility is the introduction of a more general anti-sexist law which would tackle the breadth and variety of images that degrade and undermine women and not just concentrate on pornography. It is interesting to note here the difficulties that a (proposed) bill to ban sexist advertising had in France. The bill, introduced by the French minister for women's rights, sought to 'protect the dignity of women, by making it illegal to publish images inciting hatred, violence, scorn or discrimination against women' in advertising. Its introduction was defeated by a formidable coalition of academics, intellectuals and journalists.[8]

I think it is essential that we do not get 'stuck' in pro- or anti-legislation (whatever kind of legislation that is) positions. We must not get trapped into thinking that either we're totally against pornography and are therefore obliged to follow the line of those who want to ban it or we can see no option but to let it range free and ferocious, dangerously shaping men's view of women, and their own sexuality. There is a parallel here in controversies over free speech for fascists. That debate raises similar questions about the relation between expression and action. I do not believe we should let such decisions come to symbolize and stand in for action against the problem itself. Racism in Britain has its roots not in the National Front but in imperialism, and the consistent racism of government policies. Whatever you do about the National Front, it is a political priority to tackle state racism. Similarly, although I think we should protest against pornography, it should not be our focal point in tackling violence against women, or sexism in general.

There are other forms of political action, all of which presuppose the existence of a strong, autonomous women's movement continuing to raise, and act upon, issues of violence against women. These must continue to provide concrete material help to women who are attacked by men. Allied to this, there should be a continuation (or resumption?) of direct action by women against sexist imagery of all kinds. I am thinking of the kind of acid graffiti which feminists went in for a few years ago; or sticker campaigns against offensive images; or campaigns against particular images. For instance, the Women's Media Action Group mounted a successful campaign against the Pretty Polly advertisement which showed a single 'sexy' stockinged leg. They succeeded in getting the advertiser to reconsider this image. I would like to see more socialist feminists involved in this sort of direct action and having more of an input into direct action tactics.

Attacks on outlets for pornography, sex shops and so on are more problematic. They shade so easily, or can be seen to shade, into an anti-sex 'isn't this disgusting?' stance. However, with more thought-out tactics, even this could be done. Entirely legally of course . . .

More generally, feminists should sustain a campaign within mixed institutions – ranging from political parties (what *is* the Labour Party's position on sexist advertising and pornography?) to the media unions – to maintaining sustained pressure on bodies like the Advertising Standards Authority (ASA). The Greater London Council's anti-sexist advertising policy on London Transport gave a lead here, and shows what could be done. As for the ASA, while it has no legal power it can be persuaded to push advertisers into changing the images they use to sell products. It needs a co-ordinated onslaught. In France, for example, public pressure on the equivalent of the Advertising Standards Authority led to the removal of one of the most offensive advertisements, a picture of a woman being stuffed into a hamburger.

All these kinds of actions should be more than just an attempt to change attitudes. There should be real propaganda of the word – and deed. By a combination of such strategies, by vigorous and continual pressure on the men who produce degrading images of women, the money which backs them, and the market which consumes them – we might genuinely undermine the assumptions that produce them in the first place.

References

1. Andrea Dworkin, *Pornography: Men Possessing Women*, London: The Women's Press 1981.
2. For statements on this position, see Dusty Rhodes and Sandra McNeill (eds), *Women Against Violence Against Women*, OnlyWomen Press 1985.
3. See Jean Seaton, 'Pornography and Feminism', in *New Socialist*, No. 8, November/December 1982.
4. Research studies tend *not* to be able to prove a connection between consumption of pornography and attacks against women. See *MS* magazine, April 1985.
5. See, for example, Rosalind Coward, 'Sexual Violence and Sexuality', *Feminist Review*, No. 11, Summer 1982.
6. Mandy Merck, 'Pornography', *City Limits*, 6 November 1981.
7. For full discussion of ordinances, and the pros and cons, see *Off Our Backs*, American feminist newspaper, June 1985.
8. *The Guardian*, 9 July 1985.

14. The new communications revolution

Peter Golding and Graham Murdock

Until now, socialist policy in the areas of culture and communications has been mainly concerned with the press, broadcasting, and to a lesser extent with film and the 'arts'. This is no longer adequate. Developments in technology have combined with Thatcherite policies to create new centres of cultural power and alter established communication industries in important ways. So far, thinking on the Left has lagged some way behind these changes and failed to grasp their full implications. We urgently need to make up for lost time.

Although we concentrate here on their implications for information and cultural provision, it is important to remember that communications technologies are also playing a major role in restructuring work and administration in pursuit of efficiency and profits. Current moves centre around improvements in computing and telecommunications technology and their convergence to form an integrated system which can transmit all kinds of information – speech, numerical data, written text, and visual images – over the same communications network. Applications include speeding the spread of automation in industry, rationalizing clerical work, and replacing cash and cheque transactions with electronic funds transfers.

Most organizations buy the equipment and services they need from companies specializing in advanced communications facilities, though leading firms, notably in the automobile industry, are beginning to move into these areas on their own account. In 1984 for example, the world's largest industrial company, General Motors, famous for its Chevrolet and Cadillac cars, took over the data processing company, Electronic Data Systems. Its role is to integrate all of GM's computer and telecommunications systems into one worldwide paperless network linking everyone in the corporation, from executives and product designers to dealers running local car showrooms. Then in June 1985 GM branched out into the general communications marketplace by acquiring Hughes Aircraft, one of the world's leading space satellite companies. More recently, Daimler Benz, makers of the Mercedes, have bought a controlling interest in AEG whose interests span satellites, communications and micro-electronics. The new group is West Germany's biggest industrial corporation. Similar trends are also evident in Britain. BL's information systems division for example, is emerging as an important player in the market for electronic transfers of business data.

The centrality of the new communications industries to the economic structure of advanced capitalism means that communications policy can no longer concern itself solely with maximizing the availability of cultural goods and services, promoting their diversity, and finding ways of making the cultural industries more accountable and responsive to consumer needs. These aims must remain at the core of any socialist cultural strategy, but in future they will need to be considered alongside economic goals in areas such as research and development and employment. Here we focus more narrowly on information and cultural provision, however, and in this area two sectors of the new communications industries are particularly relevant to policy: the electronic information industries and the new television industries.

The electronic information industries are based on the convergence of computing and telecommunications mentioned earier and have two main sectors: videotex and interactive services. Videotex is the generic name for any system that allows electronic information to be transmitted for display on the screen of a domestic television set, computer monitor, or visual display unit (VDU). Teletext services use the spare capacity in the standard television signal for this, while viewdata systems use the telecommunications network. At the moment, both basic teletext services (ITV's *Oracle* and the BBC's *Ceefax*) are free to anyone who has a set adapted for teletext reception, but they only operate one-way. Viewers cannot send messages back to the central information store or link up with each other. These interactive facilities are available on British Telecom's public viewdata system, *Prestel*, but access to them is much more expensive. As well as buying or renting the necessary equipment – and paying a quarterly subscription – users have to pay for the calls they make to the database, for the computer time they use and for the individual 'pages' of information they consult. Not surprisingly, *Prestel* is a luxury that most people cannot afford. At the end of 1984, there wer only 21,801 viewdata terminals in private households, compared with 2.4 million teletext sets.

At the same time, *Prestel*'s interactive facilities have a number of positive features including messaging networks that allow personal computer owners to exchange information, and home shopping services which provide the electronic equivalent of a mail order catalogue. These could be particularly useful for groups like pensioners, the disabled and low income families. At the moment many members of these groups cannot take full advantage of the cheaper prices and greater range offered by city centre supermarkets or discount stores on the edge of towns, because they find travelling to them too difficult or expensive. However it is exactly the groups most in need who are least able to enter the new electronic marketplace. Half the senior citizens currently living alone on state pensions do not even have a telephone, let alone the other equipment they require. We need to come to grips with this situation by making telecommunications a central policy concern, and by devising practical proposals for increasing the diversity of information offered over public videotex systems and widening access to interactive facilities.

There is an equally pressing need to develop a comprehensive response to the rise of the new television industries. We already live in a television-centred culture. Virtually every household in the country has at least one television set and over a third (39 per cent) have two or more. In a normal week the average adult will watch around 31 hours of broadcasting as against seven hours spent reading the daily and Sunday papers. For most people, the screen will be their major source of information about events and issues outside their local area, and their main point of access to cultural and political life more generally. They will hardly ever go to the cinema or theatre but will watch a great many feature films and drama programmes. They will almost certainly never go to a political meeting or adult education class but may watch a considerable number of current affairs and feature programmes. Until recently, everything that appeared on the television screen was either produced or purchased by one of the main broadcasting organizations. This is no longer the case. Broadcast programmes still dominate peoples' viewing but they are now competing with the options offered by the new television industries of video, cable and, very soon, direct broadcasting by satellite (DBS). Like the electronic information industries, these developments present new problems as well as new opportunities for socialist policy. However, before we can devise a coherent response to either industry, we must look a little more closely at how they are organized.

Like the older media, the new communications industries tend to be highly concentrated, with a handful of firms dominating the key markets. Indeed they are quite often the same firms, as companies with significant stakes in established areas acquire interests in emerging sectors. One of the most spectacular examples is Reuters, which has long been among the top agencies supplying news stories to the world's press. Nowadays this business, though still lucrative, contributes less than ten per cent of the company's total profits. The rest comes from its electronic information services which supply business users with economic data and allow them to deal in currencies, bullion and bonds from their terminals. W.H. Smith provides another example of the growing links between the old and new media. As well as playing a key role in determining the general availability of books and magazines through its nationwide chain of stores, it is now a major force in supplying programming for cable systems in Britain and Europe. It has a 35 per cent stake in the new Lifestyle channel, 19 per cent of Screen Sport, a substantial holding in the new Arts Channel and a significant interest in the rock video channel, Music Box, through its 30 per cent holding in Yorkshire Television, one of the three shareholders. However, the really significant players in the new communications system are the companies whose interests span the whole range of information and moving image industries, both old and new. Here again there are some very familiar names, including Robert Maxwell and Rupert Murdoch.

In addition to being the proprietor of the *Mirror*, *Sunday Mirror* and *Sunday People*, and owning publishing companies (such as Futura paperbacks) which account for 8 per cent of the British book market, Maxwell has extensive interests in electronic data services in the legal and scientific fields and significant stakes in the television industries. These include: a 13.8 per cent holding in the ITV company, Central Independent Television; 40 per cent of the independent production company, Antelope Productions; and sole ownership of the country's largest network of local cable systems. In August 1985 he extended his interests to Europe by buying a 20 per cent interest in the French broadcasting satellite TDF-1. This is due to be launched in mid-1986 with a signal capable of reaching 150 million people across the Continent through small dish receivers mounted on buildings. Rupert Murdoch is already well established in the satellite television market with his general entertainment service, Skychannel, which is piped into around 2 million households throughout Europe by local cable operators. He is now looking to expand his interests in this area through a partnership with the Belgian company, Group Bruxelles Lambert, one of the major shareholders in Radio Tele Luxembourg, another frontrunner for a channel on TDF-1. These ventures are part of Murdoch's ambitious plan to become a major force in the key markets for television-delivered entertainment. Other essential elements include: his purchase of the major Hollywood film and television studio 20th Century Fox (with its extensive back catalogue of productions); his acquisition of Metromedia, makers of the hit soap opera, *Dynasty*; his half share in one of the four major chains of American television stations; and his control of television stations in the two leading Australian markets, Sydney and Melbourne. This is in addition to owning one of the world's largest publishing empires which spans Australia and the USA as well as the *Sun*, *News of the World*, *Times* and *Sunday Times* in Britain.

Murdoch is one of the pioneers of a new style of megacorporation in the communications field, charaterized by a wide spread of interests, integrated operations, and international reach. Their rise represents an unprecedented concentration of potential control over the production and flow of information and imagery. At the same time, the countervailing power of public intervention is being steadily weakened both institutionally, through the withdrawal of public ownership and subsidy, and philosophically, through the aggressive promotion of free market principles.

The most obvious British instance is the denationalization programme. Since 1979 Conservative governments have privatized a number of public companies operating in key areas of the new communications industries. They include British Telecom, Cable and Wireless (the only company licensed to operate an alternative network to BT's until 1989), British Aerospace (the country's major satellite builder), Ferranti (the electronics company), ICL (Britain's only serious mainframe computer maker), Logica (one of the leading domestic companies in the computer software market), and INMOS (the microchip maker). Sales of shares in these companies represent a massive loss of public money at several levels.

First, there is the expense of arranging the sales themselves. It cost £323 million simply to dispose of 51.2 per cent of BT. Added to which, the shares were underpriced to attract small investors. As a result, eleven months after the sale they were worth a total of 3.4 billion pounds more than the asking price.

Secondly, there is the permanent loss of future revenues which could be used to subsidize access to telecommunications facilities and support initiatives in other areas of communications. In its first financial year as a private company for example, BT made £1.48 billion in pre-tax profits. Nor has privatization achieved the government's goal of significantly widening share ownership. In the first ten days of trading on the stock exchange 20 per cent of the BT shares allocated to individuals changed hands as people cashed in on the virtual doubling of the issue price. Most were bought by the financial institutions who dominate share ownership generally, leaving future policy goals to be determined by their corporate strategies rather than by public policy goals. According to BT's latest annual report, the insurance companies, pension funds and other large institutions own three quarters of all the publicly issued shared, but make up only 1.6 per cent of the total shareholders. This loss of direct control over a key part of the communications system makes developing an integrated public policy much more problematic.

This difficulty is aggravated by the current approach to regulating communications companies. Deregulation is not a particularly useful description of what is happening. The amount of regulation is less important than its direction. What we are seeing is a movement away from protection of the public interest and towards the promotion of corporate interests. Once again, telecommunications provides a good illustration. The main aim of current policies is to provide cheap and efficient services to business by allowing Cable and Wireless's Mercury network to compete on the best possible terms. To this end the new regulatory body, Oftel, has ruled that BT must connect Mercury's trunk network to its local and international networks and pay 50 per cent of the costs of providing any extra capacity required. The ensuing competition will undoubtedly keep costs down for business users but it will also mean higher line rentals and call charges for domestic customers, excluding even more low income households from basic telecommunications facilities. This is entirely consistent with BT's steady retreat from the historic goal of making the telephone services geographically and financially accessible to everyone. Soon after the initial decision to licence Mercury was announced, BT responded by cutting prices on the long distance and international routes most heavily used by business, increasing the price of domestic calls, and placing a question mark over the future of public call boxes in expensive-to-reach rural areas. Recent moves simply confirm the new wisdom that communication services are commodities not public utilities and that profitability takes precedence over accessibility.

This view also informs the developing cable television system. Because the present government defines cable very clearly as a commercial enterprise and not as a public service, most of the rules governing broadcasting are seen as irrelevant. Cable operators are basically in the business of selling additional entertainment channels showing sports, rock videos, feature films and mixed programming, plus additions such as arts, children's and lifestyle channels which can deliver audiences attractive to advertisers. They are not obliged to promote diversity if it does not correspond with market dynamics. There is no set limit on imported material and no positive requirement to provide reasonable access facilities or ensure that a wide range of views are presented. Cable operators may make concessions in these areas, to maintain good relations with the local community or earn 'brownie' points with the Cable Authority (who can cancel their franchise), but they are under no legal obligation to do so.

This attack on public service principles, coupled with cuts in public expenditure, is also having a powerful effect on the cultural and communications institutions that remain in the public sector. To survive in an increasingly harsh fiscal and political environment they are obliged to becme more market oriented. The push to reintroduce museum charges and make users pay for library facilities is one aspect of this. The BBC's growing commercialism is another. This is particularly significant given the Corporation's centrality to the present cultural and communications system.

Faced with the growing gap between the licence fee revenue and the costs of maintaining its present range of programming, the BBC has adopted two main strategies: cutting costs by slimming down its operations, entering into more co-financing with outside investors; and raising extra revenues through the activities of its Enterprises division. These activities include: publishing the *Radio Times* (one of the country's top selling weekly magazines); producing books and records based on programmes; selling BBC productions in overseas markets; marketing an exclusive range of pre-recorded video cassettes through Marks and Spencer's stores; providing material for the *World Reporter*, the electronic information service; selling home computers in association with Acorn; and developing a range of educational materials on videodisc. Such commercial activities are expected to make around £100 million a year that can be ploughed back into original production and used to subsidize minority interest programmes. Although this could help to extend diversity, there is always the danger that the tail will end up wagging the dog and that projects will be selected for their attractiveness to outside investors, their spin-off possibilities, their suitability for video distribution, and their chances of selling in America and other major markets. This would mean more series and made-for-TV movies rather than single plays, more costume drama rather than contemporary fiction, more documentaries on wildlife and lifestyles rather than contemporary politics and contentious issues, and more attention to the Royal Family, the aristocracy, and the landmarks, celebrities and social types that make up the televisual tourism that is so saleable internationally.

In taking full advantage of the new communications marketplace the BBC risks reducing its ability to engage with the full range of contemporary British issues and experiences. The more successful it is commercially, the greater the risk.

Cost inflation and political pressures have also prompted the BBC to compromise its commitment to universal availability. Basic licence payers no longer have access to the full range of services. The Corporation broke with this fundamental tenet of public service when it agreed to provide programmes for the experimental commercial cable service in inner London, and to take a major role in the project to offer additional national channels by satellite available only on subscription. These schemes have been shelved, but both its major ventures into the business information market, *Datacast* and *World Reporter*, require additional payments. *Datacast* uses teletext technology to provide business users with a fast, confidential and nationally available service for transmitting business data. It is expected to earn the BBC at least £2 million a year by 1987. Once again, this money could provide a useful subsidy to general production, but it is also clear that as demand expands, capacity will have to be transferred from the public teletext service, reducing the range of information it carries.

Faced with contraction and commercialization of publicly funded communications services and the rapid rise of the new mega-corporations, it is easy to lapse into pessimism. However, this misses the opportunities in the developing situation. As Geoff Mulgan and Ken Worpole argue (see pp. 136–148 above), building a socialist culture for the 1980s and beyond will entail using the full range of modern media and popular forms. Exploring the positive potential of new communications technologies is an essential part of this effort.

The possibility of using video as a cheap and flexible campaigning tool and means of expression are already widely accepted. Alternative computer applications are less well developed but potentially even more far-reaching. The scope for radical software is enormous. The possibilities of radical databases are even greater. Picture a continuously updated information store that contained and developed the kinds of materials that *Labour Research* now publishes monthly. Databases can also help to develop contact networks. In the USA for example, the National Women's Mailing List keeps a file with the names and interests of over 60,000 feminists who have agreed to be listed, making it very much easier for individuals and groups to contact people with similar interests or useful expertise. The word processing facilities of many micro computers can also be used to develop collective writing, since text can be added to, deleted or moved without having to retype. Computer networks can also be a valuable campaign tool. In the spring of 1985, for example, there were large demonstrations on campuses across America to urge university authorities to pull their investments out of companies operating in South Africa. Computer messaging was used extensively to enchange information and co-ordinate protests.

The American Airline Pilots' Association strike during the same period offers an even more elaborate example of advanced technology use. The union organized several three and a half hour long broadcasts to rally support for the strike. They used a satellite link to beam them to mass meetings in eight locations around the country, and made video recordings to distribute to members who could not attend in person. The programmes' style borrowed heavily from commercial production. They were introduced and linked by sympathetic and well-known media professionals, and featured a rock video of the strike song 'We are Family – A United Family' (based on the Sister Sledge hit, 'We are Family'). However it could be argued that this is simply a labour movement application of techniques normally used by corporate management, which reproduces the same hierarchical, top-down communications. A more radical use of satellite technology is 'space bridging'. This allows groups in widely separated locations to see and talk to each other instantaneously. The commemoration of VE Day, organized by Soviet Television and the University of California, showed some of the possibilities. It brought together American and Soviet war veterans and civilians, in studios in Moscow and San Diego, and let them talk about their experiences of working together and what it meant to them. Against the background of the official celebrations which marginalized the Soviet war effort and American support for it, this exercise in restoring popular memory was a pertinent intervention.

These kinds of alternative uses of new communications technologies are well worth exploring but they are not cheap. To make them widely available requires public financing at various levels. Subsidies to production, such as paying experienced workers to produce material or training people to make their own, providing basic equipment and facilities, and supporting particular projects, are already a well-established plank of cultural policy. Subsidies to distribution and consumption are less developed but not less essential. Like books, magazines and records most computer software and video material is distributed by large concerns who are mostly interested in mainstream commercial productions. One solution would be to subsidize shops that undertook to add the full range of local and alternative production to their shelves, though this still leaves the problem of unequal consumption.

As we noted earlier, the current costs of acquiring the necessary equipment and buying the new products and services excludes state benefit claimants and low wage earners from the new communications markets. By mid 1985, 28 per cent of households in Britain had a video cassette recorder and 14 per cent had a home computer.

Future growth is expected to be relatively slow, particularly among the poorer sections of the population who are already markedly underrepresented in both markets. One answer to this problem is to expand the scope of the library system to provide collections of alternative video material and computer software, together with viewing facilities and communal computer terminals that individuals and groups can use for word processing, messaging and accessing data banks.

These projects, however worthwhile in themselves, cannot be pursued in isolation. Any proposal for extending public provision must be measured against competing demands and considered in the context of a broadly based policy with clear aims.

To move beyond the fragmented and responsive rejection of recent privatizing and deregulatory trends to a more positive socialist policy we have to return to basic principles. The crux of such an approach is to recognize the essentially social nature of culture and communications, and to formulate mechanisms which restore the primacy of rights to communicate and to know. This can be achieved by promoting three objectives: diversity, accessibility and accountability.

Diversity has three dimensions. First, we must maximize the range, not merely the quantity, of information in circulation, in particular by increasing the visibility of the commanding heights of state and corporate power where decisions which have a significant influence over people's lives are made. Second, we must ensure that the range of viewpoints and interpretations on offer is maximized. This is crucial because information only becomes knowledge when situated in a context which allows connections to be drawn – between the particular and the general, the present and the past. Third, we should promote the widest possible range of media. This means encouraging innovation and experiment with new media, and providing space for new forms of expression.

Accessibility means ensuring that no one is barred from the means to communicate publicly or to acquire communications because of characteristics which they are powerless to influence. The aim is to maximize the range of experiences, both social and personal, that may be communicated – in other words to increase the sociability of communications, while at the same time promoting access to the full range of cultural production. In particular the aim should be to ensure that income, gender, enthnicity and location are not barriers to the full range of communications facilities.

Accountability involves developing channels through which consumers and users of communications systems can have the opportunity to make their opinions, needs, and demands felt – not only at the level of day-to-day use or consumption, but also at the level of overall policy direction.

Each of these general canons of policy naturally brings in its wake complexities and contradictions when translated into legislation or procedure. We can only point here to some of the issues raised in working towards these objectives.

Diversity of information requires strong legal guarantees of freedom of information at both local and central government level, and a strengthening of the regulations governing what corporations are required to disclose publicly. In other words pertinent legislation needs to actively promote a more open society, not merely permit it. The present government's hesitancy over such a relatively modest advance as the recent Local Government (Access to Information) Act – because it might serve as a model for subsequent legislation at national level – is an indicator of the likely scale of resistance to even marginal shifts in a more liberal direction.

Diversity also implies a change in the organization of production to allow a wider base of participation. This involves positive discrimination in recruitment to the range of relevant jobs, particularly in favour of ethnic minorities and women. It also involves opening up the production process to a wider range of inputs from outside. Tackling production practices within the core organizations of cultural production, though essential, is not the only option.

One alternative is to separate production from distribution. There are two firm precedents for this in the present system: the publishing model that informs Channel Four, and the common carrier principle in telecommunications. There is no doubt that Channel Four has succeeded in extending the range of British braodcasting, though this is only partly due to its policy of buying-in the bulk of its programming from outside producers. Cable operators do exactly the same. The difference is that Channel Four has a legal obligation to encourage innovation and pay particular attention to needs that are not adequately catered for in the rest of the system. Without strong public interest regulation and subsidies to production, simply splitting production and distribution is unlikely to extend diversity. The same is true of the historic principle that telecommunications operators provide the physical infrastructure but users determine what they want to transmit over it. As we argued earlier, subsidies are needed if the full possibilities for information exchange are to be realized.

In general the aim should be to promote more diverse production, not merely allow it. This will entail subsidies for production to ensure that opportunities are not monopolized by the larger and better financed professional groups. It will also require a more general encouragement of involvement, through more relevant media education, and local authority intervention in relevant areas of the local economy and in the support of a broad range of recreation.

Accessibility immediately throws up a dilemma for socialist strategy. On the one hand it might be argued that access to a full range of communications resources and outputs based entirely on the public sector and fully subsidized is impossible to guarantee. There will always be a market place for cultural goods however regulated and to whatever extent distorted by subsidy or control. In any case to subsidize is to promote selectively, inviting paternalism. It also implies the intrusive patronage of providing income support in the form of goods and services, not money.

The dilemma is whether we conceive communications as like health or education services, public goods whose importance and centrality in our collective lives requires social provision and guaranteed access. Or is it like food, essential but consumed in very varied ways and requiring regulation rather than public provision? Do we really want the cultural equivalent of soup kitchens? Or to take a more limited instance, would it be preferable to provide all pensioners (or indeed all the unwaged) with a free television licence or to fight for improved pensions and benefits? The former may lead down a slippery road to the provision of income in kind, a potentially punitive and controlling strategy much favoured by those who seek the extension of voucher schemes in the social security system for example. The latter alternative (they need not of course be exclusive) is a larger battle for redistribution of income, which accepts the fact of choice by purchase in the communications market place.

We need to distinguish the essential core of public sector provision from the broader range of additional services to which access can only ultimately be guaranteed by policies for income and wealth equalization. In the immediate term the priority is to defend the basic principle of public broadcasting – that all services produced should be available to everyone who has paid the basic licence fee. This means resisting attempts to introduce subscription services, and ensuring that any attempts to raise revenue through commercial activities support diversity through cross-subsidy to minority interest productions, rather than pull production towards forms and themes that offer a maximum potential for spin-offs and overseas sales. Only by insisting on this principle can we ensure that, in broadcasting at least, one core national service is available for all and, at least potentially, can provide a more or less comprehensive range of programming.

Similarly, we need to ensure that British Telecom maintains its public call-box network, and keeps local call charges to a reasonable level. For elderly and disabled people it may be worth thinking about free telephones and subsidized calls. Telephones are not often considered part of communications policy, but for many people the telephone is a key point of access to the information and advice they need to make decisions about their everyday lives and to defend their rights. Yet roughly a quarter of households in Britain are still without a telephone, disproportionately those in lower income groups.

Accountability also throws up difficult questions of strategy and practice. If we insist that the production, distribution, and consumption of communications resources and cultural goods are to be largely in the public sector then accountability must be achieved in two ways. First, communications industries and services must be, to a greater or lesser extent, integrated into the political system, at both local and national level. This will mean giving a greater role to parliament and to local authorities. Communications will inevitably become a political football, but at least in principle we will all get a kick, if only by proxy. Second, accountability will mean direct access to policy decisions and immediate opportunities for consumers to respond to production.

We can briefly illustrate some immediate targets and strategies which follow from these principles. In seeking diversity one possibility, much discussed by everyone except the last Royal Commission on the Press, is to regulate the use of revenues from advertising for cross-subsidization of less commercially viable but socially desirable production and distribution. We should also consider the possibility of extending statutory controls on advertising beyond commercial televisions (where it is subject to the Broadcasting Act administered by the IBA) to other means of communications.

This is particularly important since one of the features of the new communications marketplace is that it offers massively expanded opportunities for advertising both in terms of the amount of time and space available, and in the forms of advertising. We are no longer considering simply a 30-second slot of clearly indicated display or classified advertising, but also sponsored programmes and material, so that there will be a much more fluid line between advertising and programming or editorial matter. It will become increasingly difficult to disentangle them. Advertising features in the press will acquire a broadcast equivalent. This is significant, because one of the prerequisites of diversity is that information flows should not be unduly managed or massaged by corporations concerned to promote goods and commodities.

Diversity also requires close attention to the inadequate monitoring and regulation of monopoly. The present system is not only politically and legally weak, it remains wedded to a model of the communications industries as a set of discrete sectors, and cannot address problems of integration and cross-ownership. This will also require a careful reconstruction of the notion of the public interest in anti-monopoly legislation. In seeking to extend accessibility, immediate strategies must explore the limits of the present regulatory agencies in lobbying

Oftel to take a tougher line on pricing policy; for example the power of consumer organizations like the POUNC also needs to be promoted.

In addition, we must explore the immediate potential of existing political structures which have as yet to feel their way into communications in any serious way. Some local authorities have dipped toes tentatively into the promotion of local information technology initiatives but few have explored the possibilities of taking on a more comprehensive role in monitoring local developments and seeking the legal initiatives which would permit broader interventions in local communications systems. Equally, in the voluntary sector, community groups, tenants' and residents' associations, claimants' unions, or unemployed workers' centres, all have a great deal to offer and to gain from access to new communications resources. Much rewriting of existing legislation will be required as well as recasting of traditional initiatives such as the Urban Programme, but the possibilities are extensive.

In furthering accountability the immediate objective is to ensure that individuals and groups can correct misleading information about themselves and criticize the presentation of events and issues they are concerned with. Relevant demands include strengthening the provisions of the existing data protection legislation so that people can check on what is held on them, and extending the right of reply in the major media. Channel Four's *Right of Reply* which gives members of the audience the chance to come back at programme makers is a welcome step in the right direction. Equivalent opportunities must be introduced into newspaper publishing.

Equally pressing is the need for channels through which people can influence overall policy. We must begin with the present structure of public bodies. It is clear that relying on individuals appointed from an unpublished list of 'the great and the good' to represent the public interest is totally inadequate. Not only is such a list drawn from a very narrow range of social groups, there is also constant temptation for governments to exploit the selection process in a partisan way, as the Thatcher administration has done.

One option is to have elected bodies, with representatives drawn from major constituencies of interest and accountable to them. This throws up the problem of representing the unorganized who do not belong to any of the obvious groups – the churches, unions, consumer groups etc. Another alternative is to locate final accountability in the existing political apparatus, with only minimal use of quangos or

semi-statutory bodies. At the very least this would require reconsidering
the idea of a communications minister, and a committee structure
within local authorities which could reflect appropriate concerns in a
broader and more integrated way than conventional economic
development or recreation committees.

None of these issues is new, but the rise of the new communications
industries gives them added point and urgency. In facing up to current
developments it is important to grasp that they present opportunities
as well as problems. Innovations in computing, telecommunications
and video technology not only open up new possibilities for public
communications. By forcing us to rethink the way we approach
communications issues they give us a real chance to develop broader
and more pertinent policies.

The first step is to extend our conventional definition of public
communications to include telecommunications and the new information and television industries alongside broadcasting, film and the
printed media. The second is to see these activities as parts of an
increasingly interconnected system that can be tackled only through an
integrated programme of policies for the whole range of communications industries. As we noted earlier however, these industries are no
longer central simply to cultural life. They are also moving to the heart
of economic life, both in their own right, and through their applications
to a range of manufacturing and service sectors. As a result, future
communications policies will have to find ways of linking economic
and cultural goals and balancing the needs and rights of workers and
trade unionists against the rights and needs of consumers and users.

Recent developments also force us to confront the transnational
nature of communications. It is no longer enough just to safeguard
national production and ensure that it engages with the full range of
British experience and opinion. We need to develop policies based on
positive internationalism. The first task is to find ways of opening up
the system so that groups who are normally only spoken about can
speak for themselves and express their responses to us. The most
obvious area here is our current coverage of the Third World. The
other pressing need is to develop forms of collaboration which will
allow us to explore what we share with the rest of Europe and where
our experience differs. This means joining with other European
socialists to press for policies within the EEC and the Council of
Europe that will facilitiate these kinds of exchanges in a range of areas
from computer networking to pan-European satellite channels.

These issues may seem rather remote from the more familiar demands of the Campaign for Press and Broadcasting Freedom, but unless we come to grips with the full scale of current developments in communications, public policy can never hope to match the coherence and scope of corporate strategies, and socialists will be permanently running to catch a bus which is already full and accelerating away at increasing speed.

Part III: Campaigning for Media Freedom

15. Media freedom and the CPBF

Alan Richardson and Mike Power

The Campaign for Press Freedom was publicly launched at a TUC fringe meeting in September 1979. By the beginning of 1986, the campaign had grown to become an organization of national importance with a catalogue of successful crusades under its belt. Broadcasting had been incorporated into the Campaign's aims in 1982; the Campaign for Press and Broadcasting Freedom (CPBF), as it was renamed, had taken up and fought a range of issues, focusing initially on media treatment of trade unions, particularly during the health service dispute. As the campaign matured, its growing membership and core of full- and part-time workers and volunteers turned to wider effects of media bias. These included the Falklands war and Ireland; the way the media treated minority groups such as gays and lesbians, black people and the disabled; and of course the ever-present question of media sexism. The CPBF continues to fight on behalf of individuals and groups who suffer from the establishment press and broadcasting with the right of reply as a central theme. However trade union issues continue as a prioirity and the CPBF's most high profile role was when it supported the action of the Fleet Street unions in stopping some of the worst excesses of the national newspapers during the year-long coal strike.

The antecedents of the CPBF lay in the events of the late 1970s which raised serious questions about the social responsibility and account-ability of the press. Between December 1978 and November 1979 there was a lock-out at the *Times*, the *Sunday Times* and their supplements. Lord Thompson had sacked three thousand production and clerical staff. His aim was to introduce new technology on his own terms, an attitude that must have a depressingly familiar ring to those who had won that battle only to re-fight it in 1986 against their new proprietor Rupert Murdoch. During the winter of the *Times* lockout a vicious propaganda war was waged throughout the media against the trade union movement. The so-called 'winter of discontent', when low paid workers in public service took strike action, heralded a campaign of unrelenting vilification against individual strikers and their organizations.

Concurrently Fleet Street was conducting another campaign to promote Margaret Thatcher and her new mould-breaking monetarist ideology. They were crowned with success in May 1979 when the Tories won the general election. Clearly the Conservatives owed much to their allies who overwhelmingly dominate the national press.

There had been some activity in response to this steadily advancing right-wing and unaccountable press. Print workers had taken industrial action to obtain the right of reply for workers at Grunwick and for power workers. Women had occupied newsrooms to obtain replies to sexist coverage. Serious concern was growing inside the journalists' union, the NUJ, about declining professional standards. Plans were laid to withdraw the NUJ's representatives from the Press Council because it had proved inadequate to deal with these problems

In the wider trade union movement resentment against distorted and biased coverage grew stronger. The TUC media working party published several studies including the booklet 'Cause for Concern' which monitored two months of press reports of industrial disputes in 1979. It revealed that coverage was uniformly hostile, had become more intense, and that anti-union techniques were long standing. They concluded that the need was 'to promote constructive discussion within the trade union movement, within the media and between the two'.

Against this background the need for an organization to campaign for media freedom became clear. A small steering committee[1] was convened; it drew up a seven-point statement of aims[2] and a strategy to unite those journalists, printers, other media workers and trade unionists concerned. These proposals were discussed at a Conference on 'Democratic Accountability and the Media' held under the auspices of the Institute for Workers' Control at Nottingham in March 1979. Many who later sponsored or became active in the campaign, were present at the conference. During the next few months a list of sponsors[3] was drawn up and the aims elaborated.

Towards Press Freedom – the campaign's founding document sold 10,000 copies within three months of publication, requiring a reprint of 5,000. It noted:

It is a curiosity that among the radical, liberal, socialist, trade union groupings of British society there has been little serious intellectual research or reforming activity on the question of the press. Health, education and the arts have all been deemed suitable subjects for political debate and legislative reform. But the press, which plays a decisive role in shaping society and affects all our lives, had been left largely to its own devices.

A programme of research work and public debate was set to last at least the lifetime of the existing Conservative government. Groups were to be set up and conferences and seminars organized. Membership was offered to individuals and organizations. By April 1981, 429 individuals had joined and 334 organizations had affiliated. By March 1986, membership had grown to 932 individuals and 472 affiliated organizations.

In its first two years the Campaign took on many projects. Some issues such as the right of reply had long-term durability, while others such as the Labour daily or freedom of information have tended to ebb and flow. The TUC and Labour Party both carried resolutions committing them to policies in line with those of the campaign and assistance was given to *East End News* and *Rochdale Alternative Press*. Considerable effort was directed against the Protection of Official Information Bill, a nasty piece of repressive legislation that was hastily abandoned. In February 1980 over four hundred people attended the London launch of the campaign in Central Hall, Westminster. That meeting coincided with the first four-page edition of *Free Press*, the journal of the CPBF.

Work was in hand on a number of other areas. An enquiry into the Press Council had been set up in April 1980 and in June of that year a right of reply committee began work and drafted a pamphlet. At the same time a committee for press distribution was formed jointly with the Minority Press Group (now Comedia). Further efforts were made in relation to freedom of information, broadcasting and regional activity. However, these undertakings needed much greater human and material resources to reach the initial expectations and perceived needs of the organization. This led to a mini-crisis of ambition and possibility.

Initially the CPBF secretary was based in the Hadleigh headquarters of SOGAT, and was fully employed there, with some occasional paid help. It quickly became obvious that a regular and independent administration and office would be needed if the organization was to consolidate. As the initial euphoria and enthusiasm of the launch receded it became clear that media reforms would need long-term commitment and effort. In September 1981 the secretary noted that 'An average committee meeting can produce a dozen good ideas for further activities or new campaigning issues. The problem is that when the meeting is over we are incapable of putting the ideas into practice.' That blunt expression of the situation led to a sustained financial and organizational effort that effectively relaunched the organization. Cost free offices were established in Poland Street, London, thanks to the Rowntree Trust, and a part-time organizer was appointed by May 1982. In December 1983 a staffing grant was awarded by the Greater London Council that employed two full-time organizers and one part-time research worker. Later a temporary researcher to cover broad-casting was employed.

In Manchester the Greater Manchester Council funded employment and equipment that allowed a Northwest group to function effectively. The grants ended however, when the councils died. In the interim the CPBF pushed some of its aims into the centre of political debate, and issues such as the right of reply into popular consciousness.

The right of reply has been central to the CPBF's overall activity. Linked to this work has been the commission of enquiry into the Press Council, two parliamentary campaigns to introduce legislation and a major public debate in political, media and industrial organizations. The right of reply has always had a practical, political and ideological value in the campaign. It requires the organization of media workers so they can take action on behalf of those offended, combined with initial practical help and advice to the victims. Coupled with these efforts have been consciousness-raising amongst media workers about the wide-ranging effects of the industry which employs them and a heightened debate around the nature of the media. Much of the CPBF's aims and objectives have been neatly encapsulated in this work and many new issues have flowed from it.

One of the CPBF's earliest initiatives was to set up a Right of Reply Committee.[4] Within four months of work, the right of reply committee had provoked a public response in the press and ensured a major debate at the 1980 TUC which passed a resolution in support of the CPBF and the right of reply. Prompted by these efforts the NUJ clarified and restated its position on press freedom and its own Code of Conduct. The right of reply campaign had quickly won enthusiastic support within the labour movement. All the major trade unions organizing workers in the newspaper industry (from print-room operatives to journalists) endorsed the motion at that year's TUC. They subsequently endorsed a right of reply pamphlet produced by the sub-committee which sold 10,000 copies in a short time. In March 1982 the campaign held a major conference on the right of reply that attracted over 300 union delegates and individuals.

The right of reply is based on the simple principle that if individuals or groups have been seriously misrepresented in a newspaper or magazine, they should have a chance to put their case to the readers of that publication. The right of reply is *not* censorship; on the contrary, it extends access to the media so that more information and a wider range of views can be expressed. It does not favour 'blacking' copy, nor does it intend to interfere with the normal autonomy of editors.

The main issues came to public notice during the NHS dispute of 1982 when newspaper publishers obtained a High Court injunction against Fleet Street electricians' leader, Sean Geraghty, arising out of a 24-hour sympathy strike. The employers' action was also a counter-attack against the campaign for the right of reply. In the weeks up to the High Court confrontation, print unions affiliated to the CPBF had twice threatened industrial action to secure publication of statements supporting the health service workers' pay dispute. This was preceded by some very detailed preparation which established a model of organization used subsequently in the run-up to expected media onslaughts, especially before strikes. Health union activists met under the CPBF's auspices and decided on a publicity effort and call for solidarity for media workers. This included meetings throughout Fleet Street with union chapels, letters to editors demanding fair treatment or the right of reply and direct assistance from media union leadership to direct these efforts.

The NGA successfully demanded the publication of a statement before the proprietors' attack. The statement said the NGA fully supported the health service workers and that the government seemed set on provoking confrontation. The print workers were determined that the National Health Service workers should have a fair hearing and invoked the principle of the right of reply to secure it. The policy of the CPBF has always been to support industrial action when necessary to secure the right of reply. The newspaper employers' injunction granted on 9 August was aimed not only at stopping supportive or sympathetic industrial action. It also restrained the unions from 'interfering with the business' of newspaper proprietors, thus undermining the NGA which was about to demand publication of a statement spelling out the justice of the hospital workers' case. In the aftermath of that dispute Health Service unions funded the campaign to make a 40-minute video, *Making News*, which deals with the media treatment of the dispute.

Two years later Fleet Street's target was the striking miners and their president, Arthur Scargill. For 12 months the NUM and its leadership was subjected to an incessant barrage of abuse. From September 1983, when the NUM press officer began meeting media union leaders, regular meetings had already been taking place to prepare a counter-attack to the media's hostility. The right of reply hit the headlines during the dispute when printworkers at the *Daily Express* and the *Sun* took action to confront appalling editorial bias against the mineworkers. At the *Sun* the NGA chapel intervened to prevent publication of a front page photograph of Arthur Scargill seemingly giving a Nazi-style salute and headlined 'Mine Fuhrer'. Earlier at the *Daily Express*, after weeks of shockingly distorted reporting of the dispute, SOGAT members objected to a fabricated speech in which Arthur Scargill 'admitted' that he was lying to his members. Bill Keys, General Secretary of SOGAT, intervened to ask for the right of reply for Arthur Scargill. The editor, Sir Larry Lamb, objected to the demand for equal space and prominence for the reply and threatened to resign. The outcome of the argument was that an 'edited' version of Arthur Scargill's reply did appear the following week.

The whole story is told in the Campaign's best-selling booklet 'Media Hits the Pits' which was published immediately after the dispute ended. In an extension of the Campaign's work, a Right of Reply Unit was set up in the Spring of 1984 to allow more people to successfully challenge media bias. Since the right of reply campaign was launched it has helped people to overcome a sense of impotence which is often felt when faced with the daunting prospect of confronting the media and has also encouraged media workers to support actively right of reply demands.

The Right of Reply Unit provides a guide-to-action pack which contains the following information:

● Examples of how and where the right of reply has been won
● Information about the media policies and specific work of the media unions
● A guide to the practical steps needed to win the right of reply

- A guide to how and by whom the printed and broadcast media are produced.

Opponents of the CPBF often point to the Press Council in order to counter claims for the right of reply, and condemn trade union action in attempting to secure it. However, following widespread criticism that the Press Council had outlived its usefulness, the Campaign set up an independent Commission of Enquiry in April 1980 to examine alternatives.

Two and a half years later the commission published its report as a book, *People Against the Press* by Geoffrey Robertson who chaired the enquiry. In a thorough analysis of the workings of the Press Council – based on a consumer survey of people who had complained to it – the book presented devastating evidence of dissatisfaction with the Council's performance and procedures. Even a large proportion of *successful* complainants remained dissatisfied customers. As Geoffrey Robertson wrote: 'A remarkable picture emerged of a complaints commission whose procedures seemed to give more cause for complaint than the conduct of the newspapers it was investigating.'

However, considering the book's exposure of the Council's failure to carry out its primary functions, the conclusions of the book's final chapter did come as something of a disappointment. It argued for a press ombudsman, with statutory support, operating alongside a reformed Press Council. In contrast the Campaign's national committee at their June 1983 meeting called for a new and independent press authority with full *statutory* powers to enforce the right of reply. The Campaign believes that the Press Council as currently constituted should be boycotted, as complaining to the Press Council is actually *worse* than doing nothing. It only lends credence to an organization which has been proved to betray popular trust. The oppositional efforts of the CPBF have helped to reduce the credibility of this newspaper proprietors' lap-dog.

The CPBF's view that 'impartiality' and 'balance' in broadcasting and 'objectivity' in newspapers is a myth was presented on the BBC2 *Open Door* access slot in late 1983. As a result more than four hundred viewers wrote to the campaign for more information, many became active members and one made an anonymous donation of £3,000. The programme was called *Why Their News is Bad News* and was presented by two of the Campaign's sponsors, Julie Walters and Julie Christie.

The 30-minute programme demonstrated that those who express views at variance with the prevailing political and social consensus favoured and reinforced in the media, have a constant and unequal struggle to be heard. Julie Christie explained that:

> if television speaks to us as though we all have the same opinion, in practice it applies different rules for describing different sections of society. It depends on whether you are black or white, straight or gay, man or woman, powerful or weak. The issues that television selects, the interpretation it has of events and the comments it makes on public personalities shape our lives. Our perception of what is happening in the world is as much determined by what we don't see on television as what we do see.

Practically the CPBF has attempted to activate and involve all sections of society subject to media distortion. Specialist autonomous groups exist within the Campaign to develop work on behalf of women, gay and black people and there is a group working for the disabled. The women's group drew up a code of conduct on sexist coverage following wide consultation. The code has since been adopted by many trade unions, local authorities and others. A conference held in December 1985 attracted over 300 women and represented a highlight in feminist activity in the mid 1980s. Following the conference the CPBF published guidelines for eliminating media sexism, entitled *Women in Focus*.

The CPBF has also been active in the fight against racism in the media and in 1984 it merged with the Campaign Against Racism in the Media (CARM), which has the active participation of members from ethnic minority communities in Britain. The 1985 riots in Handsworth, Brixton and Tottenham enabled the media and, in particular, the tabloid press to run riot and keep company with Enoch Powell in his paranoia about numbers and his vision of black-created 'alien territory'. In October that year the Campaign organized a meeting in London's County Hall where black community leaders challenged media interpretations of unrest in inner-city areas. It was as unsettling for the Campaign as for the few white media representatives who attended.

Lesbians and gays are also constantly misrepresented in the media and early in 1984 a joint effort was launched by the CPBF and the NUJ gay and lesbian group. These contacts resulted in continuous activity that included attempts to advance the guidelines on coverage of homosexuality. In 1985 the popular press began whipping up anti-gay hysteria resulting from the fear of AIDS. In response to the 'gay plague' type coverage the campaign played a role in assisting gay activists in the media to promote the NUJ's guidelines on reporting of AIDS.

Links can clearly be made with the treatment of all 'dissent' by the media. Women, black, gay and disabled people have problems similar to trade unionists, peace activists and those concerned with the coverage of Ireland. In all these areas the CPBF has made an intervention. One particular occasion was early in the Falklands War. The CPBF responded to what it called 'grave fears over the mounting campaign of intimidation against covering the crisis'. The statement accused the Prime Minister of instigating intimidation of journalists, and the *Sun* and others of whipping it up. Every CPBF member received an 'appeal for urgent assistance' to counter the media witch-hunt over the Falklands. The appeal asked members, sponsors and affiliated organizations to act quickly to 'assist journalists who are being intimidated because they have been reporting faithfully on events in the South Atlantic and on differing views about the crisis. A disgusting and frightening campaign of McCarthy style witch-hunting has been mounted against honest people'.

Attention was drawn to the *Sun*'s accusation of treason against the *Guardian*, *Mirror* and Peter Snow of the BBC, and the hounding and vilification of the BBC by Tory MPs. Members were asked to write to the BBC, the *Guardian* and *Mirror* supporting those journalists who had reported honestly, and for NUJ members, branches and chapels to complement the CPBF national committee efforts by making complaints under their rules against *Sun* journalists for the 'treason' editorial and encouragement to 'sponsor a missile'. There was a substantial response to the appeal as many members and supporters reported their actions. A large number recorded their gratitude at being given leadership and the ability to join an effort against the war hysteria. An accessible and thorough analysis of media freedom and the Falklands entitled 'Rejoice' has been reprinted several times.

At the centre of the CPBF's aims has been a critique of private media ownership and a desire to develop debate around alternative forms of ownership and the feasibility of establishing a daily newspaper sympathetic to the labour movement. As might be expected there are sharp differences of opinion over the desirability of launching a national daily newspaper, so much so that over the years a lively debate has been conducted through the columns of the Campaign's journal

Free Press. In early 1984 a national conference was organized to go into the issue more deeply. The deliberations were published as 'Labour Daily? – Ins and outs of a Labour daily and other media alternatives'. The Campaign was concerned that the brief debates at the TUC and Labour Party Conference the previous year did no justice to the subject. Equally other options such as local papers, developing trade union journals and broadcasting possibilities were being overlooked.

Heightened interest in a Labour daily was aroused in the summer of 1983 when the McCarthy Report, commissioned by the TUC, established the feasibility of a new labour movement newspaper. It proposed the launch of a 32-page tabloid with a cover price of 18p and a full-time staff of 230. The newspaper would reflect the aims and interests of the labour and trade union movement. The CPBF national committee was critical of the report as it seemed to be weak in a number of areas. It was vague on editorial control, had no survey of advertisers and lacked consultation with the media unions and comparisons with international or historical experiences. However, a resolution at the 1984 annual meeting, while welcoming the principle of a Labour daily, recognized the financial obstacles to the labour movement funding the project from its own resources. The resolution also raised the possibility of a Sunday or weekend paper, an idea that had a practical echo in the proposals for a new left-of-centre Sunday newspaper to be launched in 1987. The *News on Sunday* was proposed editorially as a left version of the *Mail on Sunday*. The CPBF's 1985 AGM gave its support to the project, following a national committee decision to back the feasibility study. National committee members Mike Power and Loretta Loach joined the executive committee which supervised the study. Former Mirror Group chief Clive Thornton was also involved. In October 1985 the feasibility study was sufficiently advanced to produce 10,000 copies of a 64-page, four-colour dummy issue which provided a foretaste of the new paper's potential.

Alongside these and other practical efforts to create alternatives has gone a consistent critique of the growing monopoly control of the press. One of the earliest issues that concerned the campaign was the *Times* and *Sunday Times* lockout and the acquisition of the papers by Rupert Murdoch. At that time the Campaign stated, correctly as it turned out, that the takeover posed a grave threat to press freedom and had no confidence in the so-called safeguards and pledges of non-interference nor in the system of 'national directors'. The 1984 annual meeting denounced the joint asset-stripping of the Reuters trust by the

Fleet Street proprietors, expected to create a £1 billion windfall, as 'a cynical manoeuvre to ensure private and personal gain'. The meeting called for at least £100 million to be used as a launch fund for new media projects, adding that the press proprietors could be expected to use their super-profits to introduce new technology and break trade union strength in the newspaper industry.

The protection of trade union rights, the development of political alternatives to media domination by large corporations and support for the minority report of the 1977 Royal commission into the press, remain key objectives for the CPBF. The minority report called for the establishment of facilities for the printing, distribution and launching of new papers, as those with the least access to the mass media are usually those with the least resources. Legislation is therefore required to redress the balance.

A launch fund could be legally established through a levy of advertisements in the mass circulation press, and printing facilities established for hire through a state-owned national printing corporation. However even when launched and printed there remains the issue of distribution and retail. In order to bring this particular issue to light the Campaign along with the Minority Press Group set up a committee for press distribution in June 1980. Liz Cooper who convened the committee assisted in publishing a booklet entitled *The Other Secret Service*. This examined how the French distribution system for publishers was guaranteed by law. Equally it exposed the monopoly control of British distribution by W.H. Smith and Menzies. In recent years these companies appeared to respond to this powerful condemnation of their censorship through non-distribution by making space for a range of radical and alternative journals.

The opportunity for minority and alternative views to be expressed has made more progress on radio and television, which at least has a modicum of public accountability via parliament, unlike the privately owned newspapers. Channel Four was specifically set up to cater for minority views and its early output was welcomed as a good start by the CPBF's broadcasting sub-committee. The committee was formed following the publication of 'Changing TV'[5] as a *Free Press* supplement and some collaboration with Local Radio Workshop. The Campaign's analysis of broadcasting owes much to the work of the Glasgow University Media Group. However, complementary to the Glasgow group's theoretical efforts the CPBF has advanced debate and action on practical changes. This was reflected in the manifesto of the broadcasting sub-committee,[6] which combined an analytical overview of television and highlighted areas for reform in the broadcasting authorities' aims, control, access and finance.

Generally the Campaign has managed to work on a number of levels in broadcasting. These have included regular critiques of programme content, for example opposition to C4's *Diverse Reports* for redefining the concept of balance and thereby undermining the objective of giving space to minorities. *Diverse Reports* hit particular low points with Peter Clarke's disgraceful attack on NALGO and the Tim Brooks/Ron McKay distortions of the print union case on new technology in national newspapers. At another level the CPBF has been able to bring together groups with conflicting interests and help to resolve their differences. One such occasion followed the announcement that franchises for community radio were to be made available. Some common ground was found between the trade unions, community radio groups and other independent radio interests. This followed initial hostility between trade union delegates and community radio groups at successive CPBF annual meetings.

The Campaign has also vigorously advanced its own ideas and tactics. In December 1984 it sponsored a conference to debate the problems surrounding the right of reply in broadcasting. The radio and television chiefs who took part[7] displayed depressingly similar attitudes towards the right of reply – basically that there was no need for it. This complacent not to say pompous dismissal of the right of reply was graphically confirmed when a BBC internal policy document came into the Campaign's hands and was published as a supplement to Free Press in January 1985. The document, dated December 1981 was an abbreviated version of a report from the Assistant Director News and Current Affairs, Alan Protheroe, to the Director General of the BBC. In an accompanying memo Protheroe 'rejected outright the concept of a "right of reply". But I am equally sure we can profitably revise our attitudes to ensure a greater "opportunity" for reply when there is a proper and justifiable case for doing so.'

The Campaign's response to the Protheroe memorandum challenged the BBC's and to a lesser extent the ITV's smug philosophy that *they* know what's best for *us*. It also showed that the BBC is not quite as impervious to criticism as it seems.

Something must have shifted in the BBC in 1981. Beneath the evasions, pomposities and gusts of bombast in Alan Protheroe's report on the Right of Reply there are clear signs of tactical adjustments being made at senior levels of the BBC.

Although the concept of a 'right' of reply is flatly rejected the proposed 'opportunity to reply' is still a major concession. The fact that the question has been investigated at all should also be seen as a major advance for the CPBF and the media unions.

Two historic events occurred during 1985 that shook the complacent BBC management to its foundations. Firstly, the national strike action of its journalists and ancillary workers in protest at the banning of the *Real Lives* documentary *At the edge of the Union*. BBC executives were deeply shocked at the reaction against censorship, government interference and the supine board of governors by such differing sections of media workers. The actions represented a new stage in the struggle for media accountability.

The second event that shook the BBC was the creation of the Peacock commission to investigate the future funding of the Corporation. Professor Alan Peacock promised full public consultation and invited all interested bodies to submit evidence for or against advertising on the BBC. However, the consultative process seemed extremely narrow. Invitations to a conference on how broadcasting should be funded were only sent to advertisers, broadcasting managers and politicians. That was in spite of the fact that all the main broadcasting unions had made detailed submissions to the inquiry.

To counter this the CPBF set up its own inquiry, with researcher Janet Whyatt working on a three-pronged strategy, with academic analysis provided by the Polytechnic of Central London and a comparative study of international broadcasting systems provided by the Broadcasting Research Unit of the British Film Institute. The 'People's Peacock' set up a series of meetings, debates and think-tanks between January and April 1986.

The need to introduce legislation to encourage investigative journalism is an urgent necessity. That is why in 1984 the launching of the Campaign for Freedom of Information was warmly welcomed by the CPBF AGM which committed the national committee to work as closely as possible with the officers of the FoI Campaign. The resolution reaffirmed policies previously adopted by the CPBF in relation to official secrets. Specifically:

the immediate repeal of Section two of the Official Secrets Act; and the introduction of wide-ranging freedom of information legislation. Such legislation would place a burden on public authorities to justify the withholding of official information, and would provide for independent evaluation of the public interest in given cases of disputed disclosure.

The original CPBF freedom of information group convened by Michael Meacher merged its effort with the Labour Freedom of Information Campaign. Support was organized for the Private Member's Bill put forward by Frank Hooley. Although the 1984 FoI Campaign has rightly taken centre stage on FoI issues the CPBF has continued to respond to legal attacks on the media.

Particular concern has been expressed regarding the Video Recordings Act, in the light of which the Campaign's national committee adopted a policy of opposition to pre-censorship. The notorious Section two of the Official Secrets Act has been consistently opposed. Sarah Tisdall fell foul of the law when the *Guardian* returned, on the insistence of the High Court, the document she had leaked to the paper. The CPBF at the time appealed to the editor not to return the document in order to protect anonymous sources and so that disclosures in the public interest will continue to be made.

In its first seven years the CPBF has steadily increased the range of issues it has taken up. It has also established an organizational and political profile that has brought it increasing recognition. By mid 1986 thirty-three national trade unions had affiliated, representing $7\frac{1}{2}$ million in trade unions. Affiliations were increasing from educational institutions, political organizations and a wide range of pressure groups concerned with civil liberties, peace and animal rights. Other growth areas include academic departments and students, libraries, community printers, bookshops, publishers and general arts and media groups. These organizations alongside the individual membership represent the basis of alliance that could in a favourable political climate exert sufficient influence to make some real democratic changes in Britain's media.

The case for media reform is also being put more effectively and more often. CPBF representatives are regularly invited to participate in television and radio programmes, including chat shows and phone-ins, and to attend many conferences, seminars, and meetings. The circulation and impact of *Free Press* has grown from 3,000 at its inception to 11,000 in early 1986. Campaign fringe meetings and conferences are usually well attended.

All this bodes well for the pre-general election period when the CPBF hopes to make the media a central political issue. In 1983 some of the campaign's radical proposals were incorporated in the Labour Party manifesto (see Appendix to this chapter). That small success has prompted plans for a more substantial effort next time. The powerful vested interests of unaccountable newspaper proprietors and broadcasting chiefs may still be firmly entrenched, but thanks to the efforts of the CPBF and its supporters, their arrogant assumptions about the role of the media are challenged every day.

Notes and references

1. Consisting of James Curran, Jacob Ecclestone, Ken Fleet, Harold Frayman, John Jennings, Bill Keys, John Lloyd, Denis MacShane, Michael Meacher MP, John Mitchell, Steve Radford, Donald Ross and David White.
2. Published in September 1979 under the title 'Towards Press Freedom', 30p. By 1985 the number of aims had increased to twelve, as amendments had been made at successive annual general meetings. The full list is printed as Appendix I to this book on pp. 241–2.
3. The 64 original sponsors included the following journalists, parliamentarians, trade unionists, academics and entertainers, authors and religious people. They represent the political, industrial and social groups around which the campaign hoped to create an influential alliance to transform the media.

Neal Ascherson	Geoffrey Drain	Professor James
Joe Ashton MP	NALGO	Halloran
Ken Ashton NUJ	Katie Doyle	Keith Harper
Tom Baistow	Jacob Ecclestone	Dame Judith Hart MP
David Basnett	Udi Eichler	Roy Hattersley MP
GMWU	Moss Evans TGWU	Peter Hildrew
Tony Benn MP	Lord Gifford	Professor Richard
Lady Birk	John Golding MP	Hoggart
Ken Coates	Geoffrey Goodman	Stuart Holland MP
Harry Conroy	Richard Gott	Professor Stuart Hood
Stan Crowther MP	John Grant MP	Darcus Howe
Jonathan Dimbleby	Professor Stuart Hall	John Jackson SLADE

Lord Jacobson	Bruce Page	Mary Stott
Lord Kaldor	Dr Bikhu Parekh	Dafydd Elis Thomas MP
Bill Keys SOGAT	Christopher Price MP	John Torode
Joan Lestor MP	Lord Ritchie-Calder	Joe Wade NGA
John McGrath	Geoffrey Robertson	Keith Waterhouse
Gordon McLennan	Paul Routledge	Phillip Whitehead MP
Michael Meacher MP	Alan Sapper ACTT	Professor Raymond Williams
Eric Moonman	Vishnu Sharma	Colin Winter, Bishop of Namibia in Exile
Lionel Morrison	David Sheppard, Bishop of Liverpool	
Professor Robert Neild	Neville Smith	Audrey Wise
Owen O'Brien NATSOPA	Mervyn Stockwood, Bishop of Southwark	

4. In June 1980 the committee consisted of James Curran, Anna Coote, John Mitchell and George Jerrom. It was later expanded to include Alf Elderton, Laurie Pye and Mike Power.
5. By Greg Lanning, Alan Horrox and the Changing TV Group. The text was reproduced as an appendix to the CPBF booklet 'Labour Daily?'.
6. 'Are You in the Picture', subtitled 'An introduction to the way television works'. The sub-committee was chaired by Scarlett McGuire.
7. These included Paul Mckie, Deputy Chief Executive ITN, John Perkins, Managing Editor LBC, and Larry Hodgson, Editor BBC Radio News.

Appendix

Labour Party manifesto 1985 – The media

Our aims in the media are to safeguard freedom of expression, encourage diversity and establish greater accountability. For all the media, we will introduce a statutory right of reply to ensure that individuals can set the record straight. We will introduce stronger measures to prevent any further concentration in the media.

For the press, we will encourage diversity by:
• setting up a launch fund to assist new publications;
• ensuring that all major wholesalers accept any lawful publication,

and arrange for its proper supply and display, subject to a handling charge;
- preventing acquisition of further newspapers by large press chains;
- protecting freedom of expression by prohibiting joint control of the press, commercial radio and television;
- breaking up major concentrations of press ownership, by setting an upper limit for the number of major publications in the hands of a single proprietor or press group;
- replacing the Press Council with a stronger, more representative body.

In broadcasting, we will aim to make both broadcasting itself, and the organizations responsible, more accountable and representative – and to provide greater public access. Our aim is to promote a more wide-ranging and genuine pluralism in the media, and we set out our proposals in *Labour's Programme 1982*. We will also seek to introduce a genuinely independent adjudication of grievances and complaints. The licence fee will be phased out for pensioners during the life-time of the Labour government.

The high standards of British public service broadcasting are threatened by Tory plans to introduce cable TV on free-market principles. We will regulate satellite and cable provision and foster the same principles of diversity and pluralism as conventional broadcasting authorities. To avoid wasteful duplication, we will entrust the provision of the national cable system to British Telecom.

16. The aims of the campaign

Giles Oakley

Nowhere in the official aims and objectives of the Campaign for Press and Broadcasting Freedom (CPBF) is the term 'freedom' defined. It seems simple and obvious enough but is in fact surprisingly complex and elusive. Here I want to explore the word as a way of evaluating the broad strategies of the Campaign itself: What is meant by press and broadcasting freedom? Why is it desirable and what is being done to achieve it?

A fairly inconsequential conversation with a friend a year or so ago brought home to me just how loaded the word has become. I happened to mention that I was taking part in a conference organized by the CPBF and she, knowing my views, was somewhat surprised. 'But surely,' she objected, 'aren't they one of those nutty right-wing groups?' 'What makes you think that?' I asked. 'I thought any organization claiming the word "freedom" these days was sure to be one of those free-market economy propaganda groups.'

As she's someone who is very committed to a more free, equal and sharing society, I was bothered by her reaction. I realized, not for the first time, that the word freedom – and behind it a whole terrain of ideas – has been hijacked by the political Right. A cluster of phrases shows where the points of penetration have been: free market, the free world, freedom of choice.

Ever since the first cold war began in the late 1940s our Western model of freedom has been based on a crude notion of its supposed opposite, the societies behind the 'iron curtain', in the 'Eastern bloc', especially the Soviet Union. Unhappily for the Left this process began during the period of the 1945–51 Labour government. At that time, Labour itself came to be associated with shortages, bureaucracy and drabness, created by the necessity for economic planning, controls and rationing. No matter that the shortages were real or that Labour faced enormous problems of economic dislocation caused by the war; no matter, either, that the post-war reconstruction saw real growth, full employment *and* the creation of the free National Health Service (probably the single most liberating event for ordinary people in Britain this century). In the eyes of much of Fleet Street, especially papers like Lord Beaverbrook's *Daily Express*, Labour and hence the Left became identified with an image of state control and intervention. The Conservatives under Churchill were going to 'set the people free', just as they were again under Mrs Thatcher in 1979 when she promised to 'get the state off our backs'.

The point being made is not a party-political one about the relative merits of the 1945 Labour government and the Tory administrations that followed. More important here is to establish the recent historical context of media uses of the word 'freedom'.

The idea of freedom has deep roots in our culture, often subtly entwined with concepts of a 'free press'. Most definitions of the word embrace expressions like 'exemption from arbitrary, despotic or autocratic control; independence, civil liberty . . . The state of being able to act without hindrance or restraint, liberty of action' (Oxford English Dictionary). Numerous books deal with the competing accounts of how such freedom is best secured, but here I am more concerned with popular understandings of the word. I am less interested in the phrases used by right-wing propagandists and more in the kind of 'folk memories' embodied in phrases like 'It's a free country . . .' or concepts like 'free speech' and 'freedom of the press'.

These commonsense expressions go back a long way and are often linked with earlier historical phrases of political convulsion. Newspapers began in this country in the seventeenth century and had to have a licence from the state. It was not long before what is still accepted as a major work arguing against censorship appeared, in pamphlet form: Milton's *Areopagitica* in 1644. There was a growing conviction throughout that century and the next that the press should be free of the coercive power of the monarchy or state. By the early nineteenth century the concept of the 'fourth estate' had emerged whereby the press was seen to be part of the legitimate constitutional arrangements of the nation, alongside the Lords Temporal, Lords Spiritual and the Commons. As the economy expanded in the industrial revolution newspapers gained more advertising revenue, giving them a degree of economic independence. Increasingly the right of publishers and editors (often the same person) to say what they wanted came to be seen as a cornerstone of English liberties.

Until recently, conventional accounts of these developments, especially in school history books, have been largely uncritical. The past is presented as a succession of heroic or at least 'colourful' figures struggling to create a press that was free of state interference, buoyed up by 'cleansing' advertising money and delivering to us in the present a system that is broadly satisfactory, a solid foundation for our democracy. The durability of the myth that we already have a fully developed press freedom comes from this complacent view.

In the same way as the myths about our present media are being challenged, so their historical roots are also now being more critically scrutinized. Some historians accept that although the struggles over press rights were real enough in the past, it is more useful to see them in relation to the shifting patterns of social power at the time rather than in relation to our present needs. The claims made for a free press in the eighteenth century had less to do with abstract principles of democracy in the modern sense; they had more to do with the assertion of urban, mercantile and industrial middle-class interests. Not so much the rights of people, more the rights of property.

In relation to the aims of the CPBF these may seem remote and academic disputes. But the claim that we already *have* a free and independent press is ultimately derived from precisely these versions of eighteenth and nineteenth century history. They thus appear to have the durable imprimatur of the past and tradition.

It is at this point that the claims of present-day ideologues and the 'folk memories' intersect and reinforce each other. Private ownership of newspapers is seen as the essential guarantee of press freedom and hence by extension an equally desirable model for broadcasting and other communications systems. The 'free' play of market forces, it is asserted, ensures the public is provided with what it wants at the price it is prepared to pay. What other mechanism than the consumer expressing his or her choice through purchase can so effectively ensure the maintenance of a 'free market of ideas'? Not only is it desirable in itself as a spur to wealth creation but it remains the ultimate safeguard of all our liberties; any deviation towards regulation or control takes us down the road to serfdom. According to Nicolas Mellersh, a former Cable TV executive who advocates just such a free-market approach to the media and would like to see the BBC privatized, 'newspapers compete energetically for advertising revenue and we have in this country an overall standard of print journalism which, if it is not the envy of the world, is one of which we can be proud.' (*Sunday Times*, 24 November 1985)

Claims like this are not just made by newspaper proprietors and their allies. They are widely accepted by all sorts of people, even those who wouldn't necessarily like or admire all aspects of Fleet Street. 'Paul Collins', a fastidiously snobbish, *Daily Telegraph*-reading character in the Channel 4 soap opera *Brookside*, recently tartly declared in defence of the press: 'At least the press is independent here. None of that political bias.' It doesn't much matter if viewers were intended to laugh at him, he's clearly a recognizable type with opinions genuinely held by many people. Such views seem to be little affected by the generally low esteem afforded journalists or by the fact that most people tend to trust television more as a source of news than newspapers.

It is one of the central aims of the CPBF to challenge myths of this kind about the quality and independence of the press. It is increasingly clear that formidable pressures are building up from right-wing theorists plus powerful vested interests and their allies in government to push much of broadcasting and the other communications industries into exactly the same 'free market' mould as the press. (As someone once remarked, there are two meanings to that word mould.) So what does the media freedom *they* talk about amount to?

What supporters of the status quo mean when they say 'we' have a free press is that we don't have state-run or party-controlled newspapers. Newspaper proprietors or their editors are allowed to follow any political line they want. Constraints on the media such as the Official Secrets Act, the laws of libel, contempt and other state regulations are sometimes regarded as irksome but that is seen as a marginal rather than a central issue; accordingly there has been little press support for the idea of an American-style freedom of information bill. The fact that the vast majority of national daily and Sunday papers are strongly, even devoutly, Tory is seen as popular support for their 'commonsense' editorial positions, as registered by the fiercest body of critics of all, the marketplace. Such serious imbalance is *not* seen as damaging to democracy, nor is it seen as a weakening of the claim that we have a fully developed free press. If people *wanted* more left-wing/radical/liberal/progressive papers, they say, there is nothing to stop anyone starting a new one (as long as you have the odd £10 to £20 million to hand).

What is the CPBF reply to these views? Taking market forces first, this near-mythical 'self-regulating' system which is said to be the guarantor of our freedom has everywhere been characterized by ever-greater concentrations of monopolistic power. Despite the public rhetoric about the benefits of competition a mere five organizations control most of our newspapers. Until very recently there was an easy formula for remembering the pattern of ownership: two out of three newspapers, national and local, were owned by just three people, 'The 3 Ms': Murdoch, Maxwell and Matthews.

In the face of this, we need a concept of media freedom which goes far beyond the traditional equation of free press with private ownership. Any new definition has to take account of the growth of modern communications systems which can physically straddle whole continents through new technology and cross countless frontiers through multi-national ownership. That is a source of enormous social and political power which at the moment is held by small groups with little democratic control. The question of what constitutes media freedom cannot then be separated from wider issues about who has power in society and who has not, and about matters of national sovereignty and cultural independence. The unconstrained concentration of media power cannot be left to market forces alone to harness for the public good. If democracy is to mean anything it must mean that the power to communicate is available equally to *all* groups and classes, not just the media moguls and the mighty corporations.

What the CPBF is aiming for are mechanisms for increasing the diversity of control, the ease of public access, and the degree of democratic accountability. A litmus test for any claims for media freedom must be whether press and broadcasting accurately or fairly represent the fullest possible range of opinion and experiences from the *whole* of society. More important than the rights of a handful of arrogant media proprietors to own ever more mouthpieces for their views are the rights of the public to have access to the voices of the unheard, those who are currently excluded, marginalized or misrepresented.

As we have seen, 'freedom' is not defined in the aims of the CPBF, but its meaning can be construed from several key phrases scattered through the various clauses: 'diversity', 'diversity of access', 'plurality', 'the public interest', 'public accountability', 'fairness', 'editorial independence', 'democratic accountability'. Though not defined, 'freedom' is invoked several times, as in the central objective of working towards media alternatives 'in order to guarantee freedom from either state control or domination by business conglomerates'.

The formal aims of the CPBF are not a shopping list of demands or even a fully detailed blueprint for change. They are propositions and principles which have been gradually expanded from the original seven the CPBF was launched with in 1979. (By 1985 these had become a dozen.) In some ways they are like geological strata, some layers more active than others, some lying dormant ready to erupt when enough pressure exists.

The aims range from the general to the specific, from the principled to the practical. The most significant clauses are the most obviously ideological or political in character; it is here that the broad strategic sweep of the campaign is set out and it is these that attract most support. The first three aims all seek 'to challenge' specific dominant myths about the media, such as 'the myths of "impartiality" and "balance" in broadcasting, and "objectivity" in newspapers'. Other clauses are concerned to 'encourage debate' on such key issues as 'alternative forms of ownership and control', and 'the implications of technology advances in the media to ensure that the public interest is safeguarded and that commercial interests do not override public accountability'. There are also commitments to attack sexism in media output and in employment practices.

The aims then set out specific policy objectives, either for reform of the media or to provide mechanisms for redress following unfair media treatment. These include: the reconstitution of the Press Council; the establishment of a statutory 'right of reply'; the reform of the Official Secrets Act and other legislation restricting information; the enactment of a freedom of information bill; the establishment of a national printing corporation.

In 1984 the CPBF amalgamated with the Campaign Against Racism in the Media (CARM) and there has been a growing commitment to develop more effective anti-racist strategies and ways of getting more black people into the media. Closer links are being forged with the black communities to enable *their* needs and wishes to contribute to the formation of the Campaign's policies.

As a whole the aims may not add up to an instant plan ready for implementation as soon as some sympathetic government has been elected. But the aims *are* an important set of initiatives which have influenced the thinking not only of the Labour Party but also the Liberals, Plaid Cymru and the Ecology Party, and even perhaps the Social Democratic Party (who have vigorously challenged the BBC in its claims to impartiality in news broadcasts). In the case of the right of reply even some Conservatives have supported the idea. The campaign's aims have clearly united an astonishingly wide diversity of groups and individuals, in a way that has been mercifully free of sectarian divisions. Some have even come to see the CPBF as a prototype for the kind of social and political alliances required to take on the wider ideological challenges of the late 1980s. The alliance has brought together all the media unions together with many of the users of the 'services' they provide, plus the majority of unions affiliated to the TUC. It has also involved numerous other pressure groups such as Animal Rights, Civil Liberties, CND, women's groups, community printers, bookshops, publishers and co-operatives, various general arts and media organizations, journalists, media technicians, politicians, gay and lesbian activists, and as we have seen, various black organizations.

The CPBF is thus fulfilling a vital function in providing links between individuals and organizations at the grass-roots level where previously no lines of communication existed. It has been able to involve intellectuals as well as practical activists and efficient organizers. This extraordinary patchwork coalition, bringing together elements of the traditional labour movement and 'alternative' groupings has blossomed in a very short time and as the base of support grows new priorities will doubtless work their way through the system.

In the current hostile political climate many of the battles the CPBF has been engaged in have been essentially reactive and defensive. But the striking success of the right of reply campaign, backed by the highly effective Right of Reply Unit, has shown what democratically based ideological interventions can achieve. The concept of the right of reply has established itself securely as such an essentially reasonable and *fair* demand it would certainly survive even in the unlikely event of the CPBF closing down.

However, important though the right of reply has been in focusing attention on media abuses, effective methods of redress are only the cutting edge, the tactical point of entry for the campaign's wider strategies. It is not enough to correct individual errors or injustices. Nor would it be enough for the media simply to 'reflect' a wider range of views. We want greater and more accountable access for more people to the whole galaxy of opinion-making institutions. We don't just want a more accurate reporting of the world as it is – though we *do* want that. We also want it to be far more possible for people to actively use the media, of whatever kind, to intervene in matters affecting them or society, to set *their own* agendas, and not just respond to other people's, usually the powerful and the established. To coin a phrase, the point is not just to describe the world accurately, but to change it.

The complexity of interwoven changes in the communications industries, connecting new technologies like cable and satellite broadcasting with greater penetrations of transnational capital and increased concentrations of ownership and control mean the campaign's tactics will need further adjustment. Wider, possibly international alliances and mutual support systems will become necessary. As that happens and as Britain's economic crisis deepens, we are likely to be faced with hitherto unacknowledged conflicts of interest and contradictions. These may well require judicious handling and negotiations between our constituent groups. For example the aim of increasing the diversity of people with genuine access to the media could create problems for those people already working there, especially those with jobs *already* at risk. It is quite possible that the CPBF itself will have to take on the role of honest broker, acting as a forum for resolving conflicts through democratic debate and arriving at concrete proposals.

To a certain extent this has already happened in debates over both community radio and the future of the BBC. Deep anxieties exist over the nature of the present broadcasting institutions, as seen from the CPBF aim challenging the myths of 'impartiality' and 'balance'. There are also large question marks over the present BBC management structure as exemplified by the revelations in 1985 about MI5 security vetting of staff. On top of that, specific episodes such as the governors' craven capitulation to government pressure over the *Real Lives* programme in 1985 merely reinforced long-standing doubts about the BBC's independence. However the BBC has also been faced with unprecedented onslaughts from the government and those powerful vested interests who would like to see it opened up to market forces and privatized.

This placed some people on the horns of a dilemma. Calls by the broadcasting unions for a spirited defence of 'public service broadcasting' were initially treated with scepticism. How could people defend a concept they had long been denouncing as a smoke-screen for the establishment? How could the BBC be defended given its lop-sided coverage of the 1984–5 pit dispute? Weren't the broadcasting unions simply trying to prop up their own interests? The debates inside the CPBF were continuous but it quickly became clear that a commercialized and privatized BBC would be infinitely worse; broadcasting would be pushed further and further into an even more unacceptable

Fleet Street pattern. These fears were confirmed when the BBC announced structural changes involving the likelihood of 4,000 job losses and the casualization of sections of the labour force.

The CPBF *has* joined the fight to save public service broadcasting. It is resisting the introduction of advertising on the BBC and campaigning against the cuts. It is also setting up early lines of defence against further deregulation of broadcasting as a whole. However, it has done so not as a defence of the status quo, but in the belief that 'public service' has got to mean a move away from the elitism of the past. More has to be done to recognize that there is more than one single undifferentiated 'public', there are a series of publics, many of which feel very badly 'served' indeed. Thoroughgoing reforms are needed throughout broadcasting to ensure that the kind of access and accountability advocated by the CPBF is secured in the interest of all the public.

The test of any organization with openly declared aims is how well they withstand the pressure of events. The Campaign for Press and Broadcasting Freedom has shown that it has the flexibility to cope with contradictions and the commitment to democratic procedures to resolve them honestly and even-handedly. The trust in open debate within its own working processes is perhaps a healthy model for how the campaign would like to see the media as a whole contributing to British democracy.

17. Right of reply

Mike Power

There is no automatic right of reply to anyone. Newspapers are not debating societies. However, responsible newspapers quote Trade Union leaders during disputes and are prepared to carry letters from them, sometimes even leader page articles.

However, we would not be prepared to publish articles making claims that were not true. For example, I cannot believe many newspapers would today carry an article by Arthur Scargill because he has discredited himself. His case is based upon a series of lies which we could not assist with publishing.

Mac Keen, Assistant Managing Editor,
Daily Mail, 27 July 1984, in response to a student questionnaire

The press in Britain is much hated and with reason . . . members of the public ought to have a statutory right of reply.

Paul Johnson, feature writer,
Daily Mail, writing in the *Spectator*, 15 September 1984

The right of reply has become a popular democratic demand and the expression has entered everyday usage. This has arisen from a campaign that has the commitment of all the media trade unions and the TUC and emerged from actions taken in the national and regional press to gain redress for those whose lives and opinions have been subject to wilful distortion and abuse.

The activity has been co-ordinated by the Campaign for Press and Broadcasting Freedom (CPBF) and its Right of Reply Unit which received Greater London Council funding in 1983.

The issue of the right of reply came into prominence during the health workers' dispute of 1982; it came of age during the coal dispute of 1984–5. The antecedents of these highly organized efforts lay in the isolated challenges of the late 1960s and 1970s. Individual print workers with strong views about racism or anti-trade-union activity took responsibility for stopping the presses. They were then often subject to disciplinary measures by their company *and* their union. Since those early days a campaign has been waged to change the policies and attitudes of media unions and their members.

So effective has the struggle been that during 1985 the Fleet Street employers sought to resurrect the post General Strike agreement of 1926 in which the print unions declared they would not interfere with the editorial content of publications. While proprietors have tried to turn the clock back, editors in their newly founded guild have declared for the principle of right of reply (which in practice they seek to avoid) and divisions have opened up among senior journalists as the above quotes from *Daily Mail* journalists indicate. Enormous practical and political pressure has been exerted to bring this about. Millions of newspapers have been lost (over 45 million copies of the *Sun* alone during the coal dispute), media people in the press and broadcasting at all levels have been forced to enter the debate and act and there have been two attempts to introduce right of reply legislation since 1983. Ironically, the need for a right of reply is very well understood by the media themselves when it comes to defending their own interests. Among the stipulations laid down by ITN for use of any part of its bulletins in commentary about media coverage is that ITN should have the right of reply!

The right of reply is a democratic demand which is readily understood and widely accepted. What value is there in argument that is manifestly one-sided? What virtue in a 'free press' so often monolithic in its opinion and eager to raise a cudgel against silenced opponents? The right of reply is not a panacea that will, in itself, create more diverse media or break the grip of the monopolies, but the need for such strategic changes will gain credence if the right of reply is won. It brings together those who produce the media with their consumers, mainly under the auspices of the trade unions. Every day union members are assisting people to engage with the media to gain access and break down the frustrations and feelings of powerlessness that overwhelm those who need to make challenges. This approach creates a new and positive image of media trade unionists who have become genuinely concerned at the effect of the output of their labours. The consciousness-raising effect of this activity cannot be underestimated.

These valuable tactical advantages should not obscure the negative side of the limited right of reply demand. Clearly, different groups have more or less resources to make a challenge and a TUC-affiliated union will receive a more positive response than other economic, social or political groups.

The best possible result, achieving equal space and prominence, tends to reinforce the concept of 'balance' rather than provide for the expression of alternative views. Obviously, the reply may not be seen by those who read the original offensive piece, and there is the danger that bias can become institutionalized by merely insisting on replies. The demand for the right of reply has therefore been developed into a wide-ranging means of creatively engaging with the media and is linked to a series of strategic campaigning aims by the CPBF.

The right of reply has an urgency about it that exposes the uselessness of the industry's 'voluntary watchdogs' such as the Press Council. However, right of reply practitioners readily accept that there are fundamental differences in gaining access to the press as opposed to broadcasting.

During the first full year of the Right of Reply Unit's operation it was possible to achieve some form of satisfactory outcome in half the cases of people who asked for help in dealing with inaccurate or distorted coverage. Satisfactory outcome varied from equal space and equal prominence to the original offending item to the publication of substantial statements, lead letters, disclaimers and apologies. Direct contact with workers in broadcasting stations, both radio and television, had led to corrections in news broadcasts; complainants have also been successfully encouraged to use the facilities of Channel 4's *Right to Reply* programme and video box. Other spin-offs have included coverage of complaints and the story involved in specialist, local and alternative media. Radio phone-ins and local TV programmes have also picked up stories that began as complaints about inaccurate coverage.

One celebrated case of a small group – Teachers for Peace – who attracted the attention of the *Daily Mail* indicates the potential of right of reply. Hilary Lipkin, the secretary of the group, was visited by a *Mail* reporter posing as a prospective member of the group. The outcome was a distorted centre spread headed 'Schools most sinister lesson' which included the family's full address, plus photographs. The Lipkins' indignation was followed by threatening and abusive phone calls and letters. A first attempt to obtain some redress with a visit to the editor resulted in ejection by the police. However, after a long and fruitless involvement with the Press Council the *Mail* carried a letter from the group. More importantly, in the long run, the treatment of the

Lipkins has been raised and covered in several journals and weekly papers. They received support from many groups, including the Labour Party and National Union of Teachers. The case was also a central example raised in parliament by Austin Mitchell when introducing his Ten Minute Right of Reply Bill. Instances such as this arise constantly, creating opportunities to publicize and debate the general nature of the media. Practical and intellectual challenges of this kind avoid the charge of censorship, particularly against those production workers who have demanded disclaimers and ended up with blank spaces or no publication.

Trade unionists have recently been more prepared to take direct action to rectify distortions in the media. This change emerges partly from the general and widespread dissatisfaction that is felt with declining media standards. But, more particularly, with the constant barrage of anti-trade-union material that has become particularly virulent and extremely right-wing. The Winter of Discontent 1979, the day of action in 1980, the evidence of the Glasgow University Media Group and that of the TUC's media working group confirmed the trend. Faced with the inability to gain any genuine redress, which was highlighted particularly by the National Union of Journalists (NUJ) decision to withdraw from the Press Council in 1980, it was clearly necessary to develop new approaches. Most media workers have a long history of effective closed shop organization giving them a relatively high level of collective trade-union consciousness. This was coupled with some progressive political ideas on the media itself underwritten in official union policies giving opportunity for responses to appeal that went beyond economic self-interest. However, the full possibility of inter-union actions has only been glimpsed on rare occasions, one such being the day of action on 27 June 1984 on behalf of the miners. A joint approach by all production unions and the NUJ led to the publication of up to half-page advertisements supporting the NUM in all but three national papers which, as a result of their refusal to carry the advert, did not appear.

Professional divisions have, however, often undermined effectiveness. Many journalists felt embattled, pressurized by editorial management and production workers alike. There are many, of course, who readily self-censor and willingly ignore the NUJ Code of Conduct. Others feel constrained to accept editorial censorship, which raises the need to struggle for a right to report (which appeals to journalists' professionalism) to go hand-in-hand with a right of reply. This requires union backing for those NUJ members who are prepared to stand by their union's Code of Conduct and challenge editorial interference. Such positive encouragement would complement the role of the NUJ's Ethics Council set up in part to receive complaints against recalcitrant members. Unions have suffered considerably during the Thatcher years and resistance is to be welcomed and supported. In the media solidarity can be expressed by reacting to pleas for fairer coverage from other trade unionists currently shouldering the Thatcher burden. So, this combination of political circumstance with trade union and ideological frustration has allowed the demands for rights of reply to become high profile political issues.

The debate and actions that have flowed from the right of reply campaign have affected every part of the media. The ripples were particularly noticeable in broadcasting during 1985. Here, the events leading up to the day strike against the banning of the BBC *Real Lives* documentary was the highlight of a long period of activity. It was not accidental that members of the production unions ACTT and BETA in the BBC and Independent TV were ready to back their NUJ colleagues. The unions were committed to the right of reply both independently and generally through the TUC and they jointly sponsored a well-attended conference with the CPBF in December 1984 to put the policy into action. Delegates, who were mostly media workers, took on BBC and independent television and radio management figures, who were the main speakers. They drew attention to the right of Michael Heseltine to have a reply to *The Day After* and for the British Medical Association to have a full reply to a *Panorama* programme on brain stem death while less powerful people can be rubbished with impunity. It was noted that in the early days of Channel 4 Jeremy Isaacs had suggested that space be appended to News and Current Affairs programmes to allow people to object and explain their own perspectives. Even though that did not come about there have been two occasions on television news where opposing points of view were presented with editorial control being granted to the participants: Arthur Scargill and Ian MacGregor presented on *Channel 4 News* and Kenneth Baker and Ken Livingstone on *Thames News*. These concessions to the clamour for fairer coverage may appear marginal, but they do represent meaningful responses by the media establishment in a political environment that is hostile to such demands.

Many broadcasting workers have since held branch and shop

meetings to discuss these issues; they have considered the demand for disclaimers to be issued with hostile programmes and held joint meetings with groups such as the miners. These activities built rank-and-file support for action which was, in effect, delivered in protest at the BBC ban of *Real Lives*. The strike action therefore came as no surprise to those more aware of the mood among media workers. However, its lasting value may be that some trade unionists will reconsider their view of the media as monolithic and of their workforce as 'vermin' and 'jackals' with no place in decent society.

Solidarity actions that began with spontaneous demands for rights of reply by printworkers led to some closer understandings between trade unionists during the coal dispute. Apart from the well-known spectacular actions at the *Sun* over the Scargill Hitler-salute photograph and the *Express* 'I Lied' Scargill spoof, there were daily occurrences in the national and regional press. These actions were spurred by a soul-mate reaction following the handling that print workers received from the police in Warrington in the dispute with Eddie Shah. Printers knew from their own experience that they were not producing the truth about picket violence and gave additional assistance to the miners by donating over £2 million from Fleet Street alone and producing alternative 'right of reply' newspapers. Secondary vigilance became necessary when papers like the *Observer* and *News of the World* deliberately subverted replies carried under pressure by surrounding the reply with hostile editorial matter, cartoons and pictures. Media coverage of the coal dispute was hotly debated and acted upon during the strike and after. Many lessons have been learned on all sides. In July 1984 Kenneth Baker, the Industry Minister, accused Fleet Street unions of censorship, highlighting examples of stoppages with a blank space in the *News of the World*. He went on to say: 'Can anyone claim that the case of the miners has not been presented in our media forcefully and indeed eloquently?' Not one press report mentioned that particular part of the speech – perhaps they knew something.

Baker pointed to occasions where the right of reply had, in fact, failed because editorial management refused it and preferred to have disruption, thereby casting the unions in the role of censor. Censorship is not, and never has been, the aim of demanding the right of reply. If the 'forceful and eloquent' press coverage was really available perhaps Kenneth Baker should ask why so many organizations are spending vast sums on advertisements in order to get their cases expressed adequately. The National Coal Board, DHSS, Greater London

Council, teachers' unions, railway unions and the TGWU have all resorted to the advertising columns to guarantee publication of their statements. The TGWU case was part of the union's massive push to counter hostile and distorted coverage of ballot-rigging during the union's leadership elections. The TGWU full-page advertisements in all the national press (costing over £300,000) followed contacts with all chapels of all unions in the national and much of the regional media reminding printworkers and broadcasters of their obligations to fair coverage and to take action for replies where appropriate. Letters also went to all editors. At the *Sun* and the *Observer* the TGWU obtained the support of printworkers in obtaining substantial rights of reply. Legal action was taken against journalists on the *Guardian* and *Newsnight*. This determined and thorough no-nonsense approach had the remarkable effect of allowing the union to influence the way in which the media set the agenda on this issue. There was something resembling a respectful silence from the media throughout the re-run ballot, indicating that all was not lost, even in the present hostile media environment. The union's response was a real and effective pre-emptive strike in the spirit of the right of reply.

There is a great deal that individual unions need to do to put their own houses in order with regard to media relations. Preparation and presentation are important as the TGWU example proves. But even with this, even the most media-conscious organizations such as NALGO with a publicity staff at head office of forty people cannot get fair coverage for those they represent – witness the media vilification of social workers.

To change and diversify the British media will require more than just attention to the technical problems. It will need a continuing and much more voluble political and industrial campaign. One of the fears of the introduction of new technologies with its propensity to de-skill and de-unionize is that it will undermine the right of reply struggle. This problem was acknowledged in the 1984 TUC resolution on right of reply which accordingly called for the defence of media trade unionism. Nevertheless, even with the advent of new technologies and even greater concentration of media power with the emergence of the new-style media barons like Maxwell and Murdoch and their encroachments into electronic media, there have been small tactical acknowledgements of the right of reply arguments. Maxwell has appointed an ombudsman covering all the *Mirror* Group titles 'to give the public a fair deal'. On 15 November 1984 Hilary Benn, son of a famous father, wrote to the *Sun* complaining about an article on page 2. Two days later he opened the paper to see his statement printed in the same space, with the same prominence as the original. At the *Western Daily Press* the NGA chapel has negotiated an internal arrangement with the editor which allows for the chapel to have a statement printed on pages 1, 2 or 3 when the chapel has a grievance with the paper's content.

These actions carry the argument forward. They indicate a grudging acceptance by people with power in the media that a valid case has been made. Already in 1983 in the run-up to the general election, the journalists at the *Daily Mail* had voted at an NUJ chapel meeting by five to one, to protest at the slanted pro-Tory coverage of 'their' paper. However minor changes may appear to be they also help to further expose the role of the Press Council, a body which is bought and paid for by the press proprietors and whose findings they routinely ignore. Even the Press Council accepted the need to speed up its work when it introduced a fast track procedure to correct items of fact only. So, despite more than thirty years' existence the Council seems to be unaware that a key criticism of the media is that they report opinion as though it were fact, and vice versa. With months to wait and a little better than 4 per cent chance of a favourable adjudication there is a growing awareness of the irrelevance of the Press Council.

One solution to all these problems, it has been argued, would be for a legally enforceable right of reply. Two attempts – both unsuccessful – have recently been made to legislate in this direction: one wished to provide equal space and prominence for replies, enforced by heavy fines on reluctant editors (this mirrors the legal position in France); the other, to set up an ombudsman with the authority to instruct newspapers to give space and to protect them against possible actions under the libel laws. But either way, a new law should not be viewed as the end of the affair. A right of reply would need to be part of a series of enactments including a Freedom of Information Act that protected genuine investigative journalism. More importantly, such a law would not remove the need for industrial vigilance nor for developing enforceable codes of conduct and guidelines. A one-off right of reply law would be no more a panacea than to get a right of reply through industrial action. However, to win an argument at the statutory level would at least be progress towards our wider media objectives.

18. Freedom of information

Adrian Wilkes

Knowledge will forever govern ignorance; and a people who mean to be their own governors must arm themselves with the power which knowledge gives.

James Madison, US President, 1822

It is unacceptable in a democratic society that information is not disclosed when the only vice of that information is that it enables the public to discuss, review and criticize government action.

Democracy, being a much misunderstood and much abused concept, is constantly being defended by different political voices on differing fronts – unanimity is rare. However, a broad, nationwide, all-party coalition is now recognizing that democracy is being irrevocably eroded at its core by the disease of secrecy.

The most fundamental of our democratic rights are the right to a vote and the right to freely criticize the government of the day. Yet such rights are limited if not illusory without the right of access to public and private (as regards personal files) information. Alas, Britain is the most secretive democracy in the western world. As a result, both individuals and (as the Ponting affair illustrated) their elected representatives are unable to ensure that government avoids mistakes, injustice, unrepresentative bias or corruption.

The issue is about power. Power over our lives and over our future. Freedom of information is essential for real involvement. Government information is, and must be, public information. The emphasis here, therefore, is not on the need for a free press, but on the need for an effective, informed press.

The restrictions of secrecy on journalism

Secrecy has become a habit of public life in Britain today. It is institutionalized through the 1911 Official Secrets Act.

Section One's spying provisions, as their use in the ABC trial indicated, have a potential for the prosecution of whistleblowing journalists for communicating (to the British public, not to foreign spies) information that might be 'useful to an enemy'. Whilst the Section One charge in the ABC trial (itself an intricate attempt to silence ex-CIA agents' whistleblowing by prosecuting two British journalists) failed, the legislative formula remains so wide and unpredictable that it acts every day as a natural restriction on what articles are spiked and what books do not appear.

Yet it is Section Two that is the notoriously repressive anti-press clause. The communication of, or the receipt of, any information by a civil servant, no matter how insignificant, in the course of his or her employment, is a crime. There may be few prosecutions (though there has been a relative willingness by the present government to prosecute, until the Ponting jury highlighted Section Two's perversity) but every civil servant senses the Damoclean power of the Section Two sword.

Section Two catches all public ('official') information – there are no distinctions. Whatever its nature, whatever its importance, a blanket is thrown over every scrap of information. In principle, a civil servant cannot disclose the locations of Britain's post offices, let alone the locations of Britain's 2,000 hazardous chemical sites.

There are no voices that defend Section Two. Barring ministers, whose attitudes change according to whether they are in office or not, and a few civil service mandarins, there is virtually unanimous support for the conclusion reached by the 1972 Franks Commission: 'Section Two is a mess. Its scope is enormously wide. Any law that impinges on the freedom of information in a democracy should be much more tightly drawn.'

Lord Franks discredited Section Two prosecutions. The ABC attempt to mount a trial of journalists was a greater political and legal fiasco than the earlier prosecution of Jonathan Aitken for printing an official report on the Nigerian Civil War. Journalists have thus been tempted into a blasé attitude towards Section Two prosecutions. Journalists' sources, however, have much to be scared about. The leak enquiry has recently acquired a pernicious power.

In 1972, the Railway Gazette affair led to the interrogation and caution under the Official Secrets Act of the editor of the *Sunday Times* for publishing a report that civil servants were urging their Minister to close down 4,600 miles of the 11,600 mile rail network. In the Tisdall case the leak enquiry went so far as the Court of Appeal ordering the *Guardian* to return photocopied Ministry of Defence memos. The government's true target is not the powerful newspaper or journalist, but the scared, vulnerable, conscience-stricken civil servant, who faces up to two years' imprisonment and/or a life of unemployment. Clive Ponting was after all prosecuted *pour encourager les autres*. The question must be asked as to how much information has consequently remained behind Whitehall's closed doors.

There were also over 100 statutes that make the disclosure of information by civil servants a criminal offence. Local authorities, water authorities and health authorities are increasingly tempted to conduct their public function out of sight of their masters – the public.

In such an atmosphere, where openness attracts criminal sanctions, it is surprising that the government need say anything else to its officials. Yet there is a plethora of directives that pound secrecy into the civil servant's psyche. And of course the emphasis on secrecy finds its way into the Civil Service Pay and Conditions of Service Code.

Secrecy is thus the norm – it is the British government's way of doing its public duty. The habit is now widely denigrated by those countries that once looked to our constitution as the font of democracy.

For the British themselves secrecy precludes a free and effective press. A journalist's main source of information is not a particular civil servant with responsibility for an issue, but a departmental public relations officer – a news control agent – whose numbers have grown substantially recently, ensuring that the public hears only what is deemed wise by civil service autocrats.

Is the picture not bleak enough? Alas there are yet further bricks in the wall of secrecy hiding the clandestine workings of our government. There is advance censorship for the press on national security matters with the D-Notice system. An article which touches on military or security issues can be voluntarily spiked by editors because it may fall within one of the generalized D-Notices (issued to newspapers by the Ministry of Defence). Even the actual operation of D-Notices is a secret! Of greater concern is the fact that the phrase 'national security' is widely abused by the present government – it quite clearly now includes political embarrassment to Tory ministers. This only serves to destroy the trust of professional journalists who voluntarily work the D-Notice system. And behind the formal D-Notice system is an informal one of 'private and confidential letters' and personal chats with selected journalists.

The police too can persuade newspapers to postpone or omit details of crime, or they can simply not inform journalists about particular events. The desire of the Home Secretary to 'starve terrorists of the oxygen of publicity' led to the Liverpool police imposing a news blackout on rioting in Toxteth in summer 1985.

The BBC has not only been regularly pressurized by the government over coverage of events in Northern Ireland, but has been influenced by British Leyland to forego repeating a programme's factual condemnation of safety defects.

The civil law's armoury is also frequently utilized against the press's right to comment on matters of public concern. The law of confidence is occasionally used – most notably in the Crossman Diaries case, which was a long, laborious and cost-risky victory that uncertainly established a vague principle that the courts will only restrain publication where 'the continuing confidentiality of the material can be demonstrated'.

Our libel laws are also vague and uncertain, which again places the risk for exposing or criticizing the powerful on the journalists' shoulders. Contempt of court is another risk of potential and expensive trouble which restrains newspapers. The muddied state of the law here is little clearer after the enactment of the 1981 Contempt of Court Act.

The *Guardian*–Tisdall case highlighted the flimsy protection for newspapers from disclosure of a source of information when a 'potential threat to national security' is involved. Furthermore, the frequent use of the Act's Sections 4 and 11 bans on court reporting is justifiably raising concern at all levels of the media about the increasing degree of secrecy surrounding the administration of British justice.

The consequences of secrecy

Britain thus suffers from too much secrecy and news management. Public servants are no longer accountable, as even parliament itself is starved of so much information. The public cannot see how their taxes are spent. Public participation is seriously hampered as the public have inadequate information on which to evaluate their elected representatives. Conversely, public opinion cannot be properly gauged if the public are ill-informed. The real sources of political power and influence and their impact on government decision-making remain hidden. The Crossman Diaries proved how little learned political journalists and academics know of the machinations of policy-making in Whitehall.

Corruption and conflicts of interest are protected. Poor quality decision-making is more likely as there can be no full and effective input from people and organizations outside Whitehall or local authority policy-making circles, thus limiting the provision of more adequate information for our decision-makers. Civic and social justice is not seen to be done. Individual rights are damaged when exercised without the knowledge, in the case of discretionary decisions, of internal rules and guidelines (let alone the knowledge of what government files contain about you). And the public's opportunity to participate in the shaping of the community is yet further reduced.

Greater freedom of information is thus not only necessary as a matter of principle, but for urgent political reasons. The public, through their journalists, have a right to know what their government is doing and why. The call is for more sunshine in government.

The voices for reform

The timely launch of the 1984 Campaign for Freedom of Information breathed new life into the oft-repeated calls for greater openness in government. The problem has long been recognized (even, somewhat cynically, by the Home Secretary and the Attorney General responsible for the decision to prosecute Clive Ponting) yet the impressive and durable list of support for open government has not overcome the disease of secrecy.

The 1968 Fulton Committee on the civil service reported that 'the administrative process is surrounded by too much secrecy. The public interest would be better served if there were a greater amount of openness.' The 1972 Franks Report on the Official Secrets Act advised that 'any law which impinges on the freedom of information in a democracy should be much more tightly drawn' and called for its repeal. The EEC Council of Ministers have taken a more positive approach in accepting the right to know and urging the introduction of a system of freedom of information.

The 1977 Royal Commission on the Press reported that 'the right of access to information which is of legitimate concern to people, parliament and press is too restricted', and this combined with the general secrecy which government is conducting has caused much injustice, some corruption and many mistakes.

In 1977 the Croham Directive, from the head of the Civil Service to Permanent Secretaries, sought to voluntarily increase the flow of information. Yet the government Green Paper of 1979 acknowledged that 'administration is still conducted in an atmosphere of secrecy that cannot always be justified'.

The need for effective freedom of information legislation was recognized by Australia's Senate: 'when government is more open to public scrutiny, it in fact becomes more accountable . . . access to information . . . will lead to an increasing level of public participation.' The Canadian Commission on Freedom of Information reported that 'a reduction in government secrecy is a necessary prerequisite to the restoration of a relationship between the electorate and the government that is consonant with democratic ideals.' All of the western world's governments have accepted and acted upon the arguments for openness.

Britain's addiction to secrecy has made it into a democratic leper.

Anti-secrecy initiatives

In 1973 the Heath government accepted the Franks Report's recommendation that Section Two of the Official Secrets Act be replaced by narrower provisions, but failed to act before losing office. In 1976 the Labour government promised legislation to replace Section Two, but in so doing dropped the manifesto commitment 'to put the burden on public authorities to justify withholding information'. Despite, or because of, the ABC trial fiasco, the White Paper on reform of Section Two was not actually produced until the eve of the 1978 summer recess – it was, furthermore, only to be the basis for discussion prior to legislation after the next election. The results of the 1979 election curtailed any such plans, and also killed Clement Freud's Official Information Bill. The Thatcher governments have not considered legislating to provide a public right of access. And there matters stand.

The Thatcher government did seek to reform Section Two with its Protection of Information Bill, but it met general hostility for restrictiveness that had nothing to do with open government. Some courageous MPs have used parliament to add further vocal strength to the calls for legislation, but the major anti-secrecy initiatives have been outside Westminster or Whitehall.

The Campaign for Freedom of Information was formed in 1984 as a coalition of major national organizations, whose daily experience with secretive public officials dictated the need for a sustained effort to open up Britain's government. The need for freedom of information is so widely recognized that the campaign has, remarkably, the support of all the civil service unions as well as the support of all sides of Fleet Street and the media. All three opposition parties are committed to legislation. Certain Tory MPs have highlighted the all-party nature of the call for open government by sponsoring the CPBF's Bills on Access to Personal Files, Water Authority Meetings, Environmental Pollution Information, and Local Government Access to Information (now on the statute book as the first piece of British freedom of information legislation).

A Freedom of Information Act would recognize the right to know and thereby institutionalize a presumption that all public administration should be open. There would be, in the cases of clearly defined overriding reasons for secrecy, exemptions to protect individual privacy, to protect the community and the state, and to enable free opinion-sharing. The Act would firmly commit politicians and civil servants to implement the principles in practice. It would remove all unjustified barriers to the implementation of the spirit of the legislation and set up the administrative mechanisms whereby this can be achieved. There would have to be publicity of exactly what information exists. The public should be able to obtain information easily and quickly. There would be an avenue of appeal when information is denied. In addition, and on the assumption that matters can always be improved upon, the Act would provide for the monitoring and review of the legislation.

Secrecy is now high on the political agenda, and its ramifications are quickly being recognized by the public as well as by politicians. The case against it was put very concisely when a Bill to open up local authorities was introduced in 1960: 'Publicity is the greatest and most effective check against any arbitrary action.' The speaker was Margaret Thatcher.

19. Media bias and future policy

Tony Benn

The labour movement has long since recognized the central role that the media play in Britain, and has made it into a major issue for public discussion. We have come to recognize that the Tories have relied on the power of the media as the strongest weapon in their armoury, greater than the army or the police as instruments for getting their way. Proprietors have been ready to pay enormous salaries to employees from journalists and TV commentators to print-workers, to buy their support and acquiescence.

Our experience is of media bias which has daily become more obvious in industrial, political and military matters, denying the people the information they need for democracy to flourish, and also preventing them from hearing their own views presented fairly. But we have also learned that this power is by no means invincible. Had it been, there would have been no effective resistance to their policies by the unions or the peace movement, by women or the Irish, the blacks or embattled local authorities.

Labour has been greatly helped by the work of serious academics and by the establishment of the Campaign for Press and Broadcasting Freedom. As a result a lot of work has already been done on the policies that a future Labour government might adopt to establish a free press and broadcasting system in Britain, and many papers have been published which set out the alternatives open to us.

But there is one aspect that has not received the attention that it should: namely what we might do, here and now, before Labour returns to power which would help us to get our message across to the general public.

In recent years the new technology has opened up all sorts of possibilities some of which the movement has begun to use without necessarily recognizing their full potential.

The most obvious have been the emergence of a mass of left papers which are available if you can find them; another is the use that Labour local authorities have made of political publishing and advertising; and the third is the growth of videos produced by small but imaginative groups of producers for showing off the air.

The miners strike, the attack upon the GLC and metropolitan counties and rate-capping have given a great boost to all these enterprises and have at the same time vastly increased the demand for them. In addition a large number of books have been published about socialism, feminism, racism and peace which provide material that was never available before, and these have been supplemented by an even greater output of leaflets, posters and pamphlets which pour off the printing presses and are distributed wherever the opportunity arises.

I would like to propose seven points for discussion as to how we might develop our own resources and make them more effective.

First, we need a socialist press service to see that the existing left media get all the help possible with material that they can use; to feed out to them all the news about what is happening, and where, and what is being said, and by whom, as part of the on-going debate. It is the virtual absence of news, or serious comment about the labour movement or socialism, in the regular press that makes it so uninteresting to read, yet we have the power now to correct a part of that problem if we go about it in the right way. The appointment of press officers to unions and local parties has long been urged to keep the regular newspapers, TV and radio informed, but there is little corresponding servicing of the left press. What is needed now is the general distribution of a list of trade union and socialist newspapers, journals, video producers and publishers so that news can be passed on for publication and comment on a regular basis, and the appointment of people who will undertake that task as a special responsibility. The left media must be kept informed, both for the purpose of coverage of specific events and to give them some greater knowledge of the market that there might be for what they have already produced.

Second, we need a register of what is available to remedy some of the deficiencies that exist in the commercial distribution system by using our own, not inconsiderable, resources within the movement. One most obvious way of doing that would be to see to it that all trade union, party and community groups are able to receive information about what is available to them, perhaps by preparing a full list of their secretaries, complete with their addresses, and seeing that these are given to the publishers of all the radical papers, journals and book publishers of written and recorded material.

Third, we need our own distribution system, and for that purpose should invite all trade unions, Labour parties and Labour local authorities to set up bookstalls where socialist material could be on display, and for sale, to offset the censorship of the distributors and newsagents. There is no reason, for example, why all local councils, where Labour is in power, should not set up news-stands in all their own premises and sell Labour and socialist books and publications. Some criteria would have to be accepted to determine which of these were to go on display, but fortunately such a criterion already exists – since it would only be necessary to select those left publications that were not regularly stocked by local bookshops and newsagents. This would automatically cover almost the whole field and if there was objection on the grounds of a left-wing bias it would be open to those who complained to see to it that these same publications were sold through local commercial channels.

Fourth, we need to win the active support of all Labour local authorities which should consider giving priority to backing any group, preferably a co-operative, that was engaged in producing papers or videos for the benefit of the community, and then sustain them by advertising their own local authority services, and bulk buying the papers for general distribution in the area. Those authorities that now engage in advertising in the national or local press should consider making better use of the advertisements which they produce to include more news and comment rather than the present tendency to print slogans. It would be better still if all the advertising that they do were to be re-directed to the Labour and left press both to sustain them financially, and to encourage their wider circulation.

Fifth, we need to develop our own polling system and learn from the Tories and the business community how public opinion polls are built into press campaigns for use against the Labour movement, and then use the same techniques ourselves. At present public opinion polling in Britain is largely biased in that the questions are devised in connection with current anti-Labour press campaigns and are intended to catch, and record, opinion at the very moment when it has just been formed by those press campaigns, knowing that the proprietors will reproduce the results as confirmation of the line that they have been taking. Yet we all know that the framing of the question is the key to the whole operation and that if different questions were put the result would be much more accurate and advantageous to our view. New and different poll questions would also help to encourage people to think about a wider range of alternatives. It is perfectly open to us to devise and operate our own polls and then publish the results as confirmation of the extent of support for what we are saying, thus giving encouragement to all those who now read the commercial polls and are wrongly led to believe that their own views are in a minority.

Sixth, we need our own radio outlets and should turn our minds to the possibilities that exist for unofficial broadcasting stations as a way of getting through on the air. The problem here is that to do this is to break the present law and those who do so are running a real risk of detection and a fine, but it is being done and having heard some of the Sheffield Peace Radio broadcasts it is clear how appealing this could be as a contrast to the endless muzak pop plus political pap which is the mainstay of so many disc jockeys.

Seventh, we need to win greater workplace backing by the establishment of joint shop stewards committees and workplace branches in all newspaper and broadcasting units to report on what is happening inside them now, so that the movement is kept informed; and those inside could help deal with the publication of blatant lies and smears now put out under editorial direction. These groups might also be developing a demand now for the right to control a page of their own papers each week or day, or an hour of their broadcast output to put out the news and views as they themselves wish. Joint stewards and workplace branches would also be very valuable, in that they could help to identify the changes that will need to be made within their own organizations when a Labour government comes to power.

These are a few simple and straightforward proposals for dealing with the immediate situation, and some of them are now in operation. The skills to implement them already exist, or can be quickly developed, as we learned during the miners' strike when an endless seam of undiscovered talent in speaking, writing, organizing and dramatic or artistic ability came to the surface.

There is another reason why we should give these ideas a lot more serious attention and it is this. When Labour does come to power and we have a parliamentary majority to use in law-making and grant-giving we will want to have a number of experimental developments already under way that we can support financially and within a new framework of media and company law.

It would be relatively easy to pass new legislation requiring a right of reply, or greater industrial democracy, or to change the tax system or undermine the crude commercial sponsorship of the newspapers or TV as we have it today. But the real task cannot be merely to convert an essentially capitalist press to be fair to labour and its interests.

In any case we do not wish to control the publication of opinions that are different from our own, but to free those who hold a wide variety of quite different views from the restraints which now prevent them from getting those views across on the basis of equality.

The experience of media bias in recent years, as during the 1975 EEC referendum, the 1978–9 winter of discontent, the 1982 Falklands war and the 1984–5 miners' strike created a much more favourable atmosphere for those of us who have argued for reform and has won a wider public understanding of the danger of bias. It has also created a much larger audience for the left press, for when these papers are available views that are expressed in them can be seen to be relevant and interesting since it is in that press that the real debate is taking place.

The campaign to achieve a free press and media in Britain will be a long one. But it is now approaching its climax, and even if we have to wait for a few more years before we can carry it through to its completion, the work that has been done has already had its effect: the public are far more sceptical about what they read or are told night after night in the news bulletins.

This healthy scepticism represents an important advance for those who had almost given up hope that we would ever succeed in defeating media bias, and when people, generally, start realizing that they may have been misled the desire for change could come in a rush.

People can see what is really happening in terms of mass unemployment, poverty and hopelessness and can contrast it with the tax benefits for the rich or the build-up of nuclear weapons; and then they can see the sustained media hate campaigns against all those who stand up for the ordinary decencies of life, and draw their own conclusions. And that, when all is said and done, is all that we have asked for – that people should be able to read the facts and hear a diversity of opinions and then be able to draw their own conclusions.

Appendix I
Statement of the aims of the Campaign for Press and Broadcasting Freedom

- To challenge the myths of 'impartiality' and 'balance' in broadcasting, and 'objectivity' in newspapers by campaigning for the genuine presentation of the diversity and plurality of society.
- To challenge the myth that only private ownership of the newspaper industry provides genuine freedom, diversity or access.
- To challenge the myth that the present forms of ownership and regulation of broadcasting guarantee editorial independence, democratic accountability or high programme standards.
- To carry out research and generate debate on alternative forms of ownership and control of newspapers and broadcasting in order to guarantee freedom from either state control or domination by business conglomerates, and encourage the creation of alternative media including those sympathetic to the labour movement.
- To encourage the development of industrial democracy in the newspaper and broadcasting industries.
- To encourage debate on the implications of technological advances in the media to ensure that the public interest is safeguarded and that commercial interests do not override public accountability.
- To campaign on the general principles in the Minority Report of the 1977 Royal Commission on the Press, including proposals for a National Printing Corporation to provide a competitive public sector in the industry and a launch fund to assist new publications.
- To campaign for a reconstituted Press Council to promote basic standards of fairness and access to the press on behalf of the public. The Right of Reply is fundamental to redressing the imbalance in press bias.
- To campaign for a reduction in legal restrictions on freedom of publication and increased access to information through a Freedom of Information Bill and reform of the Official Secrets Act and similar restrictive legislation.
- To campaign for the legal right of access for publications to the

distribution system, and a guaranteed right of display.
- To work for press and broadcasting that are free of material detrimental to women and to homosexuals of both sexes.
- To seek equality of opportunity and achievement for women in the media.

Appendix II
CPBF Code of Conduct on Sexism in the Media

We resist:
- gender stereotyping, including the routine representation of women as sex objects and as 'housewives'.
- the neglect and racist portrayal of black women and women of other ethnic groups in the media.
- hostility to and misrepresentation of lesbians and gay men in the media.
- the display of women's bodies in the media to appeal to male prurience.
- the erotic portrayal of children.
- trivializing or sensational media treatment of instances in which men kill, attack or harass girls or women.

We seek to promote:
- a positive representation of women that reflects all aspects of their contribution to working, social and political life.
- a new use of language to avoid sexist terms.
- recognition in the media of the women's liberation movement as a responsible and necessary social force.

We support the implementation of this Code of Conduct. In whatever branch of the media we work, and at whatever stage of production, we will support colleagues who protest against instances of sexism in media content.

We support a Right of Reply for those adversely affected by sexist material.

Discrimination against women in the content of the media is related to discrimination against women in media occupations. The Campaign's Statement of Aims commits us to 'seek equality of opportunity and achievement for women in the media'. This itself will be a step towards ridding media content of sexism.